Mobility Justice

The Politics of Movement in an Age of Extremes

Mimi Sheller

VERSO

First published by Verso 2018
© Mimi Sheller 2018

1 3 5 7 9 10 8 6 4 2

Verso
UK: 6 Meard Street, London W1F 0EG
US: 20 Jay Street, Suite 1010, Brooklyn, NY 11201
versobooks.com

Verso is the imprint of New Left Books

ISBN-13: 978-1-78873-092-1
ISBN-13: 978-1-78873-095-2 (HBK)
ISBN-13: 978-1-78873-093-8 (UK EBK)
ISBN-13: 978-1-78873-094-5 (US EBK)

British Library Cataloguing in Publication Data
A catalogue record for this book is available from the British Library

Library of Congress Cataloging-in-Publication Data

Names: Sheller, Mimi, author.
Title: Mobility justice : the politics of movement in the age of extremes /
  Mimi Sheller.
Description: London ; Brooklyn, NY : Verso, 2018. | Includes bibliographical
  references and index.
Identifiers: LCCN 2018017911| ISBN 9781788730921 (pbk.) | ISBN 9781788730952
  (hbk) | ISBN 9781788730938 (UK ebk) | ISBN 9781788730945 (US ebk)
Subjects: LCSH: Emigration and immigration—Social aspects. | Rural-urban
  migration—Social aspects. | Transportation—Social aspects. | Social
  justice. | Environmental justice.
Classification: LCC JV6225 .S54 2018 | DDC 303.48/32—dc23
LC record available at https://lccn.loc.gov/2018017911

Typeset in Minion Pro by Biblichor Ltd, Edinburgh
Printed and bound by CPI Group (UK) Ltd, Croydon, CR0 4YY

Contents

Acknowledgments

I first want to dedicate this book to the late John Urry, who was my inspiration and mentor in so many ways, and with whom I worked, wrote, edited, and co-founded the Centre for Mobilities Research at Lancaster University in 2003, and the journal *Mobilities* in 2006. He was a model of academic commitment, collegiality, productivity, good humor, and humility. I want to thank my many friends and colleagues who continue to work on those projects, as well as those in the International Association for the History of Transport, Traffic, and Mobility (T2M), and in the Cosmobilities Network and the many other mobilities research networks around the world with whom I have shared inspiring conferences, workshops, and vital exchanges of ideas.

I first started thinking about a book on the concept of mobility justice after my experience of working in Haiti following the 2010 earthquake, where I joined in National Science Foundation–funded research with my Drexel University colleagues Franco Montalto, Patrick Gurian, and Michael Piasecki. I want to thank them, along with Jen Britton, Lavaud Vernet, Jean de Vernet, and Yves Rebecca, for our travels in Haiti in 2010. I also thank Michael Piasecki for facilitating my inclusion in another NSF project on climate change in Haiti and the Dominican Republic in 2012, with special thanks to Principal Investigator Jorge Gonzalez from City College of New York, and collaborator Yolanda Leon from the Instituto Tecnológico de Santo Domingo. My reflections on this work are gathered together in my forthcoming book *Island Futures: Global Mobilities and Caribbean Survival* (Duke University Press, 2019), which is a more empirically grounded companion volume to this one.

Building on this initial line of thought about post-disaster uneven mobilities, I gave the Distinguished Lecture entitled "Sustainable Mobility and Mobility Justice" at the University of Delaware's Transportation Center in 2011, and contributed chapters on that topic to the books *Mobile/Immobile: Quels choix, quels droits pour 2030?* edited by Christophe Gay, Vincent Kaufmann, Sylvie Landrieve, and Stéphanie Vincent-Geslin (Editions de l'Aube, 2011); and *Mobilities: New Perspectives on Transport and Society,* edited by Margaret Grieco and John Urry (Ashgate, 2012). In 2013 I gave a talk entitled "Mobility Capability: Social Justice and Counter-Geographies of Movement," at the "Differential Mobilities" Conference of the Pan-American Mobilities Network at Concordia University in Montreal, hosted by Kim Sawchuk and colleagues, where I began to see the significance of critical disabilities studies through the work of Laurence Parent; and I was invited by Inderpal Grewal to give a talk entitled "Towards Transnational Mobility Justice" for the Yale University series "Transnational feminist research and its theoretical paradigms." I thank all these hosts and audiences for the chance to grapple with these ideas and share this evolving work.

When the 2015 refugee crises associated with war in Syria, as well as the impacts of violence across North Africa, Central America, and Mexico, drove so many people to meet death while seeking safety, I began to see the need for a more general book addressing a wider global theory of mobility justice. I was also influenced by the rise of the Black Lives Matter movement and the growing protests by Indigenous people's movements against mining, hydroelectric dams, and largescale infrastructure projects around the world. I would not know about many of these mobilizations if it were not for my wonderful network of activist colleagues and, yes, thank you, Facebook friends. I also want to thank bicycling justice advocate Adonia E. Lugo, founder of the Bicicultures Network and member of the Untokening project, and Olatunji Oboi Reed, co-founder of the Slow Roll Chicago Bicycle Movement and the mobility justice advocacy group Equiticity, for introducing me to these grassroots multiracial mobility justice movements and sharing their insights and experience.

Esther Figueroa, my brilliant collaborator on *Fly Me to the Moon*, a documentary film about bauxite mining and aluminum, has also been a constant source of inspiration and encouragement in thinking about global resource extraction, human rights, and planetary ecologies. I also take inspiration from the work of Deborah Cowen, Stephen Graham, Lisa Parks, and others working so creatively on infrastructure, with special thanks to Stephen for the introduction to Verso. I want to thank Diane Davis, Neil Brenner, and Gareth Doherty at Harvard University Graduate School of Design for invitations to speak there about aluminum, infrastructure, and mobilities.

Thanks to Malene Freudendal-Pedersen and Joergen Ole Baerenholdt, I was greatly honored to be awarded the Doctor Honoris Causa from Roskilde University, Denmark, in 2015, where in my honorary address I first described the different scales of justice that became the structure of this book (and apologies to the wonderful questioner who wanted me to also cover the nano-scale mobilities internal to the human body—I could not manage to fit it all in this book!). Thanks also to Sven Kesselring and Ole B. Jensen for ongoing discussions, conversations, and invitations to participate in events you have organized.

At the Society for Caribbean Research in Hanover, I gave the keynote address entitled "Caribbean Constellations and Mobility Justice" in 2015, and another keynote address entitled "Mobility Justice and the Temporalities of Multi-Scalar Migration" at a workshop called "Mobilities and Temporalities," organized by Brenda Yeoh at the National University of Singapore in 2016. I also spoke on the topic at panels of the American Association of Geographers annual conference in San Francisco and at the T2M annual conference in Mexico City in 2016, and gave public lectures on various aspects of the book at Grinnell College in Iowa, Simon Fraser University in Vancouver, and at the Harvard Graduate School of Design. And lastly, in 2017, I gave keynote talks drawing on this book at the Australian Sociological Association, with thanks to Farida Fozdar, and on the occasion of the launch of the Australian Mobilities Network, with thanks to David Bissell. I thank the many people who have hosted me at these events, who have attended related teaching workshops, and the engaging audiences whose questions helped shape my thinking.

Other outcomes of this project include a chapter in the forthcoming book *Mobilities, Mobility Justice and Social Justice*, edited by David Butz and Nancy Cook (Routledge, 2019), who have also generously encouraged and influenced my thinking about mobility justice in global contexts. Parts of Chapter Two draw on my article "Racialized Mobility Transitions in Philadelphia: Urban Sustainability and the Problem of Transport Inequality," *City and Society*, Special Issue on Cities and Mobilities, edited by Malene Freudendal-Pedersen, Vol. 27, Issue 1, (April 2015), pp. 70–91. Parts of Chapter Four draw on my chapter "Globalizing Networked Urbanism: Frictions and Connectivity in Elite and Subaltern Mobilities," in *Exploring Networked Urban Mobilities*, edited by Malene Freudendal-Pederson and Sven Kesselring (New York and Abingdon: Routledge, 2018), pp. 19–35. Parts of Chapter Six draw on my article "Global Energy Cultures of Speed and Lightness: Materials, Mobilities and Transnational Power," in the "Energizing Society" Special Issue, edited by David Tyfield and John Urry, *Theory, Culture and Society*, Vol. 31, No. 5 (2014), pp. 127–54. I thank all of these editors for their valuable comments and journals for permission to draw on this work.

I also greatly benefited from engaging as a reviewer with the team working on the project Living in Mobility Transitions, funded by the Mobile Lives Forum, including Peter Adey, Tim Cresswell, Anna Nikolaeva, Jane Lee, Andre Novoa, and Cristina Temenos. I especially want to thank Anna Nikolaeva who inspired the concept of the mobile commons and generously shared work in progress, as well as inviting me to speak at the Cities Mobilities seminar series at University of Amsterdam in 2018.

Closer to home, institutional support for this project came in the form of a six-month sabbatical from Drexel University in 2017 and a visiting fellowship at the Center for Advanced Research in Global Communication at the Annenberg School of Communication, University of Pennsylvania, where I would like to thank Marwan Kraidy for his support. I thank my colleagues at Drexel University, especially Susan Bell in the Sociology Department, Kelly Joyce in the Center for Science, Technology, and Society, and all involved with the Center for Mobilities Research and Policy, who have supported my work in various ways. PhD student Julia Hildebrand has been especially remarkable in her service as secretary of T2M while I was president, and in her work as a research assistant. Without her steadfast work and superb organization, I would not have had the time to concentrate on writing. Many thanks also to editor Leo Hollis, my careful copy editor Angelica Sgouros, and the entire team at Verso for helping me bring this book to the light of day and find its audience.

And last, I especially want to thank my parents, as I reach a half century of life and reflect on its shape. My family has instilled in me a social justice perspective, and a love of cross-cultural knowledge, learning, and arts, that have enriched my life. My mother, Stelle Sheller, sets a constant example, from her career teaching autistic children in Philadelphia's public schools, to volunteering for the Women's International League for Peace and Freedom, to weekly service with Manna (an organization that cooks and delivers meals to people struggling with illness), not to mention her constant presence at political marches and demonstrations throughout my life.

Equally important was the influence of my father, Stephen A. Sheller, from his early legal work on civil rights cases, labor unions, and defense of consumers against corporate malfeasance, to his more recent founding, with Sandra Sheller, of the Center for Social Justice at Temple University and the Stephen and Sandra Sheller 11th Street Family Health Services of Drexel University, as well as their contributions to many other charitable institutions across Philadelphia.

Of course, my work would not be possible without the love and support of my partner Dan Schimmel, artist extraordinaire, intellectual provocateur, and self-taught theorist. His ideas spread like a fringe of turkey feather fungi, softly emanating from every page of this book. Thank you for cultivating our little patch of home. To Ally and Evie, if you ever read this book, I hope there is some glimmer of hope here for a future world still teeming with life and the pluriverse of mobile beauty. May you be part of the future mobile commons.

Preface

As I write this, the world seems to be reeling from a series of climate disasters, with the closest to home for me being the devastation of the Caribbean by Hurricanes Irma and Maria within two weeks of each other, close on the heels of Hurricane Harvey in Texas, evoking disturbing memories of Hurricane Katrina. On some islands these violent storms wiped out every home, school, and hospital; knocked out electricity, landline, and cellular phone services; ruined roads, ports, airports, and vehicles; stripped every tree and destroyed agriculture; and brought to a halt normal systems for the provisioning of food, water, fuel, and even cash. On top of these immediate impacts, there are slower crises related to delays in the arrival of aid, the inability of many people to either rebuild their lives or leave islands that are in crisis, and the mammoth task of rebuilding homes, roads, electric power grids, and economies that were already quite fragile.

This compounded disaster is in many ways a harbinger of disastrous futures to come across many parts of the world affected by climate change. These terrible events underline more than ever the problems of uneven mobilities and the need for mobility justice. Colonial legacies of fragmented sovereignty and borders have left a highly variegated terrain of social protection and vulnerability. The continuing power outage in Puerto Rico, for example, has left the elderly and ill at high risk of death. A new Harvard University study estimates that more than 4,600 people died of causes related to the effects of Hurricane Maria.[1]

Many Puerto Ricans and US Virgin Islanders, who are US citizens, feel that the United States government has abandoned them and treated them as second-class citizens. Natural disasters always have a social and political component, and uneven mobilities are a crucial aspect of their differential impact. Some are forced to move away from their homes, others are unable to escape. Such social vulnerabilities in times of crisis have deep historical roots, and often become routes for new forms of exploitation to spread, as expediency becomes opportunity for those empowered with mobility.[2]

As business tycoons and cryptocurrency millionaires descend upon the islands to reshape their economies and buy up beachfront properties, they leverage the fictive sovereignties of "offshore" financial centers in the Caribbean, which have allowed tax-free havens for capital to flourish for decades.[3] By enabling the mobility of capital and goods, while restricting the mobility of labor, these special zones allow companies to profit from low taxes and cheap workers without supporting local governments. Uneven mobilities produce these uneven spatial patterns and the ecological pressures that they bring. My work continues to highlight the injustices of differential movement within and out of the region in relation to my own privileges of mobility.[4]

More broadly, it is the excessive consumption of energy and fossil fuels in the United States that has directly contributed to the global warming and tropical storm intensification into the Category 4 and 5 hurricanes to which the Caribbean now falls victim, despite having contributed little as a region to climate change. It can therefore be argued that this hurricane season is not simply a natural disaster but a man-made disaster of *mobility injustice*. This is just one example of the many crises in the management of uneven mobilities around the world today.

How, when, and where people, goods, and capital move is, in all respects, a political question. In the face of climate disaster, it is also increasingly a moral question of the distribution of life and death. In the book *Extreme Cities*, Ashley Dawson refers to such extremes as "not a temporary aberration but an inherent feature of capitalism." He describes the side-by-side "combined and uneven" zones of "abject poverty" and "shocking affluence" as products of "centuries of imperialism and racial capitalism;" such that when natural disasters like hurricanes strike they simply gouge "the grooves of extreme inequality even deeper."[5]

Climate change is one of the extremes we live with today, but there are also other extremes of uneven mobilities. The late British social historian Eric Hobsbawm (who was one of my professors in graduate school) described the short twentieth century as the "age of extremes" in his book of that title, in which he argued: "If humanity is to have a recognizable future, it cannot be by prolonging the past or the present."[6] Given our present trajectory toward endless growth and climatic collapse, these words seem even more true today than they were in the twentieth century. In the United States, in the face of a retrograde political moment of profound backlash against all progressive policies, the current politics of mobility includes much more than ongoing efforts to reduce car dependence, change our reliance on fossil fuels, stop the building of new oil pipelines, and develop more sustainable forms of transportation and energy use.

Mobility justice encompasses these "sustainability" issues but also includes many other extremes of inequality, ranging from interpersonal bodily violence to global violations of human rights. Mobility justice in the US case includes the debates over building a border wall between Mexico and the US, and changes being made by the Trump Administration to restrict the admission of migrants and refugees to the country, and to deport others. It includes the Black Lives Matter movement protesting police shootings, detention, biased stop-and-frisk policies, and mass incarceration, as well as political debates over National Football League players kneeling during the pre-game national anthem as an embodied protest against racism in America. It includes the #MeToo movement against sexual assault, and the #NeverAgain movement against gun violence in the United States. The concept of mobility justice arises in part out of these protest movements.

As I was finishing this book I became aware of several community organizations also working on mobility justice issues. The Untokening is "a multiracial collective that centers the experiences of marginalized communities to address mobility justice and equity."[7] They developed their own Principles of Mobility Justice through a community-based discussion process, which overlaps with many of the arguments made here, and especially the notion that we need a deeper historical approach:

> Historical disenfranchisement, disinvestment, disproportionate exposure to pollution, and repressive policing in communities of color continue to negatively impact our collective health, wealth, mobility, and security . . . Mobility Justice demands that we fully excavate, recognize, and reconcile the historical and current injustices experienced by communities—with impacted communities given space and resources to envision and implement planning models and political advocacy on streets and mobility that actively work to address historical and current injustices experienced by communities.[8]

While this book lays out a framework for theorizing mobility justice, it is crucial to recognize the community-based organizing that is already happening. The Untokening held their first "convening" in Atlanta in 2016, in conjunction with the Facing Race conference. They first began using the term "mobility justice" due to dissatisfaction with existing terminology such as "transportation equity" or "bicycle justice," which seemed too restrictive.[9]

Advocacy groups like the Slow Roll Chicago Bicycle Movement, co-founded by Jamal Julien and Olatunji Oboi Reed in 2014, along with Reed's new organization Equiticity, also build on community bicycling events to advocate for "racial equity, increased mobility and racial justice to make lives better for Black, Brown and Indigenous people of color across the United States."[10] They mobilize bicycling not just as transportation, but as a tool to build community health, cohesion, and jobs, which they argue will help counter urban violence.

Above all, these groups call for space and resources for people of color, women, and others historically excluded from transport planning to envision and implement actions from their own knowledge base, and to contribute to theorizing justice as well as bringing about real transformations toward more equitable mobility and urban planning. As Emily Reid-Musson observes of these movements,

> As North American cities have started to embrace bicycling, a group of pro-bicycling advocates and researchers has argued that U.S. bicycling movements have too often ignored issues of equity and justice (Golub et al. 2016; Hoffman 2016; Lugo 2016; Stehlin 2014). While bicycling augurs more sustainable and equitable horizons, marginalized bicyclists' needs and voices need to gain more traction within bicycling movements if bicycling is to realize its potential on both social and ecological fronts.[11]

It is movements such as these, combining social justice, racial justice and climate justice lenses, that are beginning to connect neighborhood-level racial inequities (such as biased policing, transport access, and health access), to national-level migrant justice issues (such as exclusions of non-citizens from legal entitlements to freedom of mobility), to global level climate justice and human rights issues (such as land grabs for mining and oil drilling that are contributing to climate change and driving people from their homes).

Mobility justice furthermore includes the rights of women to not be subjected to sexual harassment and bodily assault in the workplace, and the rights of queer and trans people to find public bathrooms, dress as they choose to, and carry forms of non-binary identification. And it includes addressing the crises of eviction, homelessness, and urban gentrification that drives people out of city centers and leaves them without safe shelter. As The Untokening notes:

> When people live at the intersection of multiple vectors of oppression, unfettered access to mobility and public space are not guaranteed. Racism, sexism, classism, ableism, xenophobia, homophobia, and constraints imposed upon gender-non-conforming folks can make the public space hostile to many. Bodies encounter different risks and have different needs.
>
> Yet this has seldom been the starting point for envisioning more sustainable transportation. It should be. When cities plan for active transportation, low-carbon transitions, or smart mobility, these voices need to be heard.[12]

How can we begin to develop notions of mobility justice that encompass these many different vectors of class, racial, gender and other injustices across entangled scales? While climate change, migration, and urban equity may appear to be a disparate set of problems, this book seeks to show that in many ways they all come back to questions of uneven (im)mobilities. The concepts developed in this book aim to shed light on this diverse set of problems and provide new ways of thinking about their interconnectivity.

There is a relation between personal bodily vulnerabilities, the struggle for urban public space and shelter, the splintering of infrastructural systems, the management of unequal citizenship regimes and borders, and the uneven impacts of planetary environmental risks. Yet most academic research is channeled into specialist sub-fields and it is difficult to get a view of the whole terrain. Moreover, academic research has not done enough to decolonize the very approaches it employs, for example, by seeking out ideas and practices around transport and mobility from the Global South or from Indigenous knowledge or from critical disabilities scholarship.

Colombian anthropologist Arturo Escobar argues in his book *Designs for the Pluriverse*, that transformative systemic change will require autonomous thinking based in "participatory, bottom-up, situated design" from the perspective of diverse bodies and multiple places, including the Global South.[13] I will return below to his notions of Indigenous epistemologies and relational ontologies, which inform my approach. I hope mobility justice will become a concept that inspires translation, conversation, repurposing and mobilization across many borders at multiple scales.

The interdisciplinary field of mobilities research, out of which this book grows, offers an opportunity to bring arguments about these many forms of unequal mobilities into relation with each other for the first time. One social implication of mobilities research is that we need to address entire mobility systems, logistical practices, energy cultures, and the ways in which everyday mobility practices are embedded in these larger socio-technical systems that are complex, interdependent, and more-than-human. These are fundamentally political and social questions that require attention to the social injustices built into present ways of "doing" everyday life, going places, moving things, and processing mobile information.

New ways of studying mobilities focus attention on embodied and material practices of movement, digital and communicative mobilities, the infrastructures and systems of governance that enable or disable movement, and the representations, ideologies, and meanings attached to both movement and stillness. The mobilities turn also emphasizes the relation of such mobilities to associated immobilities or moorings, including the political and ethical dimensions of uneven mobility. Mobilities research is concerned not only with tracing the historical emergence of modern mobility regimes, technologies, and practices, but also critically addressing contemporary political issues such as movements for sustainable mobility, racial equity, and migrants' mobility rights, and helping to actively build everyday mobility capabilities such as physical access to the public space of the city and to transportation and communication infrastructures.

Through developing the concept of mobility justice, I seek to show how the historical development (and present effects) of interlocking systems of uneven mobility distort human relations with each other and with the world. I also hope to provoke new synergies across existing movements for mobility justice by aligning this project with existing community-based initiatives and organizations. The book seeks to develop some basic principles of mobility justice in several of the chapters, and for easier access these are collated in a single list, "Principles of Mobility Justice," included at the end of this book. I have also included a glossary of some key theoretical terms, movements, and organizations that are referred to throughout the book. Readers less interested in theoretical concerns may want to skip over chapter one and pick up the more empirical story that begins in chapter two.

The concept of the mobile commons, developed in the conclusion, I hope can point the way forward toward imagining, planning and enacting more just collective mobilities in the future. But this can only be achieved from situated, participatory processes, through which we might together contest the present and design more just futures. Thus this book is offered in the spirit of gathering together some key ideas and examples, remembering some crucial histories, and pointing toward some movements and forms of "mobile commoning" that are already beginning to mobilize for mobility justice.

Introduction: The Triple Crisis

All around the world people and governments are grappling with a series of crises related to how we move. The entire world faces the urgent question of how to make the transition to more environmentally sustainable and socially just mobilities. Too much fossil fuel–based transport is driving global warming and pushing the planetary climate toward a dangerous tipping point for mass extinctions and human non-habitability. Automobile-dependent cities are struggling with immediate environmental dysfunctions including air pollution, congestion, and failing urban infrastructure as the changing climate brings floods, blistering heat, and devastating storms. Meanwhile, the largest refugee movements since World War II, many of which are increasingly climate-related, are generating deep concerns over the closing of borders, militarized migration management, and state securitization of borders. We witness the deaths of thousands of migrants at sea or in deserts, the xenophobic treatment of foreign-born populations, the rejection of refugees and asylum seekers, the building of walls and detention centers, and the persistence of racist violence and the resurgence of ethnocentric political parties in Europe, North America, and elsewhere.

The common denominator of these parallel crises of climate, urbanization, and migration is that all revolve around questions of mobility and immobility, and together they bring into focus the unjust power relations of uneven mobility. Mobility justice is one of the crucial political and ethical issues of our day. It focuses attention on the politics of unequal capabilities for movement, as well as on unequal rights to stay or to dwell in a place. It is concerned with sexual harassment as much as transport access, and with racist violence as much as resource extraction. It allows us to think more clearly about the intertwined relations between bodies, streets, transport systems, urbanization (including not just cities but also suburbs and rural hinterlands), regional and transnational infrastructures, national borders, and wider planetary mobilities. It reveals the relation between the urban crisis, the migration crisis, and the climate crisis.

This book seeks to connect these three apparently separate crises by showing how they arise out of a common problem: the politics and power relations of (im)mobilities. The use of "(im)mobilities" is meant to signal that mobility and immobility are always connected, relational, and co-dependent, such that we should always think of them together, not as binary opposites but as dynamic constellations of multiple scales, simultaneous practices, and relational meanings. Scale is a social construction, human geographers argue, and movement is precisely that which makes and remakes space-time and entangles different scales.[1] Practices are the ways in which social relations are assembled, stabilized, and moved, involving both human actors, non-human actors and material processes in ongoing combinations. And meanings are the ways we make sense of and tell stories about the particular space-time contexts that we make, transform, and inhabit through our ongoing lived (im)mobilities.

We can re-think the politics of accessibility, transport, urbanization, infrastructure, borders, and climate in new ways by focusing on combined and uneven (im)mobilities across multiple scales at once. This approach places current debates over sustainable transportation, low-carbon transitions, urban planning, and what are usually thought of as localized urban transportation justice issues in the wider context of many different unequal mobility regimes extending from face-to-face bodily relations to extensive planetary circulation not just of people, but also of energy and resources. Many grassroots community organizations have already made these connections, for example when they connect contemporary racial inequities in mobility and urban access to long histories of colonialism, capitalist exploitation, and appropriation of land, processes that have displaced people, disrupted their forms of moving and settling, and made alternative forms of life untenable.

Mobility justice is not just about transportation within cities, though that is an important part of it, but also about the smaller micro-mobilities at the bodily scale that are inflected by racial and classed processes, gendered practices, and the social shaping of disabilities and sexualities. It is also about the rights to cross-border mobility of refugees and migrants, as well as the mobility of tourists, travelers, workers, students, and "kinetic elites."[2] And it is about the extended urban systems and infrastructural spaces that shape larger macro-mobilities at a planetary scale, such as access to water and food, and the circulations of energy and fossil fuels through pipelines and cables. And all of these are situated in relation to new technologies for digital mobility, circulations of financial capital, as well as military mobilities and logistical systems.

Elite leisure and business travel, labor migration and temporary contract work, refugee movements and migrant detention, military deployments and peasant uprooting, racist policing and sexual violence, all stand in some relation to each other, as well as to wider mobility concerns. These human mobilities are inseparable from climate change, resource extraction and urban resilience; military mobilities and global logistics chains; racial segregation and racialized problems of eviction, homelessness and mass imprisonment; access to mobility by the elderly, children, disabled people and the poor; or the normative sexual policing of everyday bodily movements of women, queer, and gender nonconforming people. The concept of mobility justice puts all these concerns in conversation with each other, transcending separate approaches that focus on each in isolation, though certainly building on the insights of transport justice, racial justice, migrant justice, sexual justice, disability justice, and climate justice movements and theories.

How can we think about these problems of the politics of uneven (im)mobilities through a common prism, showing how they not only intersect but refract and intensify each other in multiple directions at once? How can we gain leverage over each of these issues by showing its association with the others? I will draw on the new mobilities paradigm, an approach that transcends traditional disciplines and has emerged to address the complexities of the twenty-first century.[3]

The study of mobilities involves new theoretical approaches and methodological innovations for analyzing the complex movements of people, objects, and information, and the power relations behind the governance of mobilities and immobilities. It considers slowness alongside acceleration, blockages, stoppage, and friction as much as liquidity and circulation, and coerced movement as much as freedom of movement. It concerns the practices, lived experiences, representations, and meanings attached to such movement.[4]

The material turn in mobilities research calls for a critical approach to infrastructure space and the planetary geographies of uneven mobilities. By tracing connections between micro and macro infrastructures of mobility and energy, I seek to show how the mobility justice approach can open new kinds of questions and critical perspectives, including challenging the narratives, representations, and legitimations of speed, acceleration, and the elite right to movement at all costs. In this introduction, I will briefly describe the contemporary mobility crises, introduce the new mobilities paradigm, and build the foundations for thinking about mobility justice.

THE TRIPLE MOBILITY CRISIS

Climate Crisis

The first mobility crisis of the twenty-first century is the realization of climate change and the limits we must urgently place on endless growth and ceaseless movement. The Earth's climate becomes more hazardous to humans and other living things every year, with ice sheets melting, oceans warming and swelling, and extreme weather, droughts and fires, floods and storm surges affecting large swathes of the world. Innumerable scientific studies report that we are already experiencing mass extinctions and there is potential for extreme collapse of the biosphere by 2100. Yet social scientists are only just beginning to weigh in on this human-caused crisis.[5]

In July 2017, as I was writing this, the massive Larsen C ice shelf broke off Antarctica; intense monsoon rains and cyclones affected many parts of Southeast Asia, especially in Bangladesh, Sri Lanka, and Myanmar; Southern Europe and other regions experienced extreme heat waves, while California suffered up to 5,000 wildfires over the year; and floods devastated parts of Africa, especially in South Sudan, Nigeria, and Ethiopia. By September, Hurricane Harvey left large parts of Houston and Miami under water, and

Hurricanes Irma and Maria barreled through the Caribbean and Florida with 185mph winds, wreaking destruction on fragile islands, including massive destruction on Barbuda, Dominica, and Saint Martin, and inducing a severe humanitarian crisis in Puerto Rico. By January 2018, the northeastern United States and Canada were in the grip of a so-called "bomb cyclone" of frigid sub-freezing weather, while an extreme heat wave was parching Australia, and Cape Town, South Africa, was running out of water.

Climate change is a mobility crisis in at least three ways. First, because transportation-related emissions are a major contributor to global warming, accounting for approximately one-quarter of global greenhouse gas emissions according to the International Energy Association. Second, because the built environments and land uses that support current patterns of mobile life are driving global climate change and the pollution of remaining water, air, oceans, and land on which all life depends. And third, because climate change uproots people and disrupts infrastructure systems and supply chains around the world, driving environmental migration in the face of ecological and societal collapse. Climate change has instigated worldwide efforts—despite resistance in some quarters—to reduce greenhouse gases, end our dependence on fossil fuels, and fundamentally transform transportation infrastructures and the related land-use patterns that determine how people and goods move, how food is produced, and how societies are "energized."[6]

Yet the overconsumption of energy and the culturally and spatially entrenched patterns of automobility and urban sprawl in North America, Europe, and other parts of the industrial world, and their rapid growth in Asia, Africa, and Latin America, suggest that the post-car/post-carbon transition is not happening quickly enough. Climate change is not simply a technological problem that we can engineer our way out of, but is a social, political, economic, and cultural problem that we have yet to get a handle on. Even as climate change increasingly puts at risk the water, food crops, and entire biosphere on which life depends, there is a strong backlash against efforts at greenhouse gas reduction among the fossil fuel advocates, climate change deniers, and "carbon capital" oligopolies, especially those now at the heart of the Trump administration in the USA.[7]

Most of the world stands aghast as the USA withdraws from the Paris Climate Agreement, dismantles the Environmental Protection Agency, guts the Clean Air Act, promotes coal mining, opens public lands to further oil and gas exploration, approves the building of new pipelines to carry heavy crude oil, and rejects the scientific consensus around the human causes of climate change. How will we move beyond fossil fuels, automobile dependence, limitless growth, heavy industry, and high energy consumption under these political conditions? Will we ever make the transition to the much anticipated "green economy" based on clean energy, limits to the use of resources, and perhaps limits on our mobility through more localized economies?

These are social and political problems that demand more than technological fixes and policy tinkering. As Naomi Klein puts it, "This changes everything," and demands the entire remaking of our economies, polities, and ways of life, which is what makes some of those in power so scared.[8] And there is certainly a growing chorus of thinkers who are seeking new social and political models that can lead us "out of the wreckage" that we have wrought.[9]

Urbanization Crisis

The second mobility crisis we face around the world is *an urbanization crisis,* related to urban growth, the spread of automobility (referring to an interlocking system of cars, highways, fueling infrastructure, automotive companies, government policies, and car cultures) extensive urban sprawl and resource demands, and growing social inequality, splintered accessibility, land grabs, and mass evictions in the ballooning megacities around the world.[10] In many places, this has produced paralyzing traffic congestion, dangerous levels of air pollution, energy shortages, and in many cases water shortages or increased risks of flooding as sprawl has filled and paved over vulnerable ecologies.

It was claimed that more than half the human population had moved into cities by 2007, with rapid urbanization especially in China, where the urban population already outnumbers the rural population and with predictions of one billion urban dwellers in China alone by 2030.[11] Along with this urbanization, China has experienced the most rapid "automobilization" ever, as John Urry and David Tyfield point out, bringing complex system dysfunctions: hazardous air pollution, gridlock, poor road safety, stress, and social isolation. Despite efforts at technological innovation, the internal combustion engine is rapidly taking hold in China and in the Global South more generally, and remains deeply tied to common sense, everyday ways of life in the Western world, which I have referred to as "automotive emotions" that are deeply attached to the "automobilized self."[12]

These urban mobility problems are driving a global search for new forms of urban planning, transport, resource use, and infrastructure design sometimes referred to as "ecological urbanism" or "sustainable urbanism."[13] There is also a growing emphasis on disaster preparedness in the face of climate change, identifying risks and hazards to critical infrastructure, and building greater resilience into urban systems. How will the world's megacities, not to mention average cities, suburbs, and rural places outside of cities, adapt to the growing (and uneven) vulnerability to climate change, and the need to manage mobility, logistics, and settlement in new ways?

In relation to transportation, some analysts refer to a shift already occurring toward a "new mobility paradigm" based on vehicle sharing, connectivity, accessibility, "smart mobility," "the internet of cars," and "mobility as a service" (MaaS).[14] This search is not only about new technologies and innovation, however, but may also incorporate advocacy for more sustainable and just mobilities, involving active transport, bicycling infrastructure, complete streets (with room and safety features for all modes), Vision Zero safety policies (to reduce traffic fatalities to zero), and new forms of transport planning, zoning, congestion charging, and transport demand management (to reduce the over-dependence on private cars).

Some indicators suggest that in the Global North (especially in Europe) many cities have already reached "peak car" and are now starting to reduce their car use, as discussed further in Chapter 3.[15] There are car-free days, pedestrianized city centers, road pricing, reduced parking, and even in some places free public transit to nudge people toward giving up their cars. Yet, as transport geographer Tim Schwanen asks, who and what will benefit from this reinvention of a more "resilient" automobility? Do these urban mobility fixes really deal with the underlying forces that are driving the urban crisis, and the deep social rifts of uneven infrastructure and "splintered urbanism"?[16]

Despite long-running movements for accessibility, rights to the city, and transportation justice, it is unlikely to be the "mobility poor" or "kinetic underclass" who benefit, whether in the Global North or the Global South.[17] The competitive market-driven development of autonomous vehicles and smartphone-supported shared mobility also suggests a persistence of unequal and inequitable mobility, rather than the emergence of "mobility systems that genuinely redistribute life chances and well-being across the full range of urban populations."[18] How can we move toward a low-carbon transition that is both ecologically sound and socially equitable?

I argue that there is a need for a multi-scalar and mobile approach that goes beyond mobility innovation and transport justice alone (usually conceived of as a question of simply getting from A to B within cities), to address wider injustices surrounding extended urban infrastructure space and the global extraction of resources such as metals and fossil fuels across dispersed planetary geographies. Mobility justice must address how urbanization is linked to embodied power relations of (im)mobility locally and globally, including land expropriation, ecological destruction, eviction, expulsion, and the migration flows that are driving global urbanization in the first place.[19]

Refugee Crisis

Third, there is *a global refugee crisis* and deep concerns over the closing of borders, the deaths of thousands of migrants at sea or in deserts, the hostile treatment of foreign-born populations, the refusal of new refugees in many countries, and the persistence of racist violence and ethnocentric exclusions. The collapse of Syrian cities in the summer of 2015, in the midst of an intractable civil war, brought world attention to the dysfunctions of current refugee and asylum systems that left thousands of people to lose their lives trying to reach Europe or North America. While there has been a steady stream of terrorist incidents occurring regularly in war-torn countries like Iraq, Afghanistan, Somalia, and Syria, or in those fighting insurgencies or separatists such as Nigeria, Israel, Pakistan, and Turkey, a new wave of terror attacks in Western

Europe—including a series of attacks in France culminating in the November 2015 attack on the Bataclan theatre and other locations; the 2016 Brussels bombings; three major attacks in the United Kingdom in 2017; and the Berlin Christmas market attack in December 2016—all contributed to further backlash against welcoming refugees, the rise of anti-immigrant right-wing parties, and a crisis of the humanitarian asylum system.

In 2016 more than five thousand people died crossing the Mediterranean, the United Kingdom voted for "Brexit" based on anti-immigrant arguments, right-wing xenophobic political parties made gains in many European elections, and Donald Trump won the US presidential election on a nationalist platform of building a US–Mexico border wall and deporting undocumented migrants. These ethno-nationalist political polarizations continued to gain ground in 2017. Trump's executive order banning migration from seven Muslim-majority countries (Iran, Iraq, Libya, Somalia, Syria, Sudan, and Yemen) in early January 2017 elicited demonstrations at airports across the country, the firing of the acting attorney general who called into doubt its legality, and the filing of legal challenges by affected parties as well as several states. There was further outcry at his administration's September 2017 suspension of the Deferred Action for Childhood Arrivals (DACA) program, which had protected the so-called "Dreamers," a generation of young people brought into the country without documents whose lives will be shattered if they are deported to countries of origin they have never known.

Although we may hear occasional reference to "oil wars" in the Middle East, as major powers vie for control of the Iraqi and Syrian oil fields, seldom is the global refugee crisis presented as related to the problems outlined above: of automobility, climate change, urbanization, and how global energy consumption fuels social violence and the uprooting of people in many parts of the world. Of course, the language of "crisis" is one of the ways in which mobilities and security are managed under "disaster capitalism," as Naomi Klein argues in *The Shock Doctrine: The Rise of Disaster Capitalism*.[20] I, too, have examined the role of post-disaster humanitarian and non-governmental activity in responding to disasters such as the 2010 Haitian earthquake as a form of uneven mobility triggered by crisis.[21] Land grabs and calls for privatization are often associated with crisis-triggered responses to earthquakes, tsunamis, or hurricanes, and post-disaster rebuilding time and again retrenches uneven mobilities and deepens urban inequities in the name of building back better.

Despite the dangers of the language of "crisis urbanism" to feed disaster capitalism, I nevertheless believe a focus on mobility crises remains a helpful rubric with which to think across these multi-scalar political projects of managing, contesting, disrupting, and subverting unjust (im)mobilities. Because "urban crises lay bare the underlying power structures, long-neglected injustices, and unacknowledged inequalities of contemporary cities," how we recover from them reveals a lot about the reproduction of social hierarchies and power.[22] Uneven mobilities after disasters are a prime example of the social and political mechanisms by which such inequalities are reproduced in the wake (and in the name) of such crises.[23] I want to turn the language of crisis back on itself, to understand how intertwined mobility injustices jump scales, as well as to help figure out how movements building mobility justice can work against and across such crisis scenarios.

Intersectional (Im)mobilities

International migration and crisis urbanism are both at their base linked to the developmental insecurities of contemporary political economies that disrupt rural ecologies, expropriate land and water, uproot communities and displace people around the world. We should not see a migration crisis or a refugee crisis as exceptional moments, therefore, but rather as an effect of the ongoing politics of contemporary insecurities and securitization around (im)mobilities. While much attention has been given to the question of transitions in our transportation systems toward more sustainable and just forms, these concerns with transportation justice must be put in a wider context of other intersectional and cross-cutting aspects of mobility injustices and mobility politics. At the same time, questions of borders, migration, asylum, and humanitarianism must also be placed in the context of global urbanization, climate change, and transnational bodily relations shaped by racial, classed, gendered, and sexual processes that are also about the governance of (im)mobilities.

We need to theorize mobility transitions in ways that show how the production of extended urban space transforms scalar relations and remakes the contexts for movement. The triple mobility crisis cannot be solved at one scale alone, nor by technological fixes: the solutions must encompass political deliberation over how we move our bodies and the capabilities and vulnerabilities of different bodies; where we live, how we build our cities, what kinds of infrastructures we create, how we make and move things; and how we mobilize energy, water, food, and other "natural resources" around the world. Mobility justice is both a micro and a macro problem, a local and a global concern, a human and a more-than-human relation, a material problem and a moral issue.

We need to pay more attention to the interaction between urban infrastructure, land use, and connectivity across "extended urban systems" and "operational landscapes" including mining, oil production, and water and energy flows, all of which feed into concentrated urban systems via transportation and logistics networks.[24] Our old ways of planning transport and doing transport studies are certainly in need of updating, but the shift toward "smart mobility" and even the concept of "transport justice" are too limited to address the complex crises of planetary urbanization and uneven infrastructure space.[25] The concept of "spatial justice" has gone some way toward expanding our sense of these interlocking problems, but it, too, has limited analysis mainly to the urban scale and has focused on spatial forms more than on mobility itself and how it shapes wider economies and systems of political management of (im)mobilities both within the city and beyond the city.

We need a more flexible and relational sense of spatial instabilities and frictions, deterritorializations alongside territorializations, scalar shifts and entanglements, including subterranean, atmospheric, and planetary dimensions. Existing concepts of transport justice and spatial justice are simply not capacious enough to address the triple helix of mobility crises that we face. That is where the new mobilities paradigm has an important part to play.

Mobilities research has begun to analyze such systems, and even to conceive of them in a dynamic, emergent, and holistic way. It provides us with new conceptual tools to understand and analyze transport-related energy transitions, the politics of borders and migration, the circulation of energy, the uneven access differently embodied people have to urban space and political subjectivity, and the ways in which all of these are connected. It spans micro, meso, and macro levels, ranging from inter-human bodily relations, to transportation and street design, to urban and regional problems, to extended infrastructural space, transnational migration, and planetary resource circulation.

This scalar fluency will be necessary not only to address climate change and energy transitions, I argue, but also to develop the fundamental bases for mobility justice. This vision for mobility justice will offer a range of ways to move forward on a combined front toward more just socio-ecological relations that will transform not only transport within cities, but the entire system for the movement of energy, food, water, people, and ultimately carbon and the carbon-based life forms of our planet.

THE NEW MOBILITIES PARADIGM

Each of the contemporary crises around climate, urbanization, and migration are aspects of a wider disturbance in prevailing institutions, which in each case can be understood in relation to mobilities and explained through the lens of a new interdisciplinary approach called "the new mobilities paradigm." Unlike earlier studies of globalization, or late capitalism, the new mobilities paradigm does not assume movement and circulation to be a new phenomenon, nor simply a late modern global condition (as described in late twentieth-century theories of globalization). Mobilities have always been the precondition for the emergence of different kinds of subjects, spaces, and scales. Mobilities have histories, and the mobilities turn utilizes historical methodologies as much as of-the-moment mobile methods.

Not only is a focus on historically embedded and cross-cutting scales of mobilities crucial to understanding our contemporary crises, but also crucial is a cross-disciplinary theorization of mobilities based on a mobile ontology. A mobile ontology, in which *movement is primary as a foundational condition of being, space, subjects, and power*, helps us to imagine the constituent relationality of the world in a new way.[26] This approach builds on relational ontologies, in which "*nothing preexists the relations that constitute it*," as Escobar puts it. "In these ontologies, life is interrelation and interdependence through and through, always and from the beginning."[27] Rather than beginning social analysis from the sedentary perspective of nation-states and societies, or even of individuals and groups, as if these were pre-formed objects bouncing into each other like billiard balls, we can begin by trying to detect the relations, resonances, connections, continuities, and disruptions that organize the world into ongoing yet temporary mobile formations. Everything, including movement, is contingent on other moves.

Anthropologists were some of the first to question the ways that discussions about globalization in the 1990s were "founded on assumptions about movement: that movement generates change, that movement is self-evident, and that increasing mobility characterizes the present."[28] Anthropologist Bill Maurer, for example, asked whether the contemporary imagery of "quicksilver capitalism zipping around the globe in networked circuits" leaves unasked the questions that most needed answering: "What counts as capital, and what counts as movement? How do certain practices and processes constitute 'capital' such that it can 'move'? How do they also structure its 'movements' so that they can have the sorts of effects that [the] globalization literature ascribes to them?" These remain crucial questions still. Maurer suggests that when we assume that "the objects of property come first, and their movements second," we overlook the "contingent articulations that create objects of property, that underwrite different forms of 'capital,' and that permit different valences and vectors of 'movement.'"[29]

In contrast to these illusions of clean, quick, ethereal mobility, actual mobilities are full of friction, viscosity, stoppages, and power relations. We need to understand not only what is constituted as mobile, or potentially mobile, and what is not, but also where, when, and how there are resistances to that power, or counter-movements against it. Mobilities are always contingent, contested, and performative. Mobilities are never free but are in various ways always channeled, tracked, controlled, governed, under surveillance and unequal—striated by gender, race, ethnicity, class, caste, color, nationality, age, sexuality, disability, etc., *which are all in fact experienced as effects of uneven mobilities.*

Over the past fifteen years the theoretical perspective known as "the new mobilities paradigm" has developed to address such concerns. Since my publication with John Urry of a foundational article in 2006 and the launch of the journal *Mobilities*, with the editorial introduction "Mobilities, Immobilities, and Moorings," my own work has focused on themes of uneven mobility, inequality, and power exercised through mobility regimes not just in the present, but also in the past; not just in the Global North but also in the Global South.[30] I draw on that entire body of work here, and on my extensive experience in helping to form this new field through research networks, conferences, professional organizations, and dozens of publications.[31]

Mobilities research focuses on the constitutive role of movement within the workings of most social institutions and social practices, and focuses on the organization of power around systems of governing mobility, immobility, timing and speed, channels and barriers at various scales. It focuses not simply on movement per se, but on the power of discourses, practices, and infrastructures of mobility in creating the effects of both movement and stasis, demobilization and remobilization, voluntary and involuntary movement. Such discourses, practices, and infrastructures are culturally shaped by what we can think of as mobility assemblages—constellations of actors, actions, and meanings that are influenced by mobility regimes that govern who and what can move (or stay put), when, where, how, under what conditions, and with what meanings. The study of speed, its cultural valuation, and its uneven distribution has also been taken up within mobilities research, where it is explicitly linked to concerns over climate change, post-car and post-carbon transitions, and alternative mobilities.[32]

This approach originated out of the "spatial turn" in the social sciences. A key moment in a sociology of space involved debates engendered by the reception of Henri Lefebvre's *Le Production de l'espace* (1974), translated into English in 1991 as *The Production of Space*, and Doreen Massey's *Spatial Divisions of Labour* (1984) and her subsequent work. These influential texts examined the complex and varied movements of capital into and out of place, the resulting forms of sedimentation and spatial formation occurring within each place, and the struggles over space and its production. Massey's work influenced the emergence of a relational analysis of space, emphasizing that space was "the product of interrelations" and "always under construction."[33] This influenced sociologist John Urry's work, which was also concerned with space and the social relations of its production, i.e., space as a "set of relations between entities" not a container or an entity itself, an approach that would lead Urry to the ideas of "mobile sociology" and a "sociology beyond societies" at the turn of the millennium.[34]

The spatial turn took root and was deeply connected to global political economy and urban processes in the work of spatial theorists such as Edward Soja, David Harvey, Nigel Thrift, and Saskia Sassen in the 1980s to 1990s.[35] The theorizations of the spaces of "flow" and "network" became especially significant with Manuel Castells' *The Power of the Network Society* (1996), and an increasing emphasis on mobility, circulation, and flow within spatial theories of society. This led to a growing interest in scalar processes, and the new studies of place and nature as produced socio-spatial relations, envisioned as a "power geometry" of scalar configurations by political geographers such as Erik Swyngedouw, Kevin Cox, and Neil Brenner.[36] A major contributor to interest in mobility was Zygmunt Bauman who argued in *Liquid Modernity* that "Mobility climbs to the rank of the uppermost among coveted values—and the freedom to move, perpetually a scarce and unequally distributed commodity, fast becomes the main stratifying factor of our late modern or postmodern time."[37]

Urry's *Sociology Beyond Societies* (2000) helped announce mobilities as a key concept within an emerging spatial social science and humanistic inquiry. What differentiated Urry's and others' work within the mobilities turn was partly their radical emphasis on *complex mobilities* of all kinds as the ontological basis for all forms of relational space, and partly their deeper cultural analysis of how these political economic relational spaces were produced in and through social and cultural practices such as tourism, automobility, or consumption. Mobilities scholar Peter Merriman, for example, drew on process philosophy to show how places are in process, open, and dynamic spatial formations. His historical study of early practices of automobility in late Victorian Britain draws our attention to rhythms, forces, atmospheres, affects, and materialities as sensations of "movement-space."[38] Urry likewise included imaginative and virtual mobilities, as well as physical mobilities, tapping into the mobile imaginaries of all kinds of mobile subjects alongside the analysis of large-scale systems of mobility.

Mobility, in this view, is organized through specific constellations of uneven mobilities that may include transportation for daily commuting, migration, tourism, educational travel, medical travel, temporary work, smuggling, asylum seeking, military deployment, emergency evacuation, humanitarian travel, and many other kinds of human mobilities (and in many cases these overlap and occur at one and the same time). It also engages many non-human mobilities, including all kinds of logistical systems and infrastructures for the movement of things, plants, animals, weather, water, energy, and their relation to the movement of the Earth itself. And this complexity allows the field to intervene in many different disciplines and policy arenas.

The field has been influential across many areas of study, opening up many new avenues of research.[39] Within urban studies, for example, the new mobilities paradigm came to be understood as

> transforming the ways in which scholars think about space—especially urban space . . . Relational thinking about cities disrupts an overly containerized view of urban space and opens up new vistas for examining cities and their wider social relationships, connections, and flows.[40]

The mobilities turn also intersects with the field of border studies where there is a growing emphasis on bordering practices, ongoing processes of mobile border maintenance, and on new concepts such as borderscapes.[41] The study of international migration also suggests how (im)mobilities interact within a security politics focused on targeting, regulating, and intervening in circulation, such that we can think of "securitization" as a moving field of mobile practices occurring at many times and places.[42] Thus, the new mobilities paradigm also intervenes in critical security studies, and more broadly in the fields of international relations, development studies, and political economy.

Issues of uneven motility and of mobility rights, ethics and justice have become crucial to the field.[43] There has been increasing attention to concepts such as differential mobility, uneven mobilities, "motility" or potential mobility, mobility capabilities, and in general questions of power, justice, and mobility rights.[44] The governance of mobilities (or circulation) underlies the making of borders, and hence also the defining of territories and the emergence of national polities. A wide range of interdisciplinary and critical research has begun to theorize the political as mobile, or what some call "kinopolitical," a concept especially developed by Thomas Nail, which combines *kinos* (or movement, as in the word *kinesthetic*) with politics.[45]

Motility, or the potential for movement, depends on what Elliott and Urry call "network capital." All people have different capacities and potentials for movement but in general we can say that more privileged groups control more potentials, enjoy greater ease of movement, and can access a wider range of different kinds of motility. Network capital is a combination of capacities to be mobile. It includes having appropriate documents, such as passports and visas, along with money (financial capital) and qualifications such as education or professional standing (cultural capital). Having physical capacities for movement, such as shoes, appropriate clothing, good nutrition, and an environment that fits one's body, as well as vehicles and infrastructures. It also involves access to networks at-a-distance (social capital), meaning the ability to access family relations, bank accounts, or co-workers through communication devices, to find location-free information using wifi hot spots, and to have quiet and secure meeting places, as well as time and other resources for coordination.[46]

There is an uneven distribution of these capacities and forms of capital. Many people do not have access to easy mobility. They may face impairment due to design features as mundane as stairways, lack of public toilets, or inaccessible transport systems. They may face friction every time they move: cat calls aimed at women, racial aggression aimed at minorities, or rules that exclude homeless people or street vendors from sidewalks. They may be incarcerated, held in detention, or denied entry across a border. They may be forced to live far from city centers in peripheral neighborhoods lacking good transport connections, in so-called "food deserts" that lack access to social services and face high rates of eviction. And as we have seen after the recent hurricanes such as Katrina in New Orleans, Harvey in Houston, or Maria in the Caribbean, natural disasters can suddenly wipe out many forms of circulation, transportation, and communication. Those with low network capital are least able to bounce back from such interruptions or to mobilize alternative systems.

The idea of a "kinetic politics" recognizes mobilities as a constitutive political relation and even as *constitutive of* political relations. It is not just the migrant or the traveler who is mobile in these accounts, but the border itself and the infrastructure of state practices also move. There are complex combinations of movements *and* moorings within these mobility regimes that function to differentiate, channel, and separate various flows through sifting or sorting devices that speed some kinds of movement while slowing or stopping others.[47] Mobilities are organized in and through technical systems and such mobility systems presuppose immobile infrastructures. These infrastructural moorings are not only physical, but also involve embedded regulations, legal and juridical systems, bureaucracies, and social practices. The political, it could be said, is fundamentally mobile: political boundaries and identities are formed by im/mobilities.

Mobilities research also has a normative dimension: it engages not only in critical analysis of historical and existing mobility systems, but also models future transitions that might help to bring about alternative cultures of mobility. It asks how relations of (im)mobility are culturally made within and through social practices. This leads to questions such as: Who is able to exercise rights to mobility or dwelling, and who is not capable of mobility (or of staying still) within a particular situation? How have sovereign control and disciplinary systems historically produced differently marked bodies as unequal mobile subjects? How do local, regional, urban, national, and global systems for control over space, territory, communication, and speed produce differently disciplined mobilities, differentiated by race, gender, class, nationality, sexuality, etc.? What modes of counter power and subversive mobilities might inform the kinds of *moves* that can be made to resist, overturn, or escape these forms of mobile governance, territorialization, and securitization?

THE POLITICS OF MOBILITY

So far, I have argued, first, that a more robust and comprehensive theory of mobility justice can help us address the combined crises of climate change, urbanization, and global migration, as each part of a common phenomenon of unequal and uneven mobilities that impact everyday life at all scales. Second, I have suggested that the new mobilities paradigm offers a theoretical approach for addressing such multi-scalar questions, and indeed has already begun to do so. Now I want to consider how questions of justice inform this project in terms of a politics of mobility.

Mobility justice is an overarching concept for thinking about how power and inequality inform the governance and control of movement, shaping the patterns of unequal mobility and immobility in the circulation of people, resources, and information. We can think about mobility justice occurring at different scales, from micro-level embodied interpersonal relations, to meso-level issues of urban transportation justice and the "right to the city," to macro-level transnational relations of travel and borders, and ultimately global resource flows and energy circulation. This book will seek to connect these scattered histories and span these heuristic scales of the body, street, city, nation, and planet into one overarching theory of mobility justice.

Control over mobility as a form of power has deep historical roots. In her study of the liberal governances of mobility, Hagar Kotef traces the history of liberalism as a regime of movement in which the "free movement of some [people] limits, hides, even denies the existence of others." This nuanced view of freedom of movement poses some interesting conundrums for a liberal theory of mobility justice. "Control over movement," Kotef argues, "was always central to the ways in which subject-positions are formed and by which different regimes establish and shape their particular political orders." Liberal models of subjectivity, power, and freedom thus depended on the self-regulation of movement, such that "the liberal subject is essentially a moving subject, and her first and most fundamental freedom is freedom of movement."[48] However, as the liberal subject and citizen forms through rights to (well-regulated) movement, protected by the territorial state, this same process of differentiation simultaneously produces an "other" who suffers exclusion, enclosure, incarceration, and violence. This is crucial to understanding uneven and unequal mobilities today.

Kotef describes a split in early sources of liberal theory beginning with Hobbes and Locke, who each in slightly different ways, differentiate the mobility of the citizen and its others: "(I) the citizen (often a racialized, classed, ethnically marked, and gendered entity more than a juridical one), as a figure of 'good,' 'purposive,' even 'rational,' and often 'progressive' mobility that should be maximized; and (II) other(ed) groups, whose patterns of movement are both marked and produced as a disruption, a danger, a delinquency."[49] This divide, she argues, remains a split between populations today: "between those whose movement is a manifestation of liberty, and should therefore be maximized, and those whose freedom is a problem, and should therefore be tightly regulated." She develops this argument through an analysis of Israeli checkpoints and control over Palestinian mobility. But she also suggests more widely, "In our global and local travel, in patterns of migration and border crossing, in deployments of checkpoints—be it in poor neighborhoods or occupied lands—we can still witness this split."[50]

It is precisely this split that we see coming to the fore in current policies over borders and security in Europe, the United States and other white-settler nations such as Australia, but also internally in controversies over policing, racial profiling and mass incarceration of people of color. This argument is crucial for understanding why simply increasing urban accessibility is not sufficient for achieving mobility justice, even if it makes spaces of transit more accessible or inclusive. Transport justice continues to treat space as a container in which movement occurs, or, in Doreen Massey's formulation, which Kotef also cites, as a "surface on which we are placed."[51] Increasing access to transport—or to urban space more generally—will not solve the problem if we ignore the underlying processes and relations that produce mobility injustice, and which tunnel beneath transport (into the body) and beyond the city (into the world).

Kotef argues that "space becomes political via the movements it allows and prevents, and the relations that are formed or prevented via these im/mobilities." Thus, the struggle for mobility justice is a core political struggle, encompassing struggles over space, movement, and the relations of power that they enable or disrupt. "Moreover," says Kotef, "movement is one of the attributes of political spaces: political spaces are often moving spaces. Movement thereby becomes primary within the anatomy of political spheres."[52] The rights to march, to assemble, to strike, to picket, to gather, to occupy, to speak in public, and not to be arbitrarily imprisoned, are all contingent on rights to movement. This is true both within the politics internal to a city or a state, as well as external to it, including struggles over borders, citizenship, voice, and exit, incarceration, and freedom.

Who can "appropriate" the potential for mobility (including the right to stay still, as well as to move)? How can our understanding of sustainable transport and accessibility be inflected with a micro-politics of racial, gendered, (dis) abled embodiment, the meso-politics of the planning, designing, and building of infrastructures of mobility, the macro-geopolitics of migration, racialization, borders, and travel, and finally, the wider geoecological processing of energy and material flows around the world? These are not only political questions (What rights to mobility exist in a particular context and how are they exercised and protected?) but also ethical questions (What capabilities of mobility are valued, defended, and extended to all?).

Social movements have been crucial in calling attention to—and theorizing—these interconnected problems of mobility justice. From the emancipation movement to end slavery, to the transit justice struggles that began in the nineteenth century, to the bus rider protests and sit-ins of the Civil Rights Movement in the USA, for example, ongoing social movements have drawn attention to racial inequities in embodied access to spatial mobilities, which are more than simply questions of transportation. Historian Rod Clare observes that the Black Lives Matter (BLM) movement is just the latest chapter in a struggle over black mobility in the United States:

> Implicit in the rise of BLM and its attendant demands and concerns is the long-standing issue of black mobility. That is, *where* can black people go and *when* can they go there? This question is not only relevant for African Americans currently but also in their arduous history in America. The idea of black mobility has been a fundamental query since African Americans were brought to America as enslaved people. As such, their movements and associations were always strictly monitored and in many cases, prohibited by laws, slave patrols, and other means. After the end of slavery, this remained the case in the South and indeed in other parts of the country well into the twentieth century through the implementation of Black Codes, Ku Klux Klan terrorism, sharecropping contracts, city zoning laws, segregation, and various other means.[53]

Indeed, building on this perspective, I argue that the management of mobilities under post-slavery and postcolonial regimes in the liberal West is fundamental to the making of classed, racial, sexual, able-bodied, gendered, citizen and non-citizen subjects. It is not just that societies based on white supremacy happen to police black, Latinx, Asian, and Indigenous bodies, and various migrant "others," but that this constant policing of racial, gender, and sexual boundaries and mobilities is fundamental to the founding of white power through the construction and empowerment of a specifically mobile white, heteromasculine, national subject. And this power rests on the cooptation of others into supporting the dominant narratives of mobility as freedom which are embedded into Western fantasies, such as the open road, the inviting frontier, the paradise island, the conquest of wilderness, or the thrill of acceleration. Kinopolitics, in other words, is the ontological basis of present realities that waver "between freedom and unfreedom."[54]

The politics of mobility also necessarily takes other forms in non-Western cultures, and a comparative history of kinopolitics that addresses differing political cultures and "mobility regimes" governing gender, sexual, and racial differences in (im)mobilities around the world is yet to be written. There are, however, numerous new studies coming out every week of regimes of mobility in various parts of the world.[55] This present study will focus mainly on Western forms of uneven mobilities, but will try to point out the global implications of the ongoing planetary mobility crises that affect all of humanity and the non-human world.

This study also has an emphasis on urban settings and urbanization, although understanding these as extending into networked regions of rural connectivity as well as operational landscapes that draw in even remote "wilderness" areas for resource extraction. The question of mobilities within rural and remote areas raises other dimensions of unequal access that are not fully addressed here, including questions of gendered divisions of labor in farming, fishing, and food processing; the employment of temporary migrant workers in agriculture, tourism, and seasonal service work; the use of "fly in, fly out" work forces in industries such as mining and oil drilling; and the experiences of "slow mobilities" and questions of communicational connectivity in remote places.[56]

The concept of mobility justice draws on insights from arenas such as transport justice, racial justice, and environmental justice, but also differs insofar as it pertains to all forms of movement and focuses on the wide-ranging techniques for the management of different kinds of im/mobilities and mobility infrastructures. The promise of the new mobilities paradigm in the interdisciplinary humanities and social sciences is that it can bring together embodied movements for social justice (combining class, race, gender, disability, and sexuality), struggles for transport justice and accessibility, arguments for the right to the city and spatial justice, movements for migrant rights, Indigenous rights, and decolonial movements, and even dimensions of climate justice and epistemic justice—all under one common framework. This can help us to build more politically effective alliances and gain greater leverage over the urgent problems that will ineluctably shape our ways of moving, mobilizing, dwelling, and living in the near and distant future.

ALTERNATIVE MOBILITY FUTURES

Mobility Justice describes some possible visions for alternative mobility futures in which justice might pertain at multiple scales, and I make concrete proposals in each chapter for specific principles of mobility justice at each scale. These proposals take us far beyond the limited realms of transport justice as used within current urban policy making, and even beyond the notion of spatial justice, which is often attached to the city scale and the politics of localities, toward a more comprehensive and holistic paradigm in which multiple political struggles are brought together under the banner of mobility justice. In sum, a full theory of mobility justice would need to address at least the following elements of mobility injustice:

a) Injustices relating to embodied relations of gender, racialization, age, disability, sexuality, etc., keeping in mind Western capitalist histories of enslavement, resistance, racial formation, and class struggle, as well as struggles for women's emancipation, queer rights, and the rights of the disabled;

b) Struggles over "the right to the city," freedom of movement and the exercise of the right to assembly as a way of challenging unequal mobility and the uneven development of urban, regional, national, and global spaces;

c) Mobilizations relating to borders, migration, and other kinds of transnational mobility—including movements concerning the legality of slavery, human trafficking, violence against women, deportation systems, undocumented migrant arrest and incarceration, refuge and asylum policies, the creation of border walls and biometric databases, etc.;

d) The politics of the circulation of goods, resources, energy, pollution, and waste in a global capitalist system that lacks procedural justice in the deliberation over distribution of planetary matter and over the local impacts of the logistics infrastructures that move that stuff.

I argue that debates over sustainable urbanism, transport justice, and urban accessibility should be placed in the context of wider transnational mobility regimes, including questions of colonialism, borders, tourism, and migration. So, we might ask: What (im)mobilities have we given up to become "mobile" in modernity? What vectors of normative or hegemonic movement are we channeled into or conversely prohibited from exercising? What stories do we tell ourselves about the world becoming ever more mobile, and which forms of demobilization or forced mobilities do these stories mask?

Implicit in this line of argument is the recognition that mobility may not always be a form of freedom. It can also be a coercion: for those who are evicted or expropriated from their homes, who have lost their land or are rendered stateless, who are enslaved or trafficked, or forced to dwell in temporary camps with constant insecurity.[57] Mobility may even become a constraint for the privileged kinetic elite who must remain always in motion to live their "mobile lives," not to mention the restless couch-surfers and van-dwellers who, lacking affordable housing, jump from one temporary parking space to another in cities like Los Angeles, or hit the road to search for work in Amazon warehouses or in seasonal harvesting.[58] Mobility justice is as much about how, when, and where we dwell as how, when, and where we move.

Equally important, "subversive mobilities" may also be a form of resistance against dominant mobility regimes. Historian Jacob Shell has traced many practices associated with "ungovernable patterns of mobility and rebellious geographies of evasion and connection," often based around the use of subversive forms of animal mobility including camel trains in the desert, mule trains across hilly country, sled dogs in the far north, or elephant-based transport in South Asia. Anthropologist James C. Scott likewise gives a fascinating account of a vast region outside the state, known as Zomia, in the highlands of Southeast Asia where "autonomous people lived not only in the hills but also in the marshes, swamps, mangrove coasts, and labyrinthine waterways of estuarial regions." In these peripheral extra-state areas, "a zone of refuge from state power, a zone of relative equality and physical mobility," there was a constant movement of people escaping the reach of the state yet existing in relation to its modes of governance.[59]

Historians of early modern working classes describe "the unlikely ways in which the geographies of early Atlantic imperialism also provided a skeleton for the emergence of a surprising flesh of connections across vast spatial networks."[60] In the midst of slavery, dislocation, piracy, exploitation, and incarceration, argue Peter Linebaugh and Markus Rediker, there also took shape a mobile world of "sailors, pilots, felons, lovers, translators, musicians" and "mobile workers of all kinds [who] made new and unexpected connections." Taking inspiration from this, Deb Cowen finds similar processes at work in the fluid infrastructure space of the contemporary world, where "the Arab Spring, the Occupy movement, the so-called Somali pirates, a global wave of logistics labor actions, and Indigenous protests of new rounds of dispossession"—despite all their political differences—"point to the potential for a different occupation and organization of logistics space."[61] And we could add, a different politics of mobility: a kinopolitical struggle for alternative ways of moving and dwelling.

If throughout history subversive mobilities have challenged the injustices of dominant mobility regimes and offered other epistemic meanings and spatial moves, then there is hope for contemporary kinopolitical alternatives. In attempting to envision such a counter-politics of mobility, we might ask: What mobile ontologies are at play in the politics of mobility? What kinds of mobile publics might form to advocate for a more just disposition of mobilities? If the politics of mobility rests on the mobility of politics, then how can we create a new kinopolitics and with it, perhaps, a new mobile commons?

Chapter 1

What Is Mobility Justice?

Freedom of mobility may be considered a universal human right, yet in practice it exists in relation to class, race, sexuality, gender, and ability exclusions from public space, from national citizenship, from access to resources, and from the means of mobility at all scales. In many ways mobility justice is itself a mobile concept, insofar as it treats justice as an unstable configuration that moves across scales and realms. In this chapter I introduce various theorists of justice who can help us to develop a comprehensive approach to mobility justice. I trace discussions of several philosophical approaches to justice as they relate to transportation (e.g., utilitarian, libertarian, egalitarian, and capabilities approaches); elaborate on various understandings of how justice is put into practice (deliberative, procedural, participatory, etc.); and bring into the conversation the contexts in which these theories and practices of justice have been applied with a special emphasis on transport justice and spatial justice.

However, I argue that most theories of justice have been sedentary, meaning that they treat their object as an ontologically stable or pre-existing thing, which stands still before it is put into motion. In contrast, the new mobilities paradigm enables the development of a mobile ontology which not only tracks the effects of inequalities in mobility across various connected sites and scales, but also shows how justice itself is a mobile assemblage of contingent subjects, enacted contexts, and fleeting moments of practice and political engagement. Justice is not a once-and-for-all state or a series of abstract conditions that must be met, but is a process of emergent relationships in which the interplay of diverse (im)mobilities forms a foundational part. Most importantly, I argue that we cannot look at a single phenomenon like "transportation justice" in isolation. Nor is the concept of "spatial justice" sufficient to encompass all the concerns with mobility that are animating current political struggles.

Instead, we must consider how to combine the struggles for accessibility and bodily freedom of movement, for equitable infrastructures and spatial designs that support rights to movement, for fair and just forms of sustainable transport and ecological urbanism that reduce environmental harms and burdens, and for the equitable global distribution of natural resources and rights to move or dwell. Mobility (in)justices move across all of these fields of action, flowing from one into another, and often folding them all together or ricocheting across them all. Indeed, mobility injustices are not an occurrence that happens after entities "enter" a space (i.e., after travelers get into a vehicle, or people gather on a city street, or migrants enter a new country) but *are the process through which unequal spatial conditions and differential subjects are made.*

Philosophically, mobility justice is best approached through a mobile ontology that connects multiple scales and performative sites of interaction. Like many theories of justice, it is based upon an egalitarian frame concerned with fairness, equity, and inclusion, but I argue that we must also: a) extend the concept of mobility justice beyond a focus on transportation and beyond a spatial imaginary of the city scale; b) supplement it with feminist, critical race, disabilities, and queer theory perspectives on corporeality, relationality, materiality, and accessibility; and c) also bring in historical time horizons drawing on global Indigenous, non-Western, and postcolonial experiences and theoretical perspectives.

Sedentary theories of justice have not kept pace with social movements that are already cognizant of these kinds of connected scale-jumping relations and more flexible conceptual frameworks. Indigenous people's recent mobilizations against mega-infrastructure projects such as dams and pipelines across their protected lands, the international Occupy movements against social and economic inequality that began in 2011, the Black Lives Matter movement that began in 2013 against systemic racism (sparked by violence against Black Americans and especially police shootings), the ongoing transnational feminist movements for the rights of women, and earlier mobilizations like the Zapatista movement in Mexico have all demonstrated a rhizomatic form that is both locally rooted and globally mobile. Mobility justice is a way to theorize why such kinopolitical moves are necessary, how they are made, and the ways in which they might be sustained and extended in the face of entrenched neoliberal and neoimperial regimes of racialized mobility management, securitization, and territorialized injustice (e.g., extraction, exclusion, eviction, incarceration, and expulsion).

Crucially, this broader perspective on mobility justice requires more sustained attention to aspects of colonial history and an understanding of the historical formation of contemporary forms and patterns of global im/mobilities. This moves the theory of mobility justice far beyond current approaches to transport justice that have focused on day-to-day policy making around accessibility and infrastructure planning (important though that is), as well as beyond recent ideas of spatial justice that have focused on the city as a specific location, and delimited urban forms. Such nationally based, urban-focused politics of mobility have been too easily co-opted into projects of urban boosterism, "Smart Cities", "connected mobility", and gentrification through spatial fixes of the entrepreneurial city.[1]

My hope is that a more robust, multi-dimensional, and historically embedded theory of mobility justice—drawing on deeper and more far-reaching colonial, corporeal, and planetary histories and interrelations—can help us to find ways of combining political efforts and social movements that have heretofore been separated, joining them into a more powerful unified approach. It also points the way forward for an engaged social science that can more vitally help people address current political crises.

It could be argued that mobility justice most closely resembles the concept of transportation justice. The word mobility has even been used recently to simply replace transportation (e.g., "mobility services," "mobility on demand," or automobile companies like Ford declaring that they are now "mobility companies"). Alternatively, it could be argued that mobility justice most closely resembles the concept of spatial justice in its breadth and all-encompassing scales. However, I will seek to show how and why mobility justice goes beyond existing ideas of both transport justice and spatial justice, as these frameworks have not developed a mobile ontology and hence are insufficient to the task.

Existing theories of justice and applications of various critical perspectives on justice suggest how we might develop a more comprehensive, supple, flexible, and mobile concept of mobility justice. Grounding my argument in a longer view of colonial, racial, and gendered histories of unequal (im)mobilities, this chapter offers a critique of liberal theories of freedom of mobility, a critical history of colonialism and the colonial management of mobilities, and a recognition of a deeper geoecological planetary perspective on uneven and differential mobilities.

Addressing a far wider range of topics than are usually found in work on either transportation justice or spatial justice, this effort seeks to *mobilize* theories of justice. I argue that neither a liberal theory of justice nor a distributive approach to accessibility and urban space is sufficient to ensure mobility justice across all the differential bodies, uneven spaces, and entangled scales the closer analysis of which inform the rest of the book.

BEYOND TRANSPORT JUSTICE

A robust theory of mobility justice first requires understanding the relation between various philosophical approaches to justice. Acknowledging that many arguments in this field lack solid philosophical underpinnings, Anthony Perreira, Tim Schwanen, and David Banister explore the applicability of various theories of justice for thinking about transport. They consider the limitations of utilitarian, libertarian, and intuitionist theories of justice, and then develop an approach combining Rawlsian egalitarianism, based on American philosopher John Rawls's theory of distributive justice, and Capability Approaches (CA), based on the work of philosophers Amartya Sen and Martha Nussbaum.[2] While valuable in some regards (especially as pertaining to transportation), I suggest that these approaches are still too limited.

Perreira, Schwanen, and Banister draw on the work of political theorists such as Nancy Fraser, William Kymlicka, and Iris Marion Young to define justice as a broad moral and political ideal that relates to: (1) how benefits and burdens are distributed in society (distributive justice); (2) the fairness of processes and procedures of decision and distribution (procedural justice); and (3) the rights and entitlements which should be recognized and enforced.[3]

This is a useful starting point and can serve as an entry to begin to think about mobility justice. However, it is notable that in their review they admit that they set aside feminist theories of justice, which pay far more attention to questions of recognition, embodiment, and exclusion from deliberative processes (e.g., as found in Young's and Fraser's feminist philosophical approaches), and they also set aside questions of "the right to the city," which pay far more attention to spatial processes.[4] In other words, they narrow the focus to transport alone, and treat all individuals as more or less inhabiting the same bodies.

From a philosophical perspective, the utilitarian view of justice is the one most typically found in transport planning today, which takes the form of cost-benefit analysis (CBA) used to determine transportation investments. Built into CBA is the assumption that transport is about getting from point A to point B as efficiently as possible, and higher earners (and presumably tax payers) have higher priority. This generally leads to greater investment in automobile infrastructure and highways rather than in public transit and walkability, leading to the contemporary pattern of automobile dominance. "From a utilitarian perspective," argue Perreira, Schwanen, and Banister, "the eviction of, say, hundreds of families in order to expand a road would be perfectly acceptable, even if those families were not compensated in an appropriate manner."[5] Eminent domain has been used for precisely such purposes in the building of urban highways in the USA, for example, which also concentrate air pollutants in poorer neighborhoods inhabited by people of color, and often bypass the transportation needs of such communities while subjecting them to more dangerous road spaces.[6]

When transport is isolated as a matter of efficient movement, it becomes disconnected from the wider meanings of streets, neighborhoods, and communities and thereby ignores the valuation of diverse peoples' livelihoods, well-being, and health. CBA also presumes that space is an empty background that transportation infrastructure simply moves through. Maximizing the utility of some and sacrificing the space of others is part of the reproduction of power through which unequally mobile subjects are made. As Reid-Musson explains,

Car ownership and lack thereof marks extant divisions of class, gender, citizenship, ability, and race in North America [. . .]. Other research has investigated how safe and efficient travel and communications infrastructure are devised with an eye to the security of more privileged groups, providing them with spaces of movement that bypass and bisect the often insecure places where poor and racialized people live.[7]

So infrastructures for mobility that ensure the safety, security, efficiency, and comfort of the privileged may shape space in ways that not only prevent others from enjoying the same, but also actively create insecurity and discomfort by bypassing and bisecting these degraded spaces.

The distribution of mobility re-shapes space in ways that build uneven network capital such that the most powerful groups are able to occupy public space (including streets) and dominate political decision-making, while others may be marginalized, unable to assemble, or unable to stay in place because their "benefits" do not count for much and their "costs" are discounted in the aggregate analysis. When excluded and marginalized groups do enter public spaces such as sidewalks, streets, and transport corridors, they often face surveillance and suppression of their mobility, for example through policies that prevent homeless people and "vagabonds" from sitting or lying down, that force "sex workers" into delimited zones for "street-walking," that push side-walk-vendors out of prime locations, or that empower police to "stop and frisk" people of color.[8]

In contrast to utilitarianism, libertarian approaches to justice are based solely on individual rights and free market–based analytical frameworks. They assume that under ideal conditions, self-regulating markets lead to the most just outcomes. However, this is often found not to be the case, and is especially so in transportation infrastructure, which usually involves some kind of public subsidy, market failures, and non-market processes.[9] Moreover, moral philosopher Michael J. Sandel (whose famous course called "Justice" I took as an undergraduate at Harvard) argues that supposedly "free" contracts may involve large power imbalances such that it is impossible to establish free consent and choice.[10] Decisions over communal goods such as transport cannot be left to the market because those with power will utterly dominate choices, shaping the public realm in ways that prevent subordinate groups from giving free consent. The individualism of libertarian approaches may also lead to the unregulated use of public goods, "aggravating negative exter-nalities, including congestion, air pollution, and traffic accidents," according to Perreira, Schwanen, and Banister.[11]

Finally, Perreira, Schwanen, and Banister also dismiss intuitionist approaches to justice, associated with the philosopher Robert Nozick. Intuitionism is under-stood as a pluralist moral doctrine based in relativism, involving a complex balancing between differing senses of justice, such that every decision is context-dependent and ultimately arbitrary. They argue that it is not helpful to simply depend on vaguely felt intuitions in settling transport decisions amid competing moral values, and that we should be able to reach some reasoned agreements as to what is fair.

The Capabilites Approach

Perreira, Schwanen, and Banister therefore develop a Rawlsian approach to justice supplemented by a Capability Approach. John Rawls' highly influential theory of justice, first published in 1971, rests on two fundamental normative principles.[12] First, and having priority, is the principle that "the rules defining individuals' rights and liberties ought to apply equally to everyone and that individuals should have as much freedom as possible as long as this does not infringe the freedom of others." Second, the distribution of social goods (such as income, wealth, opportunities, powers, and the bases of self-respect) should "simultaneously (a) derive from a situation of fair equality of opportunity, and (b) work to the benefit of the least advantaged members of society."[13] According to this "difference principle," which sought to enshrine fairness, there may exist inequalities of opportunity and arbitrary effects; however, policies should rest on a distributive rule that seeks to maximize the minimum level of primary goods for the least well-off.

They also note the critique of Rawls by advocates of the Capabilities Approach (CA), such as Amartya Sen and Martha Nussbaum. For Sen, the distribution of resources or primary goods should not be an end in itself because it is incapable of recognizing the diversity of human needs and preferences, which concern deeply valued ends and aspirations. The Capabilities Approach takes the position that people's capacities are shaped by their opportunities, which are in turn shaped by both their internal capabilities and their external environment, including societal structures that might constrain a person's "functionings."[14] Thus, CA seeks to ensure the social provision of certain basic capabilities and minimum thresholds. Freedom of movement would be one such capability.

According to Nussbaum, a minimally just society requires that each individual has an entitlement to life, bodily health, bodily integrity, freedom of movement, and political and material control over one's environment. She describes these as capabilities, and there are many others that could be added to the list. CA has informed concepts such as "occupational justice," for example, which focuses on bodily capabilities and relates closely to feminist perspectives on justice as a bodily relation, which has often been sidelined in transport justice approaches.

Although Nussbaum's capabilities approach includes "the capabilities of being able to effectively participate in political decisions that affect one's life, to move freely from place to place, and having good health," Perreira, Schwanen, and Banister suggest that when CA is applied to questions of transport justice, the next move is usually to narrow the discussion specifically to questions of "inequalities of transport-related resources, observed daily travel behavior and transport accessibility levels."[15] Thus, rather than dealing with the full set of human capabilities to take part in moving, assembling, and decision-making, CA is narrowed to a practical question of how transportation access is distributed.

This distracts attention away from broader capabilities associated with freedom of movement, and toward a more delimited distributive approach. When applied to transportation, the notion of *distributive justice* implies not only the idea of equitable distribution of the means of transport (e.g., car ownership) and equal opportunities for access to mobility (e.g., proximity to transport services), but also the equitable distribution of the risks, benefits, and possible harms associated with mobility infrastructures (e.g., pollution, crashes). From a distributive justice perspective, poor and vulnerable populations are likely to experience not only the most limitations on access to transport, but also the greatest exposure to harm, injury, and death from unjust mobility systems, i.e., negative externalities.

For example, the poor are most likely to be excluded from access to convenient and safe forms of transportation, and suffer the highest rate of pedestrian deaths from motor vehicle collisions.[16] They are exposed to greater air pollution and health impacts of climate change. As gender, age, race, sexuality, and disability restrict movement in many ways, the least "able bodied" face major hurdles in accessing and moving through urban space, being "disabled" by built environments that prevent assisted mobility. There is also an uneven distribution of obesity and obesity-related diseases, which disproportionately affect poorer populations, including Indigenous peoples and disadvantaged immigrant populations. Thus, prevailing notions of "ability," "fitness," and "health" are racialized (as well as gendered), leading to accessibility problems with policies that focus only on "active transportation" such as bicycling.

However, transportation systems, and people's mobility more generally, cannot simply be infinitely expanded. Given the resource constraints on transport (road space, traffic congestion, energy costs) and the conflict between different exercises of "ideal" mobility (safety, pollution, greenhouse gases), it is clear that an extension of maximum mobility and speed to all (i.e., more people having access to cars, airplanes, highways, etc.), would simply increase congestion, greenhouse gases, and other environmental pollution harms. "From a social justice and environmental perspective there are considerable differences between policies that increase people's actual mobility and those that enhance people's capability to access desired destinations if they so choose," point out Perreira, Schwanen, and Banister.[17]

This is why the literature on transport justice focuses instead on *accessibility*, which "can usefully be conceptualized as the ease with which persons can reach places and opportunities from a given location and be understood as the outcome of the interplay of characteristics of individuals, transport systems, and land use."[18] Focusing on accessibility helps shift attention away from the idea of simply increasing mobility for all, leading to perpetual growth in movement and the associated problems of pollution and congestion. Problematically, though, accessibility still maintains the idea of a spatial container, focusing on the start and endpoints of such access journeys, such that mobility is seen as a means to an end. In other words, it treats space as merely an empty background for mobile activities, missing out on the ways in which mobility produces space, and the ways in which mobile subjects are relationally produced through their entanglements with each other and with spatial forms. I will return below to this concept of relational movement-space, but want to note here its absence in transportation justice theories.

From Accessibility to Equity

A key example of the focus on accessibility within transportation justice is the work of Karel Martens. In his book *Transport Justice: Designing Fair Transport Systems*, Martens argues for moving away from the focus on efficient movement in transport planning and toward a focus on the distribution of accessibility.[19] Unlike Perreira, Schwanen, and Banister, Martens draws on Ronald Dworkin's liberal political theory of justice, and concludes that a basic sufficient principle of justice is that "A fair transportation system is a system that provides accessibility to (virtually) all." Martens uses this principle to develop a measure of accessibility (based on data from Amsterdam plotting ease of movement against accessibility of jobs within thirty minutes' travel time from home).

This accessibility plot can be marked by a threshold (which is a matter of political deliberation) showing those who are in the domain of "sufficient accessibility," and those who are below the bar, in the domain of insufficient accessibility. Martens then argues that transport improvements within the domain of sufficiency should be self-financing, whereas in the domain of insufficiency, government subsidies and investments should be pursued to help lift people above the threshold. Thus he combines a kind of free market liberalism at the top end of the social hierarchy, and a state subsidized egalitarianism at the bottom end.

This leads Martens to declare three rules of people-centered transport planning: 1. Start from the people, not the system; 2. Do not assess transport interventions based on their efficiency, but in terms of their effectiveness in bringing people above the minimum threshold of accessibility (i.e., aiming for fairness in access rather than speed); and 3. Do not finance transport through car-based forms of taxation, but instead create income-based accessibility insurance schemes. These are valuable suggestions for guiding urban transport planning within the current system of European social democracies.

However, Martens assumes a rather benevolent, sensible, equity-promoting government; sets aside issues of participation in decision-making and the deliberative aspects of justice, which may exclude women, ethnic minorities, and the disabled; and presumes that changes in mobility systems will not change the urban spatial form itself, nor disrupt existing social hierarchies, nor transform relations to global sites of resource and energy extraction. This leads him to a rather limited focus on the role of urban design and policymaking, rather than questioning how superficially "fair" access to transport might be based on, and reproduce, unequal power, if it does not recognize the underlying wider politics of uneven mobilities.

Not only does this raise the question of the political viability of such a scheme in a less enlightened political arena (such as the United States, where automobility and the fossil fuel industry continue to dominate most transport planning), but it also leaves unanswered some basic philosophical questions about the ways in which mobility is deeply connected to ideas of freedom, individualism, and liberalism, ideas that have historically shaped and structured uneven spatial relations within a mobile ontology.

I propose that a wider lens of mobility justice calls for recognition, participation, deliberation, and procedural fairness to be up for discussion, adjustment, and repair. It also demands going beyond the sedentary ontology of most theories of justice, which take for granted space as background. Beyond access to transport, we need to understand the ways in which uneven mobilities produce differentially enabled (or disabled) subjects and differentially enabling (or disabling) spaces. We need a kinopolitical lens on the interdependent production of mobility spaces and (im)mobile subjects.

Transport justice, like other distributive theories of justice, presumes that there is a pre-existing space in which goods are distributed, or in which procedural justice occurs or entitlements are enforced, rather than presuming that space itself is up for grabs. Mobility justice, in contrast, built on a mobile ontology, suggests that political claims to access and goods (such as vehicles, transport, and accessibility) re-make spaces and subjects; it brings into play historical bodily relations, ecological relations, and wider global relations that inform the political arena.

Various scholars have deconstructed the problematic basis of liberal notions of unfettered mobility, ever-increasing speed, and, in general, the framing of movement as freedom, showing how meanings, symbols, and metaphors of movement, mobility, and travel are used in ways that obscure key differences of power between nationalities, classes, races, and genders.[20] Critics of distributive justice note that some forms of increased mobility participation can amount to barriers to other activities—i.e., building infrastructure for efficient automobility may limit pedestrian and bicycle access. Distributive justice is therefore insufficient to address mobility injustices.

While the shift toward a focus on accessibility goes some way to addressing this problem, transport justice nevertheless also requires *deliberation over substantive values* to determine what activities should be protected (such as funding for widening physical access to public transport systems), which activities should be reduced (such as free parking or subsidies for automobiles and highways, or more widely questioning the use of fossil fuels), and who should decide.

Deliberation over transport justice is therefore not simply about expanding mobility or even accessibility but must also concern itself with the cultural meanings and hierarchies surrounding various means of and infrastructures for mobility, including their valuation and who determines this value. In fact, it calls into question what constitutes relevant facts and meanings—i.e., are we deliberating over mobility, or health, or racial justice, or ecological well-being, and who decides? And even more radically, it would need to take into account how (im) mobilities shape space, subjects, and bodily differences in the first place.

Here, for example, is part of an Equity Statement from the Slow Roll Chicago Bicycle Movement:

> Bicycle Equity necessitates the public acknowledgment of structural, institutional and systemic racism in our society and their role in creating bicycle inequity here in Chicago. Equity is a public commitment to addressing, redressing and ultimately dismantling racism in a way which is direct and honest. Inequity experienced by some people is accompanied by unfair privilege for others who are not burdened by the same disadvantage and who benefit from a relative position of greater power than oppressed communities. Achieving bicycle equity requires the elimination of unfair privilege that has been gained via historical oppression and at the disadvantaged position of others.

> Bicycle Equity demands a public commitment to intentional diversity and radical inclusion within the bicycle advocacy, transportation and urban planning sectors as well as the broader cycling community. Equity is the promise to reflect diversity in a way which is intentional. This means achieving real inclusion is something that is beyond the realm of normal effort and is the extra effort required to be inclusive of people who have traditionally been marginalized, disadvantaged and disenfranchised in our society.[21]

This is a far more comprehensive and radical statement of what a fair movement toward mobility justice needs to achieve. It is about far more than distributive questions of access, and demands more than an egalitarian approach. Instead, it concerns overturning marginalization and disadvantage through intentional inclusion of the excluded in decision making and elimination of unfair privilege. It puts "oppressed" and "disenfranchised" groups front and center.

Perreira, Schwanen, and Banister ultimately argue that the application of the Rawlsian difference principle to transport implies prioritizing public transit, walking, and cycling in dense urban areas, and subsidizing car ownership in low-density, non-urban areas.[22] They argue for expanding the idea of mobility as a capability "into an understanding of accessibility as a combined capability," such that people are able to convert transport resources into access to "activities that are essential for meeting basic needs, such as food stores, education, health services and employment opportunities."[23] Like Martens, they argue that their egalitarian approach depends on defining certain minimum thresholds of accessibility, and establishing policies to guarantee minimum accessibility thresholds through legitimate democratic processes.

Even so, they note the difficulties in actually measuring accessibility, the tensions between focusing on person-based measures and place-based measures, and the challenges to the underlying ideas of agency and freedom of choice given the possible need for limitations on some forms of mobility to ensure greater overall fairness. It is precisely at the intersection of bodily differences in cabilities and entrenched spatial injustices that we need to shift our focus to the intersection of multiple scales and temporalities of kinopolitical processes.

Despite the important advances in using an accessibility threshold to conceptualize transport justice, therefore, the focus on minimum thresholds (and personal individual capabilities that arise in interaction with land-use patterns) overly restricts the concept of justice. Indeed, this book shows why the concept of transport justice is not capacious enough, and points toward the need for a broader notion of mobility justice, built on a mobile ontology.

FROM TRANSPORT JUSTICE TO MOBILITY JUSTICE

Mobilities theorist Vincent Kaufmann and his collaborators have defined "motility" as "the manner in which an individual or group appropriates the field of possibilities relative to movement and uses them."[24] In this regard, mobility justice involves some degree of deliberation over where to draw the limits of the field of possibilities and the limits of particular forms of using the capability for mobility. To "appropriate" mobility is to take ownership of it, to make it one's own; but perhaps in doing so we misappropriate what should be a common good.

At various times in Western democratic polities only upper-class, white, male citizens have been included, and only they have enjoyed freedom of mobility, of assembly, and of political participation.

Civic freedom requires a certain amount of freedom of mobility, but only some citizens are able to exercise this capability. As Judith Butler recently noted:

> There can be no democracy without freedom of assembly, and there can be no assembly without the freedom to move and gather. When the undocumented assemble, or when those who have suffered eviction assemble, or those who suffer unemployment or drastic cuts in their retirement, they assert themselves into the imagery and the discourse that gives us a sense of who the people are or should be ... making a demand with the body, a corporeal claim to public space and a public demand to political powers. As long as "security" continues to justify the banning and dispersion of demonstrations, assemblies, and encampments, it serves the decimation of democratic rights and democracy itself.[25]

This "corporeal claim to public space" implies that there is a mobile commons that must be protected. It is not just that the commons are shared spaces belonging to all the people, but that there must be a common right to gather and assemble: to form a commons or a plurality that can make "a public demand to political powers," as Butler puts it above.

Thus, the protection of freedom of assembly is a protection not of a specific space but of a kind of mobile commons that enjoys freedom of mobility, and that can appear anywhere: in a public square or at an airport arrivals hall, but equally alongside the Dakota Access Pipeline, in a forest to protect it from clear cutting, or at many other kinds of protest sites. Emerging applications of the Capabilities Approach to questions of transport not only emphasize the need for fairness in the distribution of transport and accessibility, but also call for greater attention to justice in transportation decision-making and participatory processes.[26]

We need to consider who is included in and excluded from transport planning and decision-making. Such *deliberative justice* should be further elaborated to take into account the potential for influence and the reasonable possibility that public input could impact the outcomes of a decision. Theorists of environmental justice such as David Schlosberg argue that efforts must be made to address pre-existing power inequalities between participants by using deliberative processes rooted in egalitarian principles (rather than pluralistic processes in which private interests compete).[27]

Deliberative processes first require *recognition*. Decision makers need to acknowledge the legitimacy of community members' participation and respect their input as an important and relevant contribution to decision-making. Building on the work of Nussbaum and Sen, as well as on political theories of recognition, Schlosberg argues that a capabilities approach to collective normative frameworks can "bring social and political recognition of specific and local vulnerabilities and the effects of climate change on the basic needs of human beings in various places and under different conditions."[28] If we extend this to considerations of mobility, then it becomes clear that we need greater political recognition of the vulnerabilities of specific groups to the harms of various kinds of mobilities (including transportation itself, but also, e.g., transport-related air pollution, greenhouse gases, and the resulting health impacts and bodily dangers) as well as the harms caused by severed neighborhoods and lack of accessibility.

This then feeds into discussions of *procedural justice*, defined as the meaningful participation of affected populations in the governance of transportation systems. This requires at least the following:

- Access to information
- Substantial understanding (which requires community-based participatory production of knowledge)

- Informed consent based on "local knowledge" not just that of experts, which must be grounded in measures to support capabilities for participation and understanding

Whereas climate justice frameworks call for broad-based stakeholder participation and a transformative approach to socio-ecological relations writ large, these have largely been absent from discussions of transport justice.[29] Procedural justice is needed to ensure the participation of disempowered groups in deliberation and decision-making processes.

Others have extended this to the notion of situated, bottom-up, interactive, participatory design, including "design for/by/from the Global South," as crucial to bringing about more just socio-technological systems.[30] Arturo Escobar links transition theories from the Global North (that largely focus on sustainability through low-carbon transitions) with feminist political ecology and Indigenous political ontologies that involve more trenchant critiques of Eurocentric capitalist modernity in the West. Procedural justice would need to ensure the possibility of opening fundamental debate over these kinds of epistemic and ontological questions.

Such processes might bring us beyond a narrow focus on transportation and accessibility, because principles of recognition and procedural justice would allow for a broader range of participants and for *other relevant topics* to be raised, such as the environmental harms of oil drilling, oil and gas pipelines, and hydraulic fracturing that support the current system of automobility, for example. These processes might also raise questions relating to the impacts of hydroelectric dams, land appropriation, and displacement of Indigenous populations; or questions of the use of fossil fuels for agro-industrial food production and circulation, and its potential social and ecological harms.

It could come into political view that not only are accessibility to transportation, jobs, education, and political participation crucial mobility justice issues, but so, too, are the conflicts over forest clearance to raise cattle for hamburgers and "fast food"; or over the Dakota Access Pipeline, Canadian tar sands exploitation, or drilling for oil in the Arctic; or over rights to refuge, asylum, and migration. More than accessibility is at stake.

The point is that these wider issues do not emerge as concerns within circumscribed discussions of transport justice, but they are crucial *mobility justice* concerns, which are fundamental to broadening the political framing and procedural issues that inform urban transport policy and planning. *Who* is recognized as a participant? *What* is recognized as a legitimate topic of deliberation? *Where* (and at what scale) should conflicts be resolved? The broader theorization of mobility justice within a mobile ontology that accepts entangled scales and fluid boundaries puts the discussion of transport justice on a different plane—or better yet, on a multi-dimensional space of quantum entanglements—that is about more than just transportation. It allows for a transit or transfer of deliberation to multiple kinopolitical issues.

Restorative and Epistemic Justice

When entire urban populations find themselves vulnerable to warfare arising from resource conflicts, and the natural disasters arising from a changing climate that threatens access to water, energy, or food, it is possible that we also need to conceive of a redress to broader mobility injustices in terms of *restorative justice*. Insofar as "kinetic elites," oil companies, and military-industrial powers have contributed far more to climate change, should they not also take responsibility for its harms on those who have contributed relatively little to global warming? When mobility becomes rationed or far more highly priced due to disruptions of infrastructure, the reaching of peak oil, or simply exercises of "austerity"-based control over "scarce" resources, then the inequalities of differential mobilities will be thrown into even sharper relief.[31] Issues of security and state securitization will increasingly come to the fore. Under such conditions the continuing harms produced by increased use of fossil fuels, harsh urban policing, and migrant exclusion, will cascade together to further exacerbate injustices of uneven mobility.

As we have seen under the Trump administration, there is a fundamental struggle over the facts underlying a whole range of policy issues, including those relating to mobility. Evidence-based policy is itself at risk. Gwen Ottinger's science and technology studies (STS) perspective on climate justice notes that relevant facts and information simply may not exist yet, as science and knowledge are emergent, may be contested, and may also undergo change over time. Efforts to include appropriate local knowledge in policy deliberations may need to go beyond procedural inclusion by opening up participation to many kinds of entities, especially if entire knowledge systems have yet to come into existence. Therefore, "procedural justice should include proactive knowledge production to fill in knowledge gaps, and ongoing opportunities for communities to consent to the presence of hazards as local knowledge emerges and scientific knowledge changes."[32] This can be referred to as *epistemic justice*, which involves recognizing and creating new forms of knowledge, new facts, and new ways of reconciling seemingly incommensurable ways of knowing.

Epistemic justice comes across very clearly in the position taken by groups working from marginalized perspectives, such as The Untokening project in their "Principles of Mobility Justice." First, they call for epistemologies arising from people of color to be brought to bear by opening information access, including the languages used in planning, and by drawing on local knowledge:

> Mobility Justice de-centers Eurocentric solutions as the default model and looks toward dynamic, grassroots approaches and solutions elsewhere, such as South and Central America, and Southeast Asia. It demands language justice and information access that does not exclude some because they speak different languages or through professional, technical, or academic jargon . . . Value the local knowledge of these communities and compensate them for sharing that wisdom.

When we rely on quantitative data to inform decision-making, or particular ways of expressing "facts," we may be "actively rejecting the knowledge and erasing the struggle and contributions of community residents."

Moreover, the "experiences and input of marginalized communities are often disputed or disbelieved by institutions of power." This leads them to call for new kinds of decision-making systems in which the marginalized can have power:

> Mobility Justice recognizes that communities are often treated as if they are unfit to design their own futures, guide public spending, or understand the "real" issues at hand—and demands that new decision-making systems and structures are created by and for these communities to center their visions and cultivate operating principles that align with their values and lived experiences. Communities must be able to reject oppressive frameworks and processes and create systems and spaces centered in our experiences. Decision-making processes must meet communities where they are, and embrace full leadership from these communities—not in ratifying or amending pre-ordained ideas but building new ways of interacting and sharing power.[33]

Mobility justice will furthermore require admission of responsibility, truth and reconciliation, as well as finding ways of making reparation to those harmed by climate change due to the excessive mobility of others, concepts which are associated with the idea of *restorative justice*. In the aftermath of Hurricanes Irma and Maria in the Caribbean, for example, the vice-chancellor of the University of the West Indies, Sir Hilary Beckles, has called for the European Union to pay for the implementation of a "new Marshall Plan" for the Caribbean, based on reparations that are owed for slavery and colonialism, as well as overwhelming responsibility for climate change. Beckles co-chaired the CARICOM Commission on Reparations, which put this case to the British Parliament, where it was roundly rejected. Yet he could directly trace the plantation-owning families and the banks in Britain today who had vast fortunes and political power arising directly out of slavery and the parliamentary compensation paid to slave owners after emancipation (for loss of their property in humans).

We might also extend this call for reparations to oil companies such as Exxon Mobil, Shell, and BP that actively profited from oil fields and petroleum refineries based in the Caribbean, making huge profits on the sale of products that contributed to climate change and directly led to climate conditions (especially warming seas) that have exacerbated hurricanes.

To summarize, I have suggested so far that we need to go beyond the current discussions of transportation justice because they are unable to capture the full multi-scalar and entangled dimensions of mobility justice as sketched above. I favor a sliding focus of attention that encompasses distributive concerns, including accessibility, but also opens the debate toward wider concepts such as deliberative, procedural, restorative and epistemic justice (see Table 1). These do not exist as a hierarchy, but as a kind of interplay in which there are interactions between narrower and wider apertures, as the focus shifts to different elements of justice within a mobile ontology.

None of these approaches to justice, however, grapples with an additional underlying problem: the spatial and geographic dimensions of mobilities. In many ways, all the theories of justice reviewed thus far are *non-spatial* or *a-spatial*. That is to say: they take space for granted as a container for social processes. One of the fundamental insights of the spatial turn in the social sciences (and of the new mobilities paradigm) is the need to move beyond a-spatial theory and toward an understanding of mobilities as performative of actually existing assemblages of spaces, practices, and material worlds.[34] Edward Soja's important theorization of "spatial justice" is useful and would seem at face value to be highly relevant for theorizing mobility justice in a way that moves beyond debates about transport alone. Spatial justice, however, also faces its own limitation of being an *immobile* ontology.

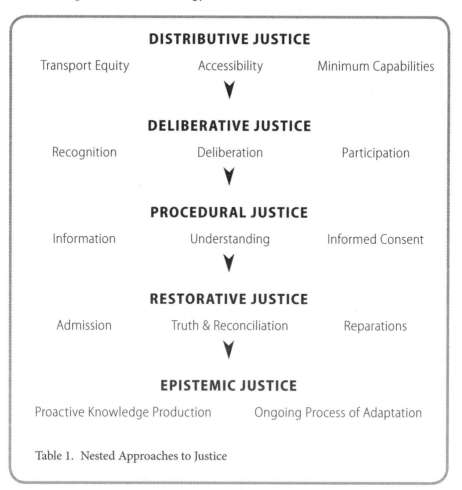

DISTRIBUTIVE JUSTICE

Transport Equity   Accessibility   Minimum Capabilities

DELIBERATIVE JUSTICE

Recognition   Deliberation   Participation

PROCEDURAL JUSTICE

Information   Understanding   Informed Consent

RESTORATIVE JUSTICE

Admission   Truth & Reconciliation   Reparations

EPISTEMIC JUSTICE

Proactive Knowledge Production   Ongoing Process of Adaptation

Table 1. Nested Approaches to Justice

MOBILIZING SPATIAL JUSTICE

One might ask why we need a theory of mobility justice when we have the very influential existing concept of "spatial justice." The concept of spatial justice has its origins in Henri Lefebvre's work in the 1960s on the right to the city (*Le droit à la ville*, 1968); and the concept of "territorial social justice" that geographer David Harvey first outlined in his 1973 essay "Social Justice and Spatial Systems" and developed further in *Social Justice and the City*. Harvey understood social justice in distributional terms, as "a just distribution justly arrived at."[35] He interpreted this concept through the spatial lens of a just "territorial distribution" in which "income," broadly understood, is fairly allocated across the population within a given territory, with mechanisms for allocating resources to the least territorially advantaged, poorest regions.

Elaborated on especially by American urban theorist Edward W. Soja, the concept of spatial justice focuses on the fair and equitable distribution of the resources of the city, including access to transportation. Yet, in Soja's telling, transport is simply a means to an end: getting somewhere to access something else (education, jobs, healthcare). His emphasis is not on mobility itself, but on the locations it connects. Ironically, although his book *Seeking Spatial Justice* begins with the example of the Los Angeles Bus Riders' Union (BRU), his approach to spatial justice in general has very little to say about either transportation or mobility more generally.[36]

The BRU was a movement in Los Angeles in the 1990s to block public investment in suburban rail projects in favor of more equitable investment in urban bus transit, which served more people and especially people of color and poor people. It was an exemplary "transit justice" movement concerned with political decision-making relating to urban transport, accessibility, and procedural fairness in determining infrastructure investments, and thus the "politics of mobility."[37] Soja's arguments help us understand this transit justice movement as part of a wider set of social struggles over urban space. Unlike the previous transport justice perspectives mentioned above, which in some respects take space and urban land use itself as a given, a spatial justice perspective such as Soja's, and before him Lefebvre's, opens up attention to questions of social power in the production of space.

Nevertheless, I argue that Soja has a very *still* concept of urban space, or at least a place-based and local perspective that reduces his interest to specific urban locales and locality-based political movements, even while recognizing the multi-scalar nature of the city. Thus, he writes:

> We can speak of unjust geographies involving the human body, as in debates about abortion, obesity, stem cell research, the transplantation of body parts, sexual practices, or the external manipulation of individual behavior. At the other extreme, the physical geography of the planet is filled with spatially defined environmental injustices, some of which are now being aggravated by the uneven

geographical impact of socially produced climate change and global warming. These two extremes, the corporeal body and the physical planet, usefully define the outer limits of the concept of spatial (in)justice and the struggles over geography *but will not be discussed any further here.*[38]

Soja quickly drops the multi-scalar understanding (which brings into view the rich intersecting mobilities of urban life, out of which uneven corporealities and planetary urbanization are themselves produced) to focus instead on "specific conditions of urban life" and what he calls "mesogeographical" struggles between the micro and the macro. He understands spatial justice as a "struggle over geography" with a focus on the specifically urban-scale space of the city, and thus, like Harvey, he generally resorts to a distributional justice perspective, in which more fair and equitable urban access would be the solution to spatial injustice.

This leads Soja to limit his analysis in ways that foreclose insights into mobility (in)justices and how they contribute to *producing differential spatial and mobility relations across many scales*. For example, in his chapter "On the Production of Unjust Geographies," Soja focuses on a series of phenomenon that relate to the occupation of territory: walls, citadels and ghettos, borderlands, and elite islands. He describes each in terms of the unjust spaces that they produce, but he fails to foreground the unjust mobilities that they depend on and reproduce. Using the example of Eyal Weizman's *Hollow Land: Israel's Architectural Occupation* (2007), Soja emphasizes the processes of home-destruction by bulldozers, and the building of new walls and barriers as a battle over space. Yet these processes are also very much battles over (im)mobilities: tunneling as an active process of moving through walls and barriers as a way of not just managing but remaking and channeling the mobilities of Palestinians. These "spatial tactics and strategies" are mobile strategies, producing mobility injustices as well as spatial injustices.[39]

Likewise, when he describes Mike Davis's *City of Quartz* (1990) on the "defensive fortressing of urban life" in Los Angeles, these gated communities, "privatopias" and "security-obsessed islands" are not just about spatial control, but also mobility control. The "imagined threats of invasion," trespassers and "incursions of the homeless and hungry," are struggles over contested mobilities—invasions, trespass, and incursions, after all, are forms of subversive movement.[40] Public space and the "commons" are not just places that we need to protect against privatization, but are suggestive of a mobile commons that goes beyond public or private property. Soja writes:

> All the publicly maintained streets of the city as well as crossroads, plazas, piazzas, and squares are part of the commons, and so too are the mass transit networks and the buses and trains (if not the automobile) that move across the city. Think not just of the Bus Riders Union case but also of Rosa Parks demanding her democratic

spatial rights to sit anywhere on a public bus. Are sidewalks part of the commons? Are beaches and parks? And forests and wilderness areas?[41]

These are all sites of mobile commons, we might say, where there have been crucial kinopolitical struggles over who can assemble and move through them, involving questions of movement that spill far beyond the city or "the urban" itself. Yet, like the theorists of transport justice discussed above, Soja also quickly reduces this to "distributional inequalities" and "discriminatory geographies of accessibility."[42] In other words, he focuses on the right to access particular places, not the right to mobility as fundamental to the production of space and mobile political subjects in the first place. He reads these inequalities of access through the lens of David Harvey's concept of "territorial injustice," linked to the "urbanization of injustice," and also relates it to "environmental justice" in terms of the location of environmental hazards in urban locations. But what if we were to shift the focus to mobility justice?

Just as theories of transport justice are reduced to questions of transport distribution and accessibility, Soja reduces spatial justice to questions of "locational bias" at the urban scale and "uneven development" at the global scale. Yet he keeps setting aside the uneven mobilities and strategies of managed (im)mobilities that shape these uneven geographies, producing excluded, disabled, imprisoned, or otherwise limited bodies whose racialization, sexualization, or "othering" shape the limits of who is a political subject in the first place, and what are the appropriate places and forms of politics.

He argues that the "geographies that we have produced will always have spatial injustices and distributional inequalities embedded within them"; yet distributing access to space would not solve the problems of mobility injustice without deeper deliberation over epistemic and restorative justice.[43] Soja is so intent on highlighting the spatial nature of these processes, that he overlooks their mobile nature. He critiques Rawls for his "fundamentally a-spatial and ahistorical notion of justice," yet Soja himself offers a sedentary notion of spatial justice, bounded by the urban limits and the localness of the urban spatial imaginary.[44]

Beyond the Western City

One of the great limitations of Soja's theory of spatial justice, moreover, is its lack of attention to colonial histories and neocolonial presents. Drawing on theorists such as Lefebvre and Harvey, he tells a story of urban crisis beginning in the 1960s and re-emerging in the 1990s. It is a history centered in Western industrial cities, from Paris to Los Angeles. When Soja argues, for example, that the "city, with its meeting places and public spaces, was the wellspring for thinking about democracy, equality, liberty, human rights, citizenship, cultural identity, resistance to the status quo, struggles for social and spatial justice," his version of Western European and North American "urban industrial capitalism" ignores other histories of urbanization in other parts of the world.[45]

What does the story of spatial justice look like from Cairo or Lagos, Jakarta or Mumbai, Rio de Janeiro or Mexico City? Even within the Western world his retelling completely erases the global struggles over plantation slavery across the Americas, and especially the significance of the Haitian Revolution as a key moment in thinking about—and advancing—democratization, liberty, equality, and the other forms of social and spatial justice such as human rights and citizenship.[46] A focus on "the city" makes such global struggles invisible, and disconnects the coerced mobilities of enslavement, colonialism, and imperialism from the broader discussion of mobility rights and spatial justice.

A more far-ranging relational and *mobile* spatial history results in a different story, at a different scale, with different time frames. Histories of slavery and anti-slavery, colonialism and anti-colonialism, are also histories of the mobilities of various kinds of labor, capital, commodities, natures, and cultures.[47] We cannot think of spatial justice as a Western, urban phenomenon without putting it into the wider, extended processes from which it arises and to which it is always related.

Such a sedentary approach to the city ignores the biopolitical and geopolitical mobilities of the city itself. Cities are made out of the mobilities of differently abled, gendered, sexualized, and racialized bodies in relation to each other. Migration remakes urban space, including not only human movements, but also the more-than-human movements of food, resources, energy, diseases, animals, pollution, waste, etc. Migrant mobilities of all these kinds are crucial elements for conceiving of mobility justice, which is lost in approaches to transport justice or spatial justice that simply look at what is happening "inside" cities at the frozen meso-geographical scale.

A theory of mobility justice is equally attentive to the regimes governing the global circulations of people *and* things, humans and more-than-humans in what some consider to be a posthuman world. Questions of mobility justice include the ontological definition of *who counts as a person*, which as we know has historically excluded women, the enslaved, queers, and the differently abled, and continues to exclude non-human animals, plants, and living entities that are in fact included in many Indigenous ontologies. Mobility justice also demands recognition of Indigenous land rights and the notion that there is an "aesthetics of community" beyond the dualisms of Western philosophy, such that all humans are part of social relations that may include the land, and other non-human entities.[48]

Mobility justice brings to light the infrastructural and logistical power that courses through transnational struggles over rights to mobility across borders, as well as the intra-corporeal powers of the body. Critical Marxist geographies of "state rescaling" and urban restructuring emphasize the historicity of social space, the polymorphism of geographies, the dynamic restructuring of scale, and the continuous remaking of state space and urban space. Neil Brenner argues that "the image of political-economic space as a complex, tangled mosaic of superimposed and interpenetrating nodes, levels, scales, and morphologies has become more appropriate than the traditional Cartesian model of homogenous, self-enclosed and contiguous blocks of territory that has long been used to describe the modern interstate system."[49] Brenner then goes on to theorize this as the emergence of a new form of "planetary urbanization" connecting together distant global regions through extensive infrastructures of resource extraction and energy transfer.[50] But there has so far been little effort to connect such theories of multi-scalar dynamics to questions of mobility justice.

Meanwhile, conflicts between migrant labor and nativist labor movements are one of the key ways in which such scalar fixes are contested. Although Soja notes the "immigrant struggles" in the *banlieues* of Paris, as discussed by Mustafa Dikej, the issues of migrant mobilities, detention, and expulsion are not central to his imagined geographies of urban politics. Soja describes the "decanting" of the urban working class from the center of Paris and the "efficiency of movement" instituted by Baron Haussmann's building of the great boulevards in the 1870s, yet never connects these aspects of the movement of populations to a question of mobility justice in and of itself, nor to the mobile ontologies by which space is produced.[51] What is the relation between the movement in Paris of workers out of the urban core, the ease of moving military troops through the boulevards, and the later conversion of these same suburbs to places of post-colonial immigrant settlement and segregation?

The city is (re)structured but it is also in play. Mobilities do not just take place, but also make place. Cities are not only sedimented spaces of injustice, but also are active mechanisms for producing uneven mobilities, unequal bodies, and unbundled infrastructures—especially colonial and postcolonial cities. Soja moves quickly through a brief section on "colonial and postcolonial geographies" that draws on Edward Said's work to argue that "the real and imagined geographies, the material, symbolic, and hierarchically organized spaces of colonial occupation along with the processes that produce them, contextualize enclosure, exclusion, domination, and disciplinary control," as well as possible forms of resistance.[52] These cases of "unjust geographies" are at their core concerned with the power to control and direct mobilities (and settlement), yet Soja focuses only on their production of unjust spaces rather than of unjust mobilities.

One of my aims in this book, therefore, is to shift our attention to the ways in which a kinopolitics of (im)mobilities is fundamental to many forms of injustice, and injustices are perpetrated and perpetuated through the control and management of (im)mobilities. We know that mobility does not always equal freedom. But is the concept of spatial justice enough? What if we understood locations or places of dwelling such as cities not simply as "spatial" but also as mobile? We could then envision space as a regime of control over movement, and we could begin to challenge mobility regimes as methods for making spatio-temporal formations of power.

Moreover, such spatial processes also increasingly involve the splintering of virtual space and uneven communication infrastructures, as much as the splintering and remaking of physical spatialities.[53] The mobilities turn in the social sciences builds on spatial theory, but also mobilizes it.[54] This subsequently can help us to mobilize the concepts of the city and spatial justice to encompass many other places that extend from the bodily to the planetary.

COLONIAL REGIMES OF MOVEMENT

The history of colonial regimes of movement and the global mobilities that colonialism entailed, have largely been invisible within discussions of transportation justice and spatial justice. Modernity, progress, and privileged forms of white masculinity have long been associated in Western thought with mobility, while immobility, stasis, and sedentary states—or "bad," irrational mobilities such as nomadism, wandering, or vagabondage—have been attributed to "backward" societies or "primitive" peoples.

We find this, for example, in the discussions of so-called Oriental despotism, Eastern serfdom, and Medieval feudalism in the works of Karl Marx, Max Weber, and Emile Durkheim, considered the founding fathers of modern sociology. The sea-faring discovery, exploration, and exploitation of the New World for "primitive accumulation," the "spirit of capitalism" associated with modern northwestern European Protestant cultures, and the American ideology of manifest destiny and the opening of the frontier are just a few of the cultural touchstones which define the West as mobile and expansionist. The iconic masculine figures of the explorer, the entrepreneur, and the frontiersman require implicit "others" who do not exercise autonomous self-directed mobility: women, children, slaves, servants, bonded workers, lazy poor, and wild natives.

What if we reincorporated colonialism as a regime of mobility control into our accounts of the problem of spatial justice? Historian Ann Laura Stoler points out that a "colony" as a common noun is "a place people are moved in and out; a place of livid, hopeful, desperate, and violent *circulation*. It is marked by unsettledness, and forced migration." Beyond that, though, a colony "as a political concept is not a place but *a principle of managed mobilities*, mobilizing and immobilizing populations according to a set of changing rules and hierarchies that orders social kinds: those eligible for recruitment, for resettlement, for disposal, for aid, or for coerced labor and those who are forcibly confined."[55]

This is a crucial point. It suggests that the theory of spatial justice would take a more mobile turn if we recognized "the city" or "the nation" not simply as a fixed place but also as a principle of managed mobilities, one that extends from the inside to the outside, from the metropole to the colony, from the local to the global, from the interior of the body to the furthest reaches of empire.

In other words, Stoler mobilizes the concept of the colony itself, destabiliz-ing it, showing its oscillations and ambiguities. She argues, "If security can in part be defined by access to 'freedom of circulation or freedom of movement,'" as suggested by Michel Foucault, "then a colony is never secure."[56] Discourses of security always rest on arguments for control and surveillance of mobility, strengthening of borders, and exclusion of dangerous "others," as we have seen in the Trump administration in the United States in 2017. Yet, "Inside and outside are mobile locations that cannot be maintained as viable borders once and for all . . . They take the form of enclosure and containment, but what and who must be kept out and what and who must stay in are neither fixed nor easy to assess. Internal enemies are potential and everywhere."[57]

And so ultimately, Stoler argues, the colony (and we could add the contempo-rary US) is full of "transgressions, escapes, flight, detention, suspicion, illicit border crossings, entrapment, and more surveillance."[58] Like the colony, we can destabilize a geographical idea of the city as a bounded spatial unit by imagining urbanization as a mobile process. Like colonies, cities today are sites of anxious circulation: "*From inside and out, a colony mobilizes fear, insecurity, and force,*" writes Stoler. "No one is immune. Colonies, designed as safety nets and havens, are never safe. Such settlements called 'colonies' are nodes of anxious, uneasy circulations; settle-ments that are not settled at all."[59] Cities, too, are not settled at all.

In many ways, the urban worlds described by Soja, as well as the borders of the US or Europe today, are just as much places of off-and-on fear, insecurity, and of unsettled and unsettling mobilities. The unjust spatialities of the city and the modern state are produced by the unjust mobilities of the world, its colonial circulations, enclosures, and containment—its fragile forms of mobility manage-ment and racialized bodies. And cities, states, and their infrastructures are constantly being remade in relation to global flows not only of people, but also of circulating bacteria and viruses, invasive species and fungal attacks, not to mention cyber threats, virtual attacks, and data leaks, with all their resulting intensification, acceleration, and securitization.

For now, my key aim in conceptualizing mobility justice far more widely than either transport justice or spatial justice can is to revisit and *mobilize* a theory of spatial justice by putting the production of space into motion. We cannot focus on questions of distributive justice alone, or even simply of expand-ing deliberative or procedural justice, without understanding the more deep-seated workings of neoliberal governances of mobility and the ways in which it orders freedom and unfreedom, centrality and marginality, recognition and expulsion. To do so entails exposing the multi-scalar processes of uneven (im)mobilities and the political and social struggles over conflicting mobilities that take place at many different scales—the mobilities of a queer body, a widened sidewalk, a complete street, an accessible public transit system; the mobilities of a tourist, a migrant worker, a refugee; or the conflicts over building of universal public infrastructures for the movement of water, energy, or communication.

Beyond that though: How do rapidly urbanizing regions in the Global South challenge our prevailing ideas of infrastructure, movement, and borders? What is the relationship between automobility, bicycling, electric vehicles, and animal-powered transport in the cities of South Asia or Africa? Is there a potential tipping point toward new modes of urbanism and transport planning beyond a cost-benefit analysis based on an imaginary model of "rational," "individual" "consumers"? What other forms of global kinopolitics are at play in the rolling out of both transportation and communication infrastructures? The sooner we begin to think about these as cross-cutting and multi-scalar transitions, the more likely we will be able to envision the social and political consequences of the (possible) end not only of automobility and its culture of speed, but of unjust mobilities of all kinds.

Disasters and the resulting disruptions of mobilities are one instance in which a range of different kinopolitical problems come into view. For example, elsewhere I have described a troubling and complex politics of (im)mobility in which the post-disaster mobilization of those with network capital produces new infrastructures, mobility systems, and logistical flows that further distort access for the very people they seek to help. Especially when those "victims" are held within the borders of an island state from which exit is tightly controlled, we can speak of an *islanding effect* in which highly motile foreign responders bring assistance to some of the affected population while holding the "internally displaced" in place. From post–Hurricane Katrina New Orleans to post-earthquake Haiti, and perhaps in post–Hurricane Harvey Texas and the post–Hurricanes Irma and Maria Caribbean islands, there is an ongoing process of serial displacement, marginalization, and containment of the mobility poor— as if they were marooned on an island of misery, even while surrounded by the coming and going of well-equipped frequent flyers.[60]

The urban is not "in between" the local and the global, or between the micro and macro, but is a relational articulation of a biopolitical and planetary urbanization that permeates and works across all scales at once. The multi-scalar approach to mobility justice that I seek to develop in this book thus includes a multi-layered politics of mobility, including at least the following: everyday embodied relations of racialization, gender, age, disability, sexuality, etc., which inform uneven freedoms of mobility and unequal capabilities; the right to the city and the mobile commons, often with a politics of occupation and presence in public space that disrupts normalized spaces of efficient flow; ethical spaces for contesting borders, migration, and other kinds of transnational (im)mobilities—slavery, trafficking, deportation, asylum seeking, etc.—in contested contexts of securitization and militarization; the just circulation of goods, resources, energy, etc., in a global capitalist system that lacks procedural justice in the distribution of planetary matter; and related struggles that connect local environmental injustices to the logistics infrastructures that move people, goods, energy, pollution, and waste around the world.

The rest of this book seeks to elaborate on this argument and develop a more comprehensive theory of mobility justice that draws on elements of transportation justice and spatial justice, but also goes beyond them and offers epistemic alternatives. I shall work across scales, starting with bodies, then transportation systems, city-scale systems and urban infrastructures, border regimes and transnational mobilities of migration and tourism, and finally planetary mobilities and geoecologies. While this sense of enlarging scale serves as an organizing rubric, clearly these scales are always entangled, intersectional, performative, and constantly being remade. If state rescaling, as described by Brenner, is itself one of the strategies of the management of mobilities, jumping across scales is not only a spatial fix for capital and a conduit for escape by the kinetic elite, but also a potential tactic of resistance by the subversively mobile who lead us toward a new kinopolitics.

Chapter 2

Bodily Moves and Racial Justice

At the scale of the body there is a kind of choreography of human movement in various assemblages and constellations. Our movements are performed in relation to other people, to vehicles, and to prosthetic technologies that assist our mobility, as well as to spatial and material affordances of the built environment that enable or prevent various kinds of movement. Humans seldom move alone, but almost always in ways that are dependent on others, connected with others, toward (or away from) others, and sometimes for or on behalf of others. It is not simply that social factors such as gender, race, sexuality, class, age, and ability shape our capacities and styles of movement in relation to other people, but rather that our capacities for movement shape our bodily experiences and identities within normative social orders and hegemonic mobility regimes. Our bodily movements in turn shape and are shaped by environments, infrastructures, and places, through our mobile desires, capacities, and limitations.

More than that, though, we perform our bodies through movement, leaving traces in spatial and social worlds. "We look, we listen, we wend our way through landscapes that continually shape and reshape our movement-abilities. These environments favor some bodies over others. We are differentially mobile," as Kim Sawchuk puts it in her thoughtful essay on "impairment."[1] Our bodies are performative but differentially empowered or impaired to be motile. Our movements make the world and make ourselves, in a dance of relational moves in which power is always corporeally in play. We can imagine the orchestration of these bodies, capabilities, spaces, and means of movement as a kind of choreography, but a highly constrained and at times even coerced dance. This movement-ability concerns not just driving, bicycling, walking, or flying, but also wheeling, crutching, wriggling, rocking, hobbling, and a whole panoply of other mobilities, some of which engender fear, recoil, and social violence.

We move within choreographies of access to different constellations of mobility, constellations that involve physical movements, their meanings and representations, and their uniquely lived experiences, as Tim Cresswell describes.[2] The concept of uneven mobility, therefore, refers, foremost, to this choreography as a terrain for movement and as experiences of moving in which there are specific embodiments, divergent affordances, routes, and pathways, differential access and means of moving, and partial assemblages of (dis)connectivity—in short, differential mobility capabilities. Second, it refers to means or modes of movement that have a greater or lesser degree of ease, comfort, flexibility, and safety with more or less friction, noise, speed, or turbulence. Third, it refers to the spatial patterns, infrastructural spaces, and control architectures that govern and multiply such relations of mobility and immobility, speed and slowness, comfort and discomfort—in other words, the governance and management of mobilities. In this chapter I will examine the bodily bases of these uneven mobilities, and the politics of resistance they elicit at the scale of the human body.

First, we must note that in general there is an absence of gender awareness and gender analysis in much of the policy discourses surrounding transportation, mobility, and issues of mobility justice. White, able-bodied, middle-class, male experts and technicians dominate transport policy and urban transit agencies, hence policy, planning, and design often overlooks women's, children's, disabled people's, and poor people's perspectives, experiences, and needs, or see them as irrelevant to the sector.[3] Likewise, there is little racial analysis of differential or uneven mobilities, and only a slight awareness of the impairment or exclusion of the differently abled, and almost no thought, until recently, to the mobility of queer and transgender people. And very seldom are these exclusions and impairments to mobility placed in the context of longer and often violent histories of patriarchy, racial domination, colonialism, sexism, and ableism as the foundations of "liberal" civil societies.

In the 1990s, feminist thinkers in some cases embraced postmodern "nomadic theories" and process theories. At the same time, however, they criticized theories of globalization for generalizing about the West and promoting generic ideas of "nomadism" that were based on blindly masculine understandings of the freedom of mobility of the white, male, privileged mobile subject.[4] Feminist theory helped to convey political economy and cultural analysis into a more multi-dimensional analytical approach to the *spatial formations* of class, race, gender, and sexual inequalities.[5]

So while many writers trace the mobilities paradigm through a Western male philosophical tradition disseminating from classical theorists such as Marx and Simmel, through postmodernists such as Deleuze and Lefebvre, and eventually through contemporary thinkers such as Bauman and Urry, a strong case could be made that this genealogy ignores the contributions of feminist philosophy and the questions it has raised about the gendered, racial, and classed scaffolding of all forms of human mobility and mobility governance. Black critical theory, black feminist theory, and postcolonial theory have received even less attention in the canonical discussions of mobility, space, and justice.

This is why the new mobilities paradigm is not simply about privileging discourses of mobility, nomadism, or cosmopolitanism but seeks to delineate the contexts in which both sedentary and nomadic accounts of the social world operate. This requires an understanding of how gendered, racialized, colonial, and neoliberal discourses of (im)mobility operate and circulate, and how they are reinforced and destabilized.

Anthropologists, especially, have called for greater attention to "bounded mobilities" and the dynamics "by which mobility becomes bounded and interacts with immobility and inequality in a variety of contexts." Nina Glick Schiller and Noel Salazar emphasize the ways in which mobility is contingent on socio-structural constraints and is always part of power "regimes" that are embedded in sociopolitical, historical and economic relations.[6]

Which mobilities are promoted and which are impaired? Whose mobilities are celebrated and whose are blocked? What kinds of mobility are seen as an inalienable right, and how are such rights stripped from some categories of people, such as women, racialized ethnic minorities, sexual minorities, or migrants and refugees? And how do the differential representations and practices of mobility interface with one another?

We can also draw on histories of colonialism and its gendered/racialized modes of governing territory and managing mobilities to show the connections between intimate moves and transnational circulations. The politics of mobility is deeply informed by colonial histories, including histories of coerced mobility, labor exploitation, sexual economies of bodily abuse, and the violent movement of white settler-colonialism and "imperial duress," as Ann Stoler calls it, around the world.[7]

A strong current of Caribbean cultural theory and postcolonial theory was also influential in this 1990s wave of critical theory, concerned with diaspora, transnationalism, and various global mobilities of people, goods, and ideas (e.g., Stuart Hall, Arjun Appadurai, Edouard Glissant, Antonio Benitez Rojo, etc.). This work recognized the founding of modern forms of mobility and immobility within the transatlantic slave trade, the plantation economy, and the forming of creole cultures and subsequent diasporic identities. Transatlantic slavery fundamentally shaped (and in many ways continues to influence) late modern systems of uneven mobility, differentiated belonging, and unequal rights to dwell and to move freely.[8]

We need a combined analysis of gendered and racialized differential mobilities, as well as of other spatial impairments to the capability for mobility, situated explicitly within histories of slavery, colonialism, and patriarchy. Uneven mobilities operate at the scale of bodily relations, taking the form of differences in gender, race, class, sexuality, and ability as they relate to regimes of mobility control. Differential capacities for movement affect what it means to be human and the ways in which people form mobile subjectivities such as the "free man" or the "slave girl," the "driver" or the "footman," the "athlete" or the "crip." Yet such bodily relations also suggest counter-geographies of subversive corporeal movement. To understand these subversive moves and new spatial possibilities, we first need to reconnect the discussion of mobility justice to the corporeal struggles over gendered, sexual, disabling, and racialized mobility regimes.

GENDER, SEXUALITY, AND BODILY MOVEMENT

The concept of "differential mobilities" has been a growing focus in mobilities research. It is widely recognized that mobilities are never free and unfettered but are striated by "a whole series of rules, conventions and institutions of regula-tion and control . . . a systematized network."[9] In particular, Kim Sawchuk recalls Doreen Massey's work on "uneven geographies of oppression" to think through how power is "evident in people's differential abilities to move."[10] Massey observed that "some are more in charge of [their mobility] than others; some initiate flows and movement; some are more on the receiving end of it than others, some are effectively imprisoned by it."[11] Gendered and sexual distinc-tions and inequalities are one of the primary sets of conventions and institutions by which bodily mobility is differentiated and unevenly enacted in processes imbued with social, cultural, economic, political, and geographical power.[12]

I want to begin with a rather stark depiction of such differentially gendered mobilities, as described by the French theorist of acceleration and speed Paul Virilio. His 1984 book L'Horizon negatif (translated in 2005 as Negative Horizon: An Essay in Dromology) opens with a section called "The Metempsychosis of the Passenger." It is a sobering account of unequal gendered mobility, which a liberal feminist might find objectionable because of its male-centered narrative and objectification of women as *vehicles* for men, while a radical feminist might recognize some resem-blance to theories of patriarchal domination. I quote it at length to get the full flavor:

> Man is the passenger of woman, not only at the time of his birth, but also during their sexual relations . . . we could say that the female is the means that the male found to reproduce himself, that is to say, to *come* to the world. In this sense, woman is the first means of transportation for the species, its very first vehicle, the second would be the horse [*monture*] with the enigma of the coupling of dissimilar bodies fitted out for the migration, the common voyage . . . At the origin of domestication, woman preceded the raised and bred animals, the first form of economy, even before slavery and husbandry. She begins this movement that will lead to the pasto-ral societies, patriarchal societies organized for war, beyond the primordial hunt . . . Patriarchy arose with the capture of women and then established and perfected itself through the husbandry of livestock. In this economy of violence that signalled the pastoral stage, beauty preceded the beast, it is the coexistence of this twofold livestock that favoured the establishment of the dominant sex . . . Some time before the pack animal, woman served as beast of burden; like the herd, she worked in the fields, controlled and supervised by men. During migrations, in the course of conflicts, she carried the baggage. Well before the use of the domesticated donkey, she was the sole "means of transport."[13]

It is significant that Virilio includes gestation itself as a mode of travel in which the unborn (male) fetus is carried by its mother, and extends his account to sexual relations in which one person (male) "mounts" or rides the other (female, in his account). In this regard, we can understand a fundamental inequality in the performance of human embodiment in which the female body is subordinated to the male body because of these profound forms of human carriage. However violent one might find this description of what he calls "the first transportation revolution," Virilio seems to have hit upon the fundamental basis of freedom of movement in the domination of the bodies of others, whether female, animal, or slave, and the relation of this domination to the means of war as a power of transportation, or logistics.

This shifts our understanding of freedom of movement away from the usual liberal narrative, which begins with presumed rights-bearing individuals who exercise their freedom of movement. Rather than the assumption that all people enjoy equal mobility, we must begin our analysis from an account of profound inequality in which the freedom of mobility is at once an exploitation of others whose self-movement is coerced by bodily control and domination in the service of others.

In the next passage, Virilio shows that men's freedom of movement rests on the "logistical support" of the "domesticated female" as a kind of "automobility" that frees men to wage war:

> The first freedom is the freedom of movement, the 'woman of burden' [*femme de charge*] provided the man of the hunt with this, but this freedom is not one of 'leisure,' it is a potential for movement that is identified with the potential for war, beyond the primitive hunt. The *first logistical support*, the domesticated female establishes war in taking over the hunter's maintenance for him; just as the territory will be laid out by the invader for the best movement of his forces, so also the woman captured and taken as a mate will immediately be changed into a means of transport. Her back will be the model for later means of portage, all automobility will stem from this infrastructure, from the pleasing conquered croup; all the desires of conquest and penetration are found here in this domestic vehicle. This woman-of-burden who will continue this portage from gestation and early infancy gives the warrior time, sometimes a *good time*, but above all *free time*.[14]

In this promiscuous passage, Virilio links together sexual pleasure, logistical power, and freedom of mobility, all achieved by and in support of violent conquest of women and of territory. Through his study of the technologies of war, and more broadly what he calls "dromoscopy," Virilio thus connects freedom of mobility directly to the means of violence and violent domination (including sexual domination) that underlie modern "civil" society.

Thus, it becomes more visible how limitations on women's mobility are closely linked to threats and practices of violence against women. Even the exercise of a "good time" is predicated on sexual domination, and "free time" is based on the exploitation of women's time, bodies, and labor. Missing from

Virilio's study, however, is any sustained analysis of colonialism as a form of violent domination over the mobilities of racialized others. This requires an intersectional analysis, for example, showing how the "liberation" of *white women* to enjoy "freedom of movement" may in fact be predicated on the subordination of women of color who become the colonized "women-of-burden".

Such an analysis might also suggest how white women's attainment of freedom of movement into the public sphere and the workplace has been policed and delimited by the exercise of masculine sexual domination. The unmasking of male sexual violence against women by the #MeToo movement at the end of 2017 (revealing ubiquitous sexual assaults across the public workplace, whether in Hollywood, Congress, television, or academia), resonates with the pervasive exercise of sexual domination as the very basis for gendered power. Yet the exposure of many more women of color, domestic workers, service workers, factory workers, migrant non-citizens, and agricultural workers to such sexual assaults in their own workplaces has elicited far less outcry than those highlighted by the #MeToo movement.

The point here is that women's day-to-day mobilities are enmeshed in the regime of control over women's racialized bodies and heteronormative sexualities within various patriarchal societies, and this, in turn, shapes wider patterns of labor control and migration in the service of the logistics of warfare and economic domination.[15] And the mobilities of bodies coded as black or brown are likewise enmeshed in histories of colonial control over differential mobilities, as well as of subversive resistance. The tensions among these managed mobilities and the resistance against them often generates frictions that take the form of interpersonal violence.

More than two decades ago, Arjun Appadurai pointed out in his perceptive essays on the cultural circulations of globalization how: "Women in particular bear the brunt of this sort of friction, for they become pawns in the heritage politics of the household, and are often subject to the abuse and violence of men who are themselves torn about the relation between heritage and opportunity in shifting spatial and political formations."[16] We might also consider stories of the surveillance and violent policing of women's mobility under various non-Western polities, which has become a standing characteristic of Western fascination.

This fascination goes back to nineteenth-century Orientalism and Hollywood portrayals of the Middle Eastern "harem," and today encompasses media depictions of Islamic fundamentalist regimes that limit women's mobility—for example stories about assaults on women using public transport in India or Egypt, the only recently won right of Saudi women to drive, the mobility constraints implied by wearing the burkha, etc., that is, stories that, when told in the Western media, also help to symbolically locate "the West" as a space in which women by definition enjoy greater freedom of mobility. A very different set of stories of "Muslim movers" emerges from scholarship engaged in "a dialogue between Islamic concepts, Muslim practices and gender and mobilities theories."[17]

If cultural judgments about the value of mobility have historically been posed in such gendered and racialized terms, it is not surprising that tropes of home and dwelling are feminized in ways that essentialize gender difference, romanticize a home-bound femininity, and often devalue the sedentary spaces and bodies associated with women.[18] Women are often defined as lacking a "mobile subjectivity," being rooted in place and home, while narratives of masculine becoming often hinge on travel, hitting the road, and escape from home. In both Western and non-Western cultures, men and women as well as boys and girls have had different patterns of access to bodily movement and to geographical travel, whether locally, nationally, or internationally. It is a question "not simply about *who* travels but *when, how, and under what circumstances?*"[19]

We can understand this as variation not only in access to mobility, but as David Kronlid argues, as a question of mobility as a "capability" which may be more or less constrained and enabled in different historical and cultural contexts. Everything from styles of clothing and footwear, use of prosthetics and mobility aids, physical abilities and limitations, all shape differing capabilities for movement. These enablements and impairments are in turn designed into clothing, dwellings, buildings and cities, as well as inflected by styles of moving or constraining bodily moves. Feminist theorists, for example, have drawn attention to social practices that teach boys to use their bodies more expansively in space, while girls are taught to restrain their movements and "throw like a girl."[20] Women cover their heads, limbs, and bodies with "modest" dress constraining their mobility. Indeed, in many countries, official dress codes prevent entry into public buildings (such as schools, hospitals, courts, and government offices) if one is wearing clothing deemed unsuitable, which might include sleeveless shirts, shorts, short skirts, slippers or flip-flops. Such dress codes become a way of excluding "undesirable" people (e.g., homeless, poor, vagrant, migrant) and especially women.[21]

Men learn to spread their legs on the subway, while women learn to take up less space and cross their legs. Boys often are accorded more freedom than girls to move around their neighborhoods, to engage in unsupervised walking or bicycle riding to meet with friends, to go camping, fishing or hiking, or to ride on public transport. The white, non-impaired, masculine body is culturally performed as a more mobile body, while the feminine body (and the non-white body) becomes more restricted and spatially circumscribed. Socialization of boys and girls, in sum, often produces a distinctive embodied *habitus* and "bodily hexis," to use Bourdieu's terms, in which boys have more latitude for movement, activity, travel across space, and risk-taking, while girls—as well as non-heteronormative boys—tend to be enculturated into more sedentary activities, more circumscribed occupation of space, and greater risk aversion (in part through threats of and actual acts of violence).[22] Such capabilities for mobility are deeply tied up with the production of white masculinity and its materialization in particular kinds of embodied agency.

Feminist theories of mobility as a relation of power suggest the fundamental relation of mobility, domination, and violence, thereby unmasking that which is invisible in contemporary liberal discourses. Stories of mobility as freedom and associated "nomadic theories" that celebrate metaphors of mobility, travel, cosmopolitanism and flight are often said to rest on a romantic reading of mobility that is highly gendered and racialized.[23] Beverley Skeggs argues that global mobility discourses more generally can be linked to a "bourgeois masculine subjectivity" that describes itself as cosmopolitan: "Mobility and control over mobility both reflect and reinforce power. Mobility is a resource to which not everyone has an equal relationship."[24] As Sheela Subramanian argues, there is a "deep link between 'race,' gender and movement in space," and gendered mobilities are always also racialized. Drawing on philosophers of embodied performance Judith Butler and Frantz Fanon, Subramanian shows how "bodies and spaces produce one another, and how the racialized [and gendered] body is constituted through immobility."[25]

Freedom of mobility is not only unevenly distributed in Western societies according to gender, age, and race, but also may in some cases occur as a kind of constraint to enact certain kinds of "good" mobility. In societies based on auto-mobility, for example, the increasing concerns for risk-management and middle-class security, combined with expectations of certain forms of "good mothering," constrain middle-class mothers into highly flexible forms of "hyper-mobility," as they feel the need to escort their children everywhere.[26] Privileged groups of highly mobile professional women may experience "the gendered difference in caring for social relations," such as caring for elderly parents, which over their life-course restricts their mobility as "gender gives shape to mobility and migration" among all socioeconomic groups.[27] Boyer, Mayes, and Pini argue that "narrations of mobility and fixity are used to reinforce not only the normative striation of women's movement but gender binarisms themselves in which women are positioned as fixed and men as mobile," although such dualisms might also suggest potential for destabilization within everyday practices and non-binary frameworks.[28]

More generally, as Robyn Law has shown, binary gender differences profoundly structure mobility and limit the social meanings attached to movement.[29] But this also implies their potential for transformation. In challenging both the naturalization of dominant narratives and the gendered binaries on which they rest, the new mobilities paradigm can contribute to destabilizing such binaries and the unequal power relations that they constantly perform and reproduce. We might mobilize our bodies to leverage other relations with space: "If to change ourselves is to change our worlds, and the relation is reciprocal, then the project of history-making is never a distant one but always right here, on the borders of our sensing, thinking, feeling, moving bodies," as feminist philosopher J.K. Gibson-Graham put it.[30]

How we move might move how the world is made. Many cultures through-out the world have limited or circumscribed women's ability to travel and to move. Religious practices associated with female modesty (such as veiling, *purdah*—a form of female seclusion practiced among Muslims in South Asia— or general separation of the sexes) have prohibited women's travel or made it possible only if escorted by male relatives. Cultural fashions such as foot-bind-ing in China, corsets in the Victorian era, or high-heeled shoes in the modern global city also are understood as limitations upon female mobility, and even as a fetishization of female immobility. In other respects, though, we might note that foot-binding or the wearing of high heels are a signal of the elite status of those privileged women who will no longer carry burdens, but will instead be served by other subordinates to carry them. Either way, there are potentials for resistance to these embodied practices and sexual geographies.

Critical geographer Katherine McKittrick crucially calls attention to black women's geographies not only as spaces of resistance and negotiation of these moves but also as "areas of working toward more just conceptualizations of space and place."[31] She pays attention to a range of sites that contribute to a discussion of "the connections between justness and place, difference and geog-raphy, and new spatial possibilities." She calls our attention to under-recognized spaces of black women's bodily resistance, including the "space between her legs," the slave auction block, and the attic garret as a hiding place for runaways. This radical geography offers "a different way of knowing and imagining the world"—and a different way of imagining movement through it. It opens an entire terrain of "black moves," which potentially subvert the control of bodily mobility capabilities, and challenge the sexual violence of the patriarchal mili-tary state through forms of "citizenship from below" and embodied freedom.[32]

Women's sexual mobilities are a site of profound social contestation, long linked to concerns over prostitution and other forms of sexual economic trans-action that take place outside the home. In recent times this set of concerns has been caught up in movements against "trafficking," in which men are assumed to be the "traffickers" of women; but international sex work often involves complex intersections among migration, mass media, tourism, and diaspora.[33] Women may experience the mobilities associated with migration and with tour-ism as simultaneously liberationary and coercive, enabling new projects of the self, yet constraining them into particular gendered/racialized performances.

Tourist fantasies and seductions of the exotic just as strongly influence Western women's expressions of sexual desire through travel—in which poorer black and brown men have also participated in sex work—raising questions about "mobile sexualities" and the construction of racialized bodies in "hot" locations such as the Caribbean.[34] As Appadurai noted, deterritorialized money, commodities, and persons intersect with the "mediascapes" of film, entertainment, and pornography to produce "loops which tie together fantasies about the Other, the conveniences and seductions of travel, the economics of global trade and the brutal mobility fantasies that dominate gender politics in many parts of Asia and the world at large."[35] Sexuality, in other words, is always kinopolitical.

Queer migration politics have helped to show how sexuality is constructed and managed through the control of mobilities at the border and within the nation, and is in fact crucial to the formation and stabilization of national identities. Recent studies of "queer migration" have built on earlier work such as Gloria Anzaldua's influential *Borderlands/La Frontera: The New Mestiza*, to destabilize the binary constructs of male/female, native/foreign, home/away that have long informed the construction of national borders and heteronormative identities.[36] An entire field of sexual geographies has also begun to trace the many ways in which "multifaceted movements—migration, physical and social mobility, and motility—underpin the formation of gay enclaves and recent transformations in sexual and gendered landscapes."[37]

In sum, feminist, black, and queer studies have offered remarkably productive new conceptualizations of the politics of mobility at the intersection between bodies and the production of space. Gender, race and sexuality are stabilized and destabilized through kinopolitical struggles over (im)mobilities, shaping potentials for movement as well as physical, psychic, cultural, and environmental impairment.

IMPAIRMENT AND DISABLING ENVIRONMENTS

Unjust mobility regimes are also expressed in built environments, streets, borders, and cities that impair some kinds of movement while enabling others. Critical disabilities scholar Laurence Parent argues that, "Despite the growing literature on walking practices, mobile methods, differential mobilities, and mobility justice, little is known about what it means to move through cities using a wheelchair."[38] The field of critical (and queer) disability studies has been crucial in drawing attention to the varied forms of inaccessibility built into our cities, and the intersectional ways in which these limit and constrain diverse kinds of bodily mobility. This work offers another crucial dimension to the theorization of mobility justice.[39]

Disabling environments are a kind of violence, dehumanizing the differently abled (and indeed all of us) much in the same way that Virilio's account shows the dehumanizing of women, and critical race theorists show the dehumanizing of racial others. In each case, domination is achieved through control over the mobility and immobility of subalterns, advantaging some while impairing others, and leaving our common humanity under erasure. The movement for universal access has sought to transform built environments, as well as to draw attention to the injustices of our current transportation and communication systems, and wider urban environments and public spaces. This is a fundamental basis for mobility justice.

Theorists of disability understand bodily impairment as part of a *disabling effect* of the capitalist city and a form of social oppression that is not located in the body but is built into the architectural and spatial environment. Brendan Gleeson, for example, argues that:

> disability as a specific socio-spatial experience, is a critical feature of the capitalist city . . . A powerful disabling feature of capitalist cities is their inaccessible design. This means that the physical layout of cities—including both macro land-use patterns and the internal design of buildings—discriminates against disabled people by not taking account of their mobility requirements.[40]

From a mobility capabilities perspective, then, the impairments produced by non-universal designs are a question of mobility justice. Geographer Rob Imrie likewise argues that, "assumptions of unrestricted movement and mobility in contemporary Western societies are hegemonic in prioritizing specific bodies and modes of mobility and movement."[41] Mobility justice requires designing for the movements of all kinds of bodies and this has entailed broad social movements by those who are impaired to demand more inclusive and universal spaces.

Geographer Tim Cresswell likewise reads disability theorist Michael Oliver to show how practices of walking tap into "a set of meanings associated with being human and being masculine. Not being able to walk thus falls short of being fully human."[42] Thus we see scholars call for moving beyond the linguistic category of the "physically disabled" to instead imagine the "mobility impaired." While there is much debate over the term "impairment," it is clear that over the life-course we are all to some degree "prosthetic citizens" whose capacities for mobility "depend on the constraints" and affordances "of the public sphere."[43] As the ancient Sphinx's Riddle demanded for entrance to the Greek city of Thebes: "What is the creature that walks on four legs in the morning, two legs at noon and three in the evening?" Oedipus is said to have correctly answered, it is "Man", who over the course of his life also usually experiences variable degrees of loss of eyesight, hearing, and physical capability, through which the mobility impairments of our physical environments become more obvious. These impairments may relate to aging or injury, but not necessarily, and may be linked to structural inequalities that expose poorer populations to higher rates of mobility impairing diseases such as asthma and diabetes.

Whatever the cause of impairment, it is clear that the privileged subject in the mediascapes and the physical environments of the city is the enabled, autonomous, and individual mobile subject—often male, often upper middle class, often white. Not only do individuals have different kinds of mobility capabilities (and stories), but they also have different degrees of access to participation in decision-making about urban design and transport planning. Mobilities of transport and mobilization for political protest are closely related: without bodily freedom of mobility there may be no way to disrupt the ruling mobility regime and its kinetic elites.

Despite emphasis on the politics of mobility in work by Cresswell, Adey, and others, mobilities researchers have not spent enough time showing how forms of knowledge production shape the ways in which embodied differences of uneven mobility are orchestrated, choreographed, and governed in ways that produce differences of class, gender, race, ethnicity, nationality, sexuality, and physical ability. Critical disability studies have shown us how mobility infrastructures are not only "splintered" between favored elite and disfavored non-elite spaces, but also produce deeply "differential mobilities." Sawchuk argues that "the term 'differential mobility' is germane for thinking of how some movement-repertoires give preference to bodily norms that create hierarchies of corporeal differences that are structured into the built environment." Such structures are also a kind of infrastructure in which some people may "find themselves distanced from the 'able bodied' and excluded from the world that does not allow them to move through with any ease."[44]

In contrast to privileging efficient flows of traffic and unfettered mobility, whether for the fast-moving pedestrian or the rush-hour automobile commuter, we might argue that there are "vital frictions" that take place within the uneven terrains of corporeal mobilities, for example as diverse people pass on a sidewalk, as they mix, slow, and pause for social encounters of conviviality or conflict.[45] Spaces of uneven mobility and differential impairment are always contested through a micro-politics of proximity and crowding. The marginalized (including those whose mobility is impaired in various ways) might leverage the blockage of movement to create a politics of occupation as a presence in public space that disrupts "normal" and normalizing mobility spaces and offers epistemic alternatives by physically enacting differential mobilities. Such assemblies create a kind of mobile commons. Whether assembling in a street, building an off-grid communications network, or creating a protest camp at a pipeline construction site, there are many ways to mobilize a kinopolitics that reclaims mobility space from the kinetic elite.

The Slow Roll Chicago Bicycle Movement, for example, makes a point of bringing together otherwise fragmented communities around casual, slow, cycling events that purposely deemphasize cycling as transportation. As co-founder Reed explains it, the aim is to bring communities together in a ritual of social cohesion, where they can move together in public space, share stories, and in doing so improve individual health, as well as rebuild community trust in neighborhoods shattered by violence. Once people build trust and cohesion, they are more likely to come out and support local businesses, thereby creating local jobs and helping to suppress violence on their streets. As their motto puts it "We ride bikes to make our neighborhoods better."[46] This communal self-mobilization (which could also include people rolling in wheelchairs, moving slowly, or moving together in diverse ways) serves as a model for what I will describe below as the mobile commons.

Public infrastructure investment and transport planning can be made into a site of political battle over other more subtle restrictions on the right to the city. Urban streets and public transit are places where differential bodies on the move come up against the obduracy of infrastructural space in their daily lives, making urban mobility a matter of public contestation and conflict. Disability activists have done "wheel ins" in which they gather at the platforms of inaccessible subway stations and, by blocking access by others, embody how they are literally stuck there. The production of unexpected delays, mixed crowds, interstitial publics, and newly punctuated temporalities can leverage uneven mobilities for a politics of empowering the marginalized. Such stoppages and counter-moves can also enact a kind of epistemic justice by shifting the sites for the production of knowledge and political action.

In addition to the gendering and impairing elements of built environments, one of the most crucial aspects of American cities (and those in other white-settler societies and many postcolonial societies) is the racialization of mobilities. Black social movements and subversive embodied movements to occupy or claim space—or what we might call "black moves" in a kinopolitical framework—have been crucial to contesting the injustices of white, colonial, and capitalist mobility regimes, both historically and today.

BLACK MOVES 1: FUGITIVE SUBVERSIVE MOBILITIES

Despite the attention paid to how multiple and disparate im/mobilities shape politics, surprisingly little scholarship currently focuses on the intersections of kinopolitics with systems of racialized/gendered/sexualized hierarchy. We could say that all racial processes, racialized spaces, and racialized identities (including whiteness) are deeply contingent on differential mobilities. Racial boundaries are formed, reformed, and transformed through mobile relations of power. Race is a performance of differential mobilities. And racial projects are concerned with the management of mobilities. The freedom to remain somewhere, to dwell in place, and to determine one's own personal and familial movements are all fundamental elements of mobility justice.[47]

How can a deeper history of colonial and postcolonial mobility regimes help to inform how we understand mobility justice today? Caribbean theorist Sylvia Wynter refers to some spatializations of difference as "archipelagos of poverty." She links struggles over race, class, gender, sexual orientation, and ethnicity with struggles over the environment, global warming, severe climate change, and the "sharply unequal distribution of the earth's resources." This is an important starting point for multi-scalar approaches. These geographies, she writes, are "defined at the global level by refugees/economic migrants stranded outside the gates of the rich countries, as the postcolonial variant of Fanon's category of *les damnés*." It is significant that she includes in this group not only "the criminalized majority of Black and dark-skinned Latino inner-city males now made to man the rapidly expanding prison-industrial complex," but also "a global archipelago, constituted by the Third- and Fourth-World peoples of the so-called 'underdeveloped' areas of the world."[48] These spaces, in other words, are connected.

Unequal relations of power always make mobilities racially and sexually loaded (through social controls over segregation, human reproduction, and population control). Such relations of mobility management have long been contested through embodied encounters that draw on a deep understanding of the histories of the colonial corporeal politics of (im)mobility. Here, I briefly consider the origins of Western kinopolitics in systems of slavery, and the struggle against it through subversive mobilities.

Historians now better understand how the Atlantic slave trade "stood at the basis of creating the systems of financial capitalism . . . as 'spaces of flows' . . . a movement that relied on violence to generate and secure it, which provoked violence to usurp it or resist to it, and which was a mode of violence." As Kotef argues, the "freedom of the sea" that benefited the British Empire and other colonial empires, "was also a principle of violence" and a place of "accelerated movement of both trade and violence."[49] In this sense the foundational freedom of mobility of capital through which the modern capitalist world system was built was secured through limiting the mobilities of racialized others, and especially those who were enslaved in the service of plantation capitalism and its domestic reproduction.

Not only were people violently torn away from their homes and sent in chains across the Atlantic, but each day slave catchers, masters, and overseers forced captive people to carry out work, to schedule their time, and to move their bodies in ways that were not voluntary. And at the same time this coerced mobility was also a form of immobility, keeping people in chains, or on plantations, in barracks or locked in prisons, brothels, or bedrooms.[50] The sovereign power of "mastery" was built upon the repeated daily denial of others' personal freedom, and when slavery finally was overthrown it was the personal mobility of the freed people that was experienced as especially galling and fearful to whites, leading to post-emancipation systems of coercive control over free black mobilities.[51]

Nevertheless, the history of the transatlantic system of slavery also crucially reminds us that despite African people being captured, imprisoned, and transported across the Atlantic for capitalist profit, they also moved throughout the Americas in a vast system of subversive counter-movements. What sociologist Orlando Patterson calls personal freedom, the freedom to self-determine the movements of one's own body, was fundamentally destroyed by enslavement while also becoming a core value that freed people struggled for.[52] Although enslavement generally implies the loss or impairment of autonomous bodily mobility, people caught up in its violent grip nonetheless created some degree of mobility capabilities for themselves.

There were black traders or sailors (like Olaudah Equiano, who wrote a famous account of his travels) who were able to move along routes of commerce and earn money to purchase their own freedom. There were runaways and Maroons for whom self-emancipation from enslavement depended on their capability to move away from the plantation zone, to hide in remote places such as mountains and swamps, and to escape the slave patrols that sought after them.[53] The Maroon capability to move through these difficult terrains and survive deep in the wilderness, drawing on Carib and Taino knowledge and Indigenous cultural practices, along with making occasional raids on the plantations, underlines their success in exercising autonomous mobilities. Sometimes welcoming runaway slaves, or trading with pirates and buccaneers, Maroon communities existed on the fringes of often transient and precarious colonial settlements to whom they presented an existential threat.

In the United States, the history of the Underground Railroad famously commemorates the hidden mobilities and secret "stations" through which thousands of people escaped slavery as a kind of extensive transport infrastructure comparable to the steel tracks of a railway. Historians have also uncovered the ways that enslaved people used spaces such as provision grounds and open-air marketplaces to create "a *rival geography* that defied the spatial confines of enslavement." They created "alternative ways of knowing and using plantation . . . space that conflicted with planters' ideals and demands." Such alternative knowledges formed into rival mobilities: "Where planters' mapping of their farms was defined by fixed places for plantation residents, the rival geography was characterized by motion: the movement of bodies, objects, and information within and around plantation space."[54]

Caribbean political philosopher Sylvia Wynter referred to this as the contest between plot and plantation, whereby enslaved people used their small plots and provision grounds to create a counter-space of non-capitalist economies and community reproduction, which in some cases became a form of common land after emancipation. Escape from the coercive control of bodily freedom that was the basis of slavery also occurred in more fleeting forms, known as *petit marronage,* which anthropologist Richard Price describes as "repetitive or periodic truancy with temporary goals such as visiting a relative or lover on a neighboring plantation."[55] The small exercises of autonomous mobility within *petit marronage* are just as significant as the more permanent geographical escape of *grand marronage,* for understanding the foundations of mobility justice upon the self-determination of autonomous bodily mobility. This form of occasional *marronage* was especially utilized by women, giving a measure of control over their familial and sexual relations, if not a permanent escape from slavery.

By bringing into view the violence that shaped black lives especially, we can gain an acute understanding of the "difficulty of life in freedom" for those who "escaped" slavery or were "emancipated"—both terms suggesting forms of mobility away from something or someone. Freedom of mobility remains enmeshed in kinopolitical struggles that involve racialized/sexualized bodies and spaces, and the oppressive racial/gender/sexual projects of colonial-capitalist white-settler states. Even with its abolition, the system of slavery did not simply disappear overnight, and black mobility became one of the key sites for contesting black freedom.

McKittrick notes that "black Atlantic Cultures have always had an intimate relationship with geography" including "the naturalization of identity and place, the spatialization of racial hierarchies, the displacement of difference, ghettos, prisons, crossed borders, and sites of resistance and community."[56] Here she deftly links the historical patterns of mobility politics to those of the contemporary moment, from colonial geographies to prison reform movements. All of these are also sites of uneven mobilities and struggles for mobility justice. Critical black theorist and poet Fred Moten, with collaborator Stefano Harney, also fleetingly invokes the ways in which what they call "the undercommons" arises out of "black study" of the histories of the fugitive, the runaway Maroon, the bodily touch that arises out of "the hold" of the slave ship and the "hapticality" of being.[57]

Like the sensing, thinking, feeling, and moving bodies that Gibson-Graham described, these writers all recognize the moving "interface between self and world as the site of becoming of both."[58] It is these embodied moves, these furtive kinopolitical movements of bodies with other bodies, that challenge unjust mobility systems in the most immediate sense. Subversive movements and the haptic politics of the slave hold reverberate through the world-making of black moves which brought new ways of feeling, sounding and moving into being.

BLACK MOVES 2: FURTIVE MOVEMENTS

Racialized mobility systems in the United States originate in the system of slavery and its coercive and violent controls over black bodies and mobilities. But modern unequal mobility regimes are also grounded in the reactions against the abolition of slavery and the backlash against the Reconstruction era, which produced efforts at segregation codified as Jim Crow laws. This led into a long history of conflicts over freed peoples' mobility and access to urban space. Segregated street cars and public transit were contested in the nineteenth century and into the twentieth century. The Great Migration out of the South brought black populations into the Northern cities in the 1920s–30s, with the Pullman Porters becoming the largest black employer in the country. The crucial struggles of the Civil Rights era to gain equitable access to urban transit systems and public spaces along with voting rights, education, and other elements of full citizenship are exemplified by the figure of Rosa Parks and many others who challenged mobility restrictions.

Jim Crow pervaded all aspects of life, but especially forms of transportation. Even bicycling clubs began with bans on African-American cyclists, with the first club during the bicycling boom of the 1890s, the League of American Wheelmen, explicitly positioning bicycling as "a white, masculine nationalist project . . . in a period that defined bicycling, and by extension personal and public mobility, as an exclusive privilege reserved for middle- to upper-class whites."[59] Both bicycling, and later driving, were formed within social hierarchies that could dictate which bodies could operate a bicycle or drive a car, and could stigmatize others (by class, race, and gender) as second-, third-, or fourth-class citizens. The impairment of black mobilities continued legally well into the twentieth century in the United States and many argue continues informally today through policies such as stop and frisk, the over policing of those "driving while black," and the discrimination against border crossers with brown skin.

The question of reparations for slavery still animates calls for reparative justice today and could conceivably be extended to calls for freedom of movement and the abolition of borders. Biometric control in airports has deep links to these racialized forms of surveillance. Simone Browne has powerfully shown "how contemporary surveillance technologies and practices are informed by the long history of racial formation and by the methods of policing black life under slavery, such as branding, runaway slave notices, and lantern laws."[60]

American historian Cotten Seiler suggests that "Too often scholars discuss mobility in the abstract, assuming or omitting the highly consequential matter of the identity of those who move and its effects on how they move." He refers to the "racialization of mobility," meaning the ways in which "the modern practices and institutions of mobility have been and remain highly racialized."[61] Legal scholar Michelle Alexander likewise has made the powerful case that there is a system of racialized social control in the United States that has perpetuated the racial inequities of the system of slavery through their transformation first into the Jim Crow system of racial segregation and restrictions, and more recently through the racialized system of mass incarceration.

In her influential book *The New Jim Crow*, she argues that the so-called "War on Drugs" that began under the administration of President Ronald Reagan (and continues today, when Attorney General Jeff Sessions has called for reinstating minimum sentencing laws) has normalized the creation of a "racialized caste system" in which warrantless searches are conducted on black motorists, pedestrians, and transit passengers, sweeping a vastly disproportionate number of black citizens into a court system with a lack of legal representation, unaffordable bail, rigid minimum sentencing laws, aggressive prosecutors, and unforgiving prison and parole systems.

Although Alexander's focus is not on mobility per se, we can see that the police practices of warrantless searches, racial profiling, and stop and frisk are built around control over black movement in public spaces, sidewalks, streets, and highways. Emblematic of such racialized (and gendered) mobility regimes are the massive use of stop-and-frisk powers by US police forces against young black (and brown) men. In 2013 an investigation by the American Civil Liberties Union (ACLU) revealed that the New York Police Department (NYPD) has conducted more than four million stop and search procedures since 2002. Nine out of ten of those who were stopped were completely innocent. Around 54 percent of those stopped were black (another 31 percent were Latino). These figures were remarkably consistent over the period 2003–2014 with the percentage of those stopped being black ranging between 53 percent and 56 percent in any given year. These numbers are clearly out of sync with the general demographics of New York City.

Across the United States, poorly specified forms of "deviant" bodily mobility have been used to stop and search African Americans under charges known as "Manner of Walking" which are used disproportionately against African Americans, such as the infamous "manner of walking along roadway" municipal ordinance in Ferguson, Missouri, associated with the fatal police shooting of eighteen-year-old Michael Brown in August, 2014.[62] A federal report found that ninety-five percent of such charges in Ferguson were against African-Americans.

In the case of *Floyd v. City of New York*, the plaintiffs argued that stop-and-frisk procedures of the NYPD should include "reasonable suspicion" and should be enacted without regard to race. The judge was highly critical of the kinds of reasons given on the official police forms that were used when stops were made, such as "furtive movements." Furtive movements, in the view of the judge, could not be reasonable grounds for suspicion. As the police officers testifying explained,

> "furtive movement is a very broad concept," and could include a person "changing direction," "walking in a certain way," "[a]cting a little suspicious," "making a movement that is not regular," being "very fidgety," "going in and out of his pocket," "going in and out of a location," "looking back and forth constantly," "looking over their shoulder," "adjusting their hip or their belt," "moving in and out of a car too quickly," "[t]urning a part of their body away from you," "[g]rabbing at a certain pocket or something at their waist," "getting a little nervous, maybe shaking," and "stutter[ing]." [The] officer explained that "usually" a furtive movement is someone "hanging out in front of [a] building, sitting on the benches or something like that" and then making a "quick movement," such as "bending down and quickly standing back up," "going inside the lobby . . . and then quickly coming back out," or "all of a sudden becom[ing] very nervous, very aware." If officers believe that the behavior described above constitutes furtive movement that justifies a stop, then it is no surprise that stops so rarely produce evidence of criminal activity.[63]

This transcript is an account of particular ways in which young, urban black and brown men move, in which various seemingly innocuous forms of bodily movement can be coded as "furtive." Anyone's movements might become suspect under these conditions. The judge thus found that the NYPD had enacted a form of racial profiling that had resulted in the disproportionate stopping and frisking of black and Latino citizens, infringing on personal liberty.

Floyd v City of New York "draws our attention to several aspects of the politics of black mobility," argues Cresswell, and the ways in which control over black and brown bodies is ingrained in the American justice system. "Most obviously, the case is about the application of differential amounts of friction," which implicitly rests on white *ease* of movement.[64] Black people—particularly young black men, but we might also add queer and transgender people of color—are prevented from moving far more often than anyone else in the United States, while white men typically experience unchallenged movement through public space (although this may vary by class position). This is far more than an inconvenience for a racialized minority; it is humiliating and demeaning. It also leads to high rates of arrest, as well as death. These issues came to a head with a series of highly publicized and controversial police shootings of black men and boys, including Michael Brown, Eric Garner, and Tamir Rice in 2014, followed by Eric Harris in 2015, Alton Sterling in 2016, and many others highlighted by the Black Lives Matter movement.

Racial profiling is especially associated with discriminatory stops of motorists. A study conducted in New Jersey and Maryland in the 1990s, for example, found that "only 15 percent of all drivers on the New Jersey Turnpike were racial minorities, yet 42 percent of all stops and 73 percent of all arrests were black motorists—despite the fact that blacks and whites violated traffic laws at almost exactly the same rate."[65] This racial profiling, commonly known as DWB ("Driving While Black" or "While Brown"), and sometimes DWI ("Driving While Indian"), describes the frequency with which non-white automobile drivers are stopped by police, detained, and sometimes searched. A US Department of Justice investigation of the Ferguson Police Department after the police shooting of Michael Brown found that African Americans made up 67 percent of Ferguson's population yet accounted for 85 percent of traffic stops.

Although recognized since the 1990s, it was after the rise of social media that people were empowered to share mobile video recordings of such traffic stops, leading to national attention to the deaths of Philando Castile, Walter Scott, and Sandra Bland, all of whom died at the hands of police following minor traffic stops. In 2016 the ACLU even created an app called Mobile Justice in which users could record and upload videos of police traffic stops. A whole series of mobile phone videos revealed controversial police stops in which black motorists were violently arrested and in some cases shot. These repeated injustices became one of the key grievances of the Black Lives Matter movement.

Protests around police shootings brought attention to how mobility and race intersect, and connected it to deeper historical antecedents in slavery and the control of black mobility.

Protests around such racialized mobility regimes have long involved subversive moves, from the marches and sit-ins of the Civil Rights Movement, which claimed a right to move and to stop in public space, to the marches and protests of Black Lives Matter, and even the movement started by NFL football star Colin Kaepernick (and others) to kneel during the playing of the national anthem. Kaepernick first did so in August 2016, protesting the deaths of Alton Sterling and Philando Castile, but in September 2017 it swept across the NFL in reaction to President Trump and the recent conflicts in Charlottesville, Virginia, where several hundred white nationalists and white supremacists marched as part of a "Unite the Right" rally at the University of Virginia in August 2017, that resulted in violence and three deaths, while revealing the strength of neo-Nazi groups in the US.

These corporeal choreographies sparked a national debate about embodied protest, and the limits placed on black political expression. Whether marching, standing up, sitting down, or kneeling, movements for racial justice in the United States have mobilized subversive bodily moves against dominant racial mobility regimes. These examples tell us something about the intertwining of power and coercion in the shaping of bodily freedoms, and the deep relation between mobility and immobility as gendered, sexed, classed, disabling, and racialized practices. The history of bodily freedom of mobility is perpetually accompanied by unfreedoms, limitations, and impairments—but also intertwined with resistances, counter-movements, and subaltern moves.

HABEAS CORPUS

At the scale of the body, we can posit that all people have a right to freedom of bodily movement, without undue constraint imposed from outside. A core foundation for the legal protection of freedom of movement and prevention of unlawful detention is the writ of habeas corpus, grounded in British common law. This recourse in law allows a prisoner to report their unlawful detention or imprisonment before a court, and thereby to establish the legal authority of the custodian to detain the prisoner. While it dates back to seventeenth-century England, the writ of habeas corpus was most famously used in the 1792 *Somersett's Case*, in which the court ordered an enslaved African to be freed upon reaching England, where holding people in slavery was not legal. Similar protections against deprivation of liberty are found in other European bodies of law drawing on Roman law, and were enshrined in the Constitution of the United States and in the Universal Declaration of Human Rights.

However, there is also generally a provision for the suspension of habeas corpus during times of war or uprising. After the September 11, 2001, terrorist attacks, for example, US president George W. Bush tried to suspend the provision by placing detainees in the military prison camp at Guantanamo Bay, known as Camp X-Ray. This attempt to remove prisoners to outside of the jurisdiction of habeas corpus was overturned by the Supreme Court in *Boumediene v. Bush*. More recently, habeas corpus has been used during deportation proceedings as a legal recourse to challenge unlawful pretrial detention and detention by the US Bureau of Immigration and Customs Enforcement (ICE). The June 2018 political outcry over the Trump administration's separation of families at the US-Mexico border—detaining parents and placing more than 2,400 children in federal custody (many of them held in a former Walmart warehouse)—exemplifies the lack of due process at the border and the ways in which regimes of mobility management can put human rights in jeopardy. While freedom from illegal detention can be considered the foundation of personal freedom of mobility, there are other ways in which freedom of movement should be legally protected at the personal bodily scale yet which are very much in jeopardy today.

In the United States, despite extensive liberties and protections of individual rights to personal freedom, there continue to be differential gendered, racial, and sexual mobilities in which white men have greater capabilities for mobility than women, in which women and girls in public space often experience sexualization and sexual harassment, and in which people of non-binary sexualities and non-normative gendered embodiments are stigmatized for how they move, and at times violently attacked when occupying public space. The Black Lives Matter movement was quickly joined by the "Say Her Name" protests which increased attention to the female, queer, and transgender victims of police shootings and assaults.

Secondly, there is a racialized mobility regime in which racialized minorities cannot exercise full freedom of mobility, being constantly impeded by police stops, searches, arrests, police shootings, and imprisonment without due process and protection of the law. The intensification of deportations by ICE has also led to a situation in which undocumented immigrants find themselves unable to appear in court either as plaintiffs or witnesses, since they might be taken into custody and deported. Even legal migrants are reluctant to get involved with the law or with political action as their family members may be affected by investigations. As Dawson notes, "The United States deports nearly 400,000 people annually. The US prison-industrial complex keeps over 2.3 million people in cages; in any particular day, 19,000 people are in federal prison for criminal convictions of violating immigration laws, and an additional 33,000 are civilly detained by the Immigration and Customs Enforcement (ICE) agency."[66] This is a massive "detention and deportation regime," exercised in the name of national sovereignty, "but its practices extend far beyond the borders of the nation-state."

Thirdly, there are impairments of physical mobility of all people through the design of the built environment and public spaces, especially the non-accessibility of public transportation, despite the requirements of the crucial Americans with Disabilities Act, which requires access to public facilities. Such exclusions also take more social forms, with normative practices that fail to pay attention to accessibility, for example, by not asking about access needs when events are planned, by relegating the differently abled to time-consuming work-arounds, or with assumptions about walking and bicycling as "good mobilities" or that public transit is for "every-body" even though many people are excluded.[67]

Uneven and differential mobilities as experienced at the interpersonal scale of the body involve choreographies of differential access to mobility and performances of differently disciplined mobile subjects. The concept of uneven mobilities signals both the means or modes of movement that have a greater or lesser degree of ease, comfort, flexibility, speed, and safety, as well as *the disciplining of mobile subjects* through affective experiences of moving with more or less friction, danger, fear, or turbulence. We need to be cognizant of the spatial restrictions imposed by such uneven and differential mobilities, and to begin our project for building mobility justice from the ground up: where social and structural violence shape the ways in which bodies meet, the ways in which we move, and the ways in which our movements shape space.

In the face of these injustices we can therefore propose some of the following principles that would be necessary for mobility justice at the bodily scale, before we even begin to address issues such as transportation and urban form:

- Each person's freedom of mobility shall be constrained by the rule of mutuality: i.e., not trampling, endangering, or depriving others of their capability for mobility.
- Individual mobility shall not be involuntarily restricted by threats of violence, either physical or symbolic, including enforced forms of clothing, segregated means of movement, or unevenly applying temporal or spatial limits on mobility.
- Gender, sexual identity, and other markers of identity shall not be used as the basis for restricting mobility or exclusion from public space.
- Racial, ethnic, religious, or national profiling (including Indigenous identities) shall not be used to police entire groups or stop individuals from exercising freedom of movement.
- Universal design should be required in all public facilities to ensure accessibility to all people and especially access to all modes of public transportation and public media.
- Children's rights to mobility and the rights of the elderly, pregnant women, and those needing assisted mobility should be protected and included in design and planning.
- Protections of habeas corpus shall extend to all people, both citizens and non-citizens, and there shall be no forms of state detention without legal representation, due process, and judicial appeal.

The capacity to move and the coercive power of stopped movement, deten-tion, or imprisonment are fundamental dimensions of human rights and justice. Mobility, indeed, is crucial to politics, power, and resistance. Existing social movements have begun to make these scale-jumping connections, from the racial justice movement to the migrant justice movement, from refugee protec-tion to Black Lives Matter, anti-border-wall protests and queer activism.[68] Tamara Vukov has written recently about the political implications of this strug-gle for mobility justice, and offers some ideas toward a vision of mobility justice, including first, "the building of a world in which safe, accessible, and just forms of movement and dwelling are open and available to all." She incorporates not only transportation justice, but also concerns related to dwelling, such as equi-table policies around homelessness, and rights to occupy and remain in place, such as equitable policies around residency and citizenship, which are more associated with struggles for spatial justice.

Secondly, Vukov calls for "an end to the many macro and micro forms of *forced* mobility and displacement (from colonial and war-based displacements to deportation and evictions due to gentrification)." Here, too, we see a combi-nation of scales, a sensitivity to colonial histories but also to contemporary urban issues such as eviction, connecting the macro and meso level of mobility justice struggles and visions of "altermobilities." And finally, she also calls for "The dismantling of imposed forms of immobility, including detention, incar-ceration, the legacy of colonial confinement (such as reservations) and separation walls and barriers."[69] While certainly not easy to achieve, these prin-ciples at least lay out a set of ideals against which we can measure our progress toward mobility justice. We can now turn to transportation itself.

Chapter 3

Beyond Automobility and Transport Justice

In his writings around the turn of the millennium, sociologist John Urry defined automobility as a complex dominant system. In our co-authored article "The City and the Car" (2000), we described automobility as the "quintessential *manufactured object*" of Western capitalism, the "major item of *individual consumption* after housing," an "extraordinarily powerful *machinic complex* constituted through the car's technical and social interlinkages with other industries," the "predominant global form of 'quasi-private' *mobility* that subordinates other 'public' mobilities of walking, cycling, traveling by rail and so on." It is the "dominant *culture* that sustains major discourses of what constitutes the good life, what is necessary for an appropriate citizenship of mobility, and which provides potent literary and artistic images and symbols." And finally, it is the "single most important cause of *environmental resource-use*."[1] This multi-dimensional characterization of automobility remains seemingly locked in place and has proven difficult to transform.

Historians have long noted the many problems generated by the shaping of American cities in the mid to late twentieth century by a system of automobility.[2] The problems associated with automobility range across all the scales of spatial formation, from bodily harm, community decay, and urban failure, to global pollution and economic injustice. Numerous commentators have shown the ways in which car-based cities reduce community. Systems of automobility overrun and over-pave physical space, which has detrimental impacts on other kinds of movement through cities. Car crashes cause massive numbers of fatalities (being the leading cause of death among young people). Globally there are nearly 1.3 million people killed in road crashes each year, and an additional 20 to 50 million injured or disabled. In the United States, around 37,000 people die in car crashes every year and, between 2009 and 2016, the number of pedestrians struck and killed by cars increased by nearly 50 percent, from around 4,000 to nearly 6,000.[3] The use of fossil fuels, furthermore, contributes to excessive levels of air pollution, and leads to economic instability of oil dependent economies.[4] As historian Zack Furness argues, "The postwar redevelopment of the United States was problematic not only because it helped transform the metropolis into an *auto*polis but also because simultaneously it facilitated both mass suburbanization at home and the geopolitical policies necessary to ensure steady supplies of oil from abroad."[5]

During the last decade (and longer) when many critical commentaries have been written about these multiple problems associated with automobility, global passenger car numbers have nonetheless climbed from 679 million in 2006 to just under 1 billion by 2016.[6] The USA still "drives almost a third of the world's cars and produces nearly half of the world's transport-related carbon emissions."[7] According to the United States Department of Energy, the US produced 25 percent of all GHG emissions worldwide and consumed 23 percent of the world's oil annually in 2011 despite having only 4 percent of the global human population. There was a slight decrease by 2016, when the United States consumed a total of 7.21 billion barrels of petroleum products, and consumed 20 percent of the world's oil, still outstripping China which consumed only 13 percent.[8] About 34 percent of US GHG emissions are from the transportation sector, with the vast majority being from passenger vehicles. After a slight dip during the recession, since 2014 the rate of new car purchases in the US has again begun to increase, lead by the purchase of fuel-hungry light trucks and sport utility vehicles (SUVs), which drove down the overall energy efficiency of the US transportation fleet.[9] Sprawling suburbs have continued to attract population in the US and in 2017 outstripped urban growth—suggesting that entrenched patterns of automobile dependence will continue.

Transport scholars Stephen Gosling and Scott Cohen propose that there are actually "taboos" on particular transport policies, making them impossible to even bring up because they are so politically risky. Especially significant is the political unwillingness to acknowledge that "there are huge differences in the power geometries of individual mobility, with a minor share of highly mobile travelers being responsible for a significant share of the overall distances traveled, as well as emissions associated with this transport."[10] A small proportion of privileged travelers (generally white men earning high incomes) engage in frequent and long-distance travel, even what might be called "binge-flying," as well as driving large-engine luxury cars, overall producing hugely disproportionate amounts of greenhouse gases and other pollutants. Car use and parking by such kinetic elites also generally takes up more urban space, as compared to those who use public transit or bicycling. But what politician is willing to raise this point? Road pricing policies, taxation, or other austerity measures simply give these users even greater motility by excluding others.

Living in this deeply dominant system of automobility, it is often difficult to see how we will move beyond it, despite some efforts in that direction.[11] The United States has been much slower than other industrialized countries to implement many changes in transport practice, in part because of its entrenched policies supporting a culture of automobility, but also because of the power of "carbon capital." Even before the appointment of climate change "deniers" and oil industry executives like Rex Tillerson (former CEO of Exxon Mobil, who briefly served as secretary of state) in the Trump administration, low oil prices were already contributing to renewed growth in the purchase of less fuel-efficient SUVs and light trucks. Now there is an even stronger resurgence of pro-car and pro-fossil fuel interests in government, allied with anti-regulation states-rights conservatives and explicit supporters of white supremacy who oppose the environmental regulations of the Obama administration.[12] Policies, cultural shifts, and environmental regulations that had briefly slowed the growth of automobility in the US in the prior decade are again in retreat.

Even when the BP Deep Water Horizon exploded in 2010, spewing 5 million barrels of oil into the Gulf of Mexico, nothing changed. Even when the automobile-driven suburban sprawl of Houston, Texas, one of the petroleum production capitals of the world, contributed to the massive flooding of the area by Hurricane Harvey in September 2017, nothing changed. It seems that Americans will continue to live in car-dominated environments that perpetuate what Rob Nixon calls the "slow violence" of fossil fuel capitalism.[13] The minority of humanity who live their lives as "high emitters" of carbon dioxide are complicit in the slow violence of climate change, as are those living in petroleum producing, refining, and exporting economies—from Trinidad to Norway—however "green" they might claim to be, since we all continue to burn "energy without conscience."[14]

Nevertheless, the past teaches us that even mobility systems that have been around a long time will eventually be replaced. Despite the entrenched infrastructure of fossil fuels and the power of "Big Oil," there are still various mobility transitions happening around the world today, advancing along varied pathways toward "post-car" cities.

Beyond Mobility?

In one of the most up to date textbooks in urban planning, *Beyond Mobility: Planning Cities for People and Places* (2017), Robert Cervero, Erick Guerra and Stefan Al make the case for city and regional planners to focus more on place-making and less on mobility. The core premise of the book is that "improving mobility (i.e., the efficiency of motorized travel) has overly dominated past planning practices." They want to recalibrate planning and cityscapes to prioritize places and people rather than (motorized) mobility and traffic flow. While this sounds good in principle, and aligns with sustainable urbanism agendas, there is a problem with pitting "mobility" against "place."

First, this dualism sets up a problematic interpretation of "mobility" as simply meaning motorized transportation, and ignoring the need for deliberation over and improvements to other kinds of mobility (walking, wheeling, bicycling, transit). If we are called upon to shift "beyond mobility," how can we advocate for better, fairer, more just mobilities? It would be more accurate to call the approach "beyond automobility," since it favors active transport and "green mobility" such as public transit, yet the authors seem to tactically avoid challenging automobility, and even claim that "we are not out to remove cars from city streets."[15]

Second, the focus on place-making is heavily justified throughout the book due to its contributions to economic growth, job creation, and raising real estate values. Yet these rising prices and "land price premiums" near walkable, transit-oriented developments are known to lead to extremely problematic processes of gentrification and uneven development of "green" and "sustainable" cities or neighborhoods. The track record for so-called place-making and creation of "live, work, play" districts is that it displaces the poor and pushes racial and ethnic minorities out of newly "desirable" (to whites) neighborhoods.

The authors of *Beyond Mobility* do not deeply enough consider the need to improve mobility for the mobility poor and to limit the kinds of place-making that attracts gentrification and improves mobility only for the kinetic elite. Their chapter on "Global Cities" is the only one that does mention improving accessibility for the working poor living in informal settlements in suburban peripheries of burgeoning global cities, yet it is precisely well designed BRT systems that are crucial, not place-making. Improving mobility and equity for the poor is not based on policies "beyond mobility": it is squarely focused on improving mobility and accessibility.

Only in the final pages on "Inclusive Cities" do these leading urban planners bring up the problem that "urban betterment is often followed by higher land prices that end up pricing out the poor and often even middle-income people. In any city, there's a finite, limited supply of real estate with good access to transit, safe and walkable neighborhoods, and animated, vibrant streetscapes. Invariably well-off segments of society outbid others for these choice areas, displacing long-time residents and the working class." Yet they still follow this observation by claiming that "actions that reduce the dominance of private cars help the poor," with no clear evidence of how, given the real-estate price effect. Moreover, they suggest that "urban planners are well positioned to make cities more socially inclusive through their oversight of building codes and design standards" and through promoting "equitable TOD" of which the examples they give are Hong Kong and Singapore, places with extremely high real estate prices, not known for equity and social justice.[16]

This "beyond mobility" strategy is at odds with the evidence of existing cities, where urban planning has led to growth of places with extreme wealth concentration and income inequality. Unfortunately, despite good intentions and an extensive literature review of some of the best practices in urban planning, *Beyond Mobility* falls short on actually addressing the deep mobility injustices that are built into our urban environments. These shortcomings in place-based urban planning will be as inequitable as earlier mobility-based planning regimes if planners fail to understand *the connection between mobilities and places, between mobilities and immobilities, and between such relational (im)mobilities and power.*

Future scenario envisioning is one way to try to capture complex dynamics of change. In his work for the Institute for Social Futures, Urry describes four scenarios for the transformation of automobility, which he labels Fast-mobility City, Digital City, Livable City and Fortress City. The first scenario of the

"Fast-mobility City" would mean the intensification of existing speedy and extensively mobile lives through innovations around vertical urbanization, driverless cars, and drone delivery, but is only possible with rapid innovation in the viability of some post-carbon fuel such as hydrogen, and will also intensify existing social inequalities. The second scenario of the "Digital City" would depend on the rise of digital communication and virtual experience as a substitute for physical movement, along with digital lives, digital fabrication, Smart Cities, and sentient robots. The third, the "Livable City," implies smaller-scale, more localized, and lower-energy practices emerging, along with greater vehicle sharing and mobility as a service. The final neo-Medievalist model of the "Fortress City" implies rich economies breaking away from the poor, retreating into privatized, fortified, armed enclaves protected from the "wild zones" of violence and danger left outside the walls. All of these trends are present in some ways already, in various combinations, and will each influence future trends.

One trajectory toward the future is the disruptive business innovations occurring around smartphone-connected shared mobility, and what has come to be known as "mobility as a service." Connected, autonomous, shared, electric (a.k.a. CASE) mobility has become a buzzword of consulting firms and business modelers, who predict a huge shift taking place in the car market, as privately owned internal combustion engine cars are replaced. James Arbib of RethinkX, a not-for-profit think tank on non-linear technology disruptions, predicts that "transport-as-a-service" using electric, shared, and automated vehicles will lead to a 70 percent decline in new vehicle sales within ten years, contributing to job losses and a collapse of oil demand, but more positively (he suggests) making cities more livable and freeing up people's time and income.[17]

Steve Buckley, manager of the northeast US planning, environment, and traffic practice of one of the leading global engineering firms, WSP Parsons Brinkerhoff, notes that we already have a private-ownership model of incrementally automated vehicles developed mainly by the existing auto industry (e.g., Volvo, Toyota) and new entrants such as Tesla. But WSP predicts that by 2025, non-automotive sector tech companies (e.g., Alphabet/Google, Amazon, Apple, or perhaps even new tech giants emerging in China) will spearhead the creation of an increasingly shared transport network model that depends on full automation. With costs estimated to be as low as fifty cents per mile for driverless cars, this is predicted to become a $2 trillion market by 2030.[18]

As technology theorist Adam Greenfield trenchantly observes, however, such predictions of the future are ideologically driven, especially when coming from actors with deep investments in such futures. Automation, machine learning, algorithmic control, and artificial intelligence are all interconnected developments that may be highly socially disruptive, but their direction depends on how they are enacted, regulated, and made real. Their outcomes are not inevitable. We need to pay attention to the ways in which a company like Amazon, for example, is seeking to "consolidate its investments in logistical innovation, deploying a mesh of autonomous trucking, mobile ware-housing and drone-based delivery assets, knit together by network-analysis and demand-anticipation algorithms."[19] This ongoing colonization of everyday life by information technologies demands rethinking our future forecasts around all forms of transport.

Second, city governments and transport agencies are having to rapidly adjust to these changes by continuing to advocate for human-centered public approaches which are often swept aside in the rush for new technology. Linda Bailey, executive director of the National Association of City Transportation Officials (NATCO), argues that we need to make automated vehicles work for cities by regulating them in ways that promote health and safety, equity and access. We can only capture the benefits of reduced traffic violence, decreased travel costs, and freed-up public space if cities redevelop rights of way for humans, design for safety, insist on shared data, move more people and fewer vehicles, and "code the curb." "Coding the curb" would mean regulating and pricing the amenity of curb space to avoid what she calls the "tragedy of the commons" in today's appropriation of streets and curb space by transport network services such as Uber or by private bus services for tech compa-nies like Google, who use public bus stops without paying for them.[20] But cities will need to do far more than that to protect the public realm, as the full implications of CASE "mobility as a service" unfold. A 2017 study of traffic in New York City, for example, found that app-based ride services had put 50,000 additional vehicles on the road over the prior four years, added 36 percent to the total miles traveled by for-hire vehicles, and added to a 15 percent increase in passenger trips.[21]

Third, there has been extensive promotion of transport policy packages known as "Complete Streets," "Livable Cities," "Transit-Oriented Development," and "Vision Zero"—all of which seek to restrain automobility in various ways. These initiatives combine elements of both sustainability and transport equity. Social movements are continuing to challenge the dominant cultural frames that legitimize certain forms of mobility valuation (e.g., economic rationality, utility, economic growth, security, 'smart' technology) with counter-frames that promote alternative mobility practices and values (e.g., sustainability, environ-ment, health, relationality, sharing, the mobility commons). Streets must be for people, not just vehicles.

It has long been known that the fatality rate of car crashes can be sharply reduced by enforcing slower speeds. Cars going over 25 mph are far more lethal. This means slow speed is important, and in some design solutions this includes the promotion of walking and biking through better infrastructure design, the use of shared space (where cars are not given priority), flush surfaces (where all street pavement and curb surfaces are level) that can be easily crossed especially by wheelchair users, and low-tech accessibility for lower income groups to be able to access information. Yet if we focus solely on place-making, and not on more equitable mobilities, we will simply design the poor out of the way, turning livability into a luxury for those with high network capital.

There are many pressures on the existing dominant system of automobility and its associated forms of transport planning, as well as new opportunities. However, all such socio-technical transformations involve complex systems distributed across many different locations and affecting many different scales. The societal challenge consists in democratically transitioning toward both sustainable and socially just mobility systems in the face of looming threats such as global climate change, increasing natural disasters, and resource shortages. Sustainable mobility and transportation justice together are crucial to these transitions in mobility, and the two problems are fundamentally interconnected. But we must also envision this as a mobility transformation that goes far beyond automobility and involves far more than questions of transportation.

There is growing recognition that transitions in urban transport systems depend not just on individual choices, good design, technological transformations, or economic forces, but also on changes in entire mobility cultures and the kinopolitics surrounding every mobility practices. Theorizing the relation between sustainability and mobility justice requires recognizing that not just the built environment, but also the cultural landscape, the economy, and the entire political system in many countries is deeply enlaced with dispositions toward automobility that envision personal mobility as a freedom and individual right. These dominant practices of a kind of automobile citizenship are not only linked to race, gender, and class identities, but also deeply embedded in wider energy cultures that are themselves grounded in global inequalities.[22]

We will not understand the transitions that are happening (or might happen in the future) unless we integrate a multi-scalar theory of embodied relations of (im)mobility and extended infrastructural spaces of planetary urbanization into our models of mobility transition. Mobility transitions do not just happen "inside" cities, nor do they involve transportation alone. They cross micro, meso, and macro fields of relations, engaging complex arrays of political actors, and transforming social, economic, and cultural fields of power. As we re-make mobility we also re-make space, and transform ourselves.

CREATING TRANSPORT JUSTICE

Whether dealing with the freedom to move, or the right to stay in place, race, class, and gender have been crucial factors to the uneven distribution of community transport access and individual transport poverty, as well as harmful exposures to transport externalities such as air pollution and unsafe roads. Movements for "transportation justice" have highlighted the inequitable distribution of transport access, including racial, ethnic, age, ability, and class barriers to mobility. Yet analysts of automobility still underemphasize the extent to which historically dominant forms of *white, male, elite* automobility shaped modern infrastructures of urban mobility, and limited the access of others to its privileges.

The field of transportation equity especially highlights the inequitable race and class distribution of transport access in the United States.[23] This literature on transportation equity originates in the transportation-based actions of the Civil Rights movement of the 1960s, but gathered force due to the impacts of "urban renewal" and highway building on black communities in the late 1960s and early 1970s. In some cases transport justice advocates also adopted the radical anti-capitalist egalitarian philosophies of the 1970s, which criticized American car culture, consumerism, and suburbanization. Since the 1990s, more formal academic literature has developed the concept of "transport poverty," which is defined as a combination of the inability to meet the cost of transport, lack of access to (motorized) transport, lack of access to key life activities due to lack of transport, and exposure to transport externalities.[24]

Transport justice has also been taken up within mobilities theory that focuses on the relation between high and low "motility" or potential for movement.[25] Motility offers a way of measuring capabilities for movement, highlighting the ways in which movement depends on the "affordances" of the environment in which we find ourselves, in combination with our own abilities. There are many injustices built into current transportation systems, whose inequalities have splintered cities and unevenly distributed transport, mobility access, harms such as air pollution, and access to basic services that are considered fundamental to human flourishing (e.g., food, healthcare, education, employment opportunities).

The spatial forms of new infrastructures often create barriers and social exclusions, epitomized by what Tim Cresswell calls the "mobility poor" who in the United States are predominantly black, Latino/a, and racialized immigrant populations.[26] While developed Western countries may once have had national visions and urban centralization of public infrastructure projects, they have long been racially exclusive, classed, and gendered, and have since become increasingly fragmented and splintered.[27] These patterns of uneven development are even more pronounced in rapidly growing global cities.

Racial Mobility Regimes

There is a long history in the USA of racial and class discrimination in mobility rights and freedoms, which carried over into the age of automobility and were built into racially segregated cities and suburbs.[28] Historians such as Kathleen Franz and Cotton Seiler have detailed specific regional histories of the racial politics of automobility and public transit systems in the United States, highlighting the experience of African Americans. Segregation, exclusion, and struggles for access characterize this history. In the nineteenth century, for example, whites used streetcar segregation to establish racial categories and boundaries, and shape urban space. These innovative "clean" vehicles linked whiteness with new technology, speed and industrial modernization. "The measure of control that streetcar companies and conductors exerted over the streetcars was an effort to reproduce white dominance and privilege by making these benefits appear to be a natural part of the social and technological organization of the city."[29]

We can trace racialized mobility regimes in the wider patterns of US urbanization and suburbanization including the unequal investment in highway and automobile infrastructure at the expense of public transit, privileging white suburban automobility over other forms of mobility; the 1950s Federal Housing Authority subsidies for suburban home ownership that contributed to "white flight" from the de-industrializing cities of the postwar era; the urban renewal policies of the 1960s–70s that created ghettos of public housing projects with limited means of transport access in contrast to the white suburbs mainly accessible by car; the urban zoning codes and parking minimums that required car-dependent development; and even the repeal of the federal 55 mile-per-hour speed limit in 1995, which was said to be responsible for 12,545 deaths and 36,583 injuries in fatal crashes between 1995 and 2005, as well as significantly reducing fuel economy and contributing to greenhouse gases.

In the late twentieth century, whites used automobility to "secede" to the suburbs. Sikivu Hutchinson shows how transport planning paradigms marginalized low-income and minority bus riders in favor of white commuters, leading to higher risks of exposure to pollution and dangers to health and safety for residents of low-income neighborhoods lacking in transport infrastructure. The LA Bus Riders Union successfully waged a battle against such differential and uneven transport policies.[30] Racial profiling of drivers, commonly known as DWB ("Driving While Black" or "While Brown"), describes the frequency with which racialized automobile drivers are stopped by police, detained, and sometimes searched. This surveillance practice, instigated by small infractions from broken taillights and turning without signaling to tinted windows and loud radios, impedes the automobility of specifically racialized non-white drivers and ascribes criminal intent. Over the last decade this has resulted in a crisis of police shootings of black motorists, contributing to the emergence of the Black Lives Matter movement.

Gendered Mobility Regimes

Patterns of transportation use and access have been fundamental to the making of American patterns of racial segregation, as well as the gendered segregation of the suburban "housewife." Race and class, of course, are always also intersectional with gender and sexuality, which have equally shaped the uneven access to space, place, and mobilities. Reading the literature on gendered mobilities, feminist historian of space Dolores Hayden observed that "if the simple male journey from home to job is the one planned for" by transport planners, then "the complex female journey from home to day care to job is the one ignored."[31]

Sociologist Judy Wajcman also found that "women have traditionally moved in different rhythms to men, for various reasons to do with childcare, employment, and social routines" and that their journeys were "often shorter in terms of distance and the time taken to travel," more frequent, and occurred at different times of day."[32] There are also major distinctions in white, black, Asian, and Latina women's patterns of mobilities, due to racially segmented job markets and systemic racial/gendered discrimination. Many non-white domestic service workers, hotel workers, and building cleaners, for example, must travel to and from work after dark or before dawn, on inadequate and slow public transit, suffering greater exposure to potential crime.

Dominant transportation systems planned around the white, male, able-bodied, individual, middle-class, rush hour commuter therefore have generally marginalized or discounted women's transportation needs, but also subordinated other non-normative mobile subjects. Imrie argues that transport policies premised upon a "universal, disembodied subject which is conceived of as neutered, that is, without sex, gender, or any other attributed social or biological characteristics" produces the disabled subject whose needs have not been considered.[33]

Mobility, gender, and race have intersected historically, and they intersect today, in unequal relations of power that make mobility into a racializing, gendering, and (dis)abling process. Uneven and differential mobility produces racialized/gendered/disabling spaces and identities, including the dominant positioning of able-bodied, white masculinity as the default mobile subject whose needs are designed for. Ease of mobility, speed, efficiency and comfort are deeply contingent on differential mobilities and power over the mobilities of subaltern others, exercised through the shaping of spaces of movement and their (in)accessibility.

There is also an articulation of urban mobility regimes with transnational mobility regimes that bring immigrant populations into urban peripheries and certain types of suburbs, which often lack good transit connections. It is often *non-citizens* who must take buses with inadequate stops and schedules, and risk dangerous walks and bike rides along unsafe roadways with inadequate cycling infrastructure to get to jobs which lack employer subsidies for transportation, in contrast to those who arrive by car along subsidized highways to free parking places and are given tax breaks for car commuting.

These inequities have public health implications, with air pollution and noise pollution from roadways, airports, and ports having the most detrimental health impacts on poor communities of color. Thus, issues of health equity, measured for example by Michael Marmot's work for the World Health Organization, are also crucial to establishing fair and just mobility systems. As his research suggests, "Cycling, walking, and the use of public transport promote health in four ways. They provide exercise, reduce fatal accidents, increase social contact, and reduce air pollution."[34] Such factors interact with other factors such as unemployment, social exclusion, stress, and poor nutrition to compound the effects of unequal mobilities on the public health of the poor.

This leads to policy recommendations including reducing car use and encouraging cycling and walking in part through changes in land use such as: "converting road space into green spaces, removing car parking spaces, dedicating roads to the use of pedestrians and cyclists, increasing bus and cycle lanes, and stopping the growth of low-density suburbs and out-of-town supermarkets, which increase the use of cars." However, reducing car use will not improve equity if it simply makes driving increasingly expensive and livable cities increasingly expensive.

How can we connect urban sustainability transitions and transport justice into a broader frame that recognizes the historical formation of unequal mobilities and urban spatial forms as processes of racial injustice? Such an analysis of the racialized politics of mobility extends to other white-settler societies such as Australia, Canada, and South Africa, which share similar patterns, and to various similar class inequalities and ethnic inequalities in capabilities for mobilities that extend this kind of analysis across Europe, as well as to other parts of the world.[35] There will be no mobility transition until we face the racialization of (sub)urban space, the unequal rights to the city—and to the car—and the determinative impacts this has on human health and thriving.

Global Mobility Regimes

Building on his earlier influential work on the "splintering" of urban infrastructure, geographer Stephen Graham observes that the recent boom in building elevated highways and "flyovers" in economically developing global cities is producing deeply unequal spaces. Newly built expressways in sprawling megacities like Chennai, Mumbai, Manila, and Jakarta connect the archipelago landscapes of splintering urban forms:

> They lace together the securitized enclaves of residence, work, leisure and mobility that constitute the archipelago of urban life for the wealthy car-user. Indeed, the routes of elevated freeways, so often used as cordon sanitaires to separate and isolate districts within racialized or class-based planning regimes (Bullard, Johnson, and Torres 2004; Henderson 2006), are also sometimes deliberately designed to necessitate the demolition of informal cities of the poor.[36]

The division of urban space, the forcible eviction of poor residents, and the demolition of their informal neighborhoods are all key forms of accumulation by dispossession, supporting the "premium mobilities" of elites. Thus, the modernizing goal of gleaming flyovers and the economic growth they are purported to support only accrue benefits to the kinetic elite and often directly harm the mobility poor.

Even in seemingly egalitarian spaces, such systems rely on the "everyday infrastructure" of the queue as a kind of "control architecture" that patterns stop-and-go mobility. There is a daily dance with inherent power relations in the organization of waiting: "If speed and movement is a commodity, then delay is the control," Gillian Fuller argues, such that "for some, with smart technologies and good salaries, queues can be jumped, for others they are unavoidable."[37]

Waiting is also an effect of disabling environments in which one cannot physically gain access to stairways, entrances, or means of transport. And waiting may also be encoded into modes of social power that require gendered or racial deference, and speedier access by elites (often white and male) whose time is considered more valuable. Rush hour road pricing gives quicker city center access to such kinetic elites, while the mobility poor in many sprawling cities are often relegated to long pre-dawn commutes on multiple slow bus lines, or in meandering informal shared taxis, such as Matatu in Nairobi, Kenya, or Tap-Taps in Port-au-Prince, Haiti, or exposed to dust and danger on the back of motorcycle taxis.

Having to wait, while others "speed" past, is a form of power, for instance, experienced daily by car drivers who jump into the electronically tolled EZ-Pass "fast lane" in the USA, or who get on the privately tolled "expressways" that have recently been built in cities such as Santiago, Chile, or the North–South Highway in Jamaica. Such exclusive roadways reshape social and geographical space by giving those who can afford it greater access via "time-space compression."[38] Simultaneously, people living near these roads find themselves cut off from their normal access and often having to risk their lives crossing highways (illegally).

Transport inequity also accompanies and fundamentally supports the global ecological unsustainability of the entire system of automobility. Forms of racialized labor, racial embodiment, and state racial projects are closely tied to economic structures that rely on cheap energy and that produce racially segregated urbanism, suburbanization, and a heavy carbon footprint linked to long commutes by car, large energy-hungry suburban houses, and status competition to drive ever larger or more powerful cars. While China is quickly growing its car culture, the United States remains one of the most energy-consuming countries in the world and contributes about one-third of transport-related greenhouse gas (GHG) emissions globally.

The Fifth Assessment Report (AR5) of the Intergovernmental Panel for Climate Change (IPCC) estimates that GHG emissions from transportation "have more than doubled since 1970 to reach 7.0 Gt CO_2eq by 2010 with about 80 percent of this increase coming from road vehicles." With no mitigation measures, "the current transport sector's GHG emissions could increase by up to 50 percent by 2035 at continued current rates of growth and almost double by 2050."[39] This continuing growth in road vehicles contributes to global warming which has negative impacts on some of the poorest and most vulnerable parts of the world.

Having covered these issues of transport injustice, we can now turn to current transitions in automobility that appear to be occurring in many countries. By some measures it could be construed that we may be moving away from the dominant twentieth-century system of automobility toward something else— although what exactly remains to be seen. This transition, however, must be assessed not only in relation to overall patterns of automobility within specific cities, but also in relation to wider questions of differential mobility and mobility justice. What are the implications of a decline in automobility in contexts of deeply racialized, classed, gendered, and international inequities in mobility capabilities?

THE DECLINE IN AUTOMOBILITY

As cities across the world face the effects of climate change, congestion, pollution, health inequity, and insufficient transport accessibility, it is increasingly evident that our old ways of moving are broken, or at the very least are reaching limits of capacity and sustainability. One key arena of active intervention and experimentation in urban planning and policy is the effort to replace the current dominant system of automobility (based largely on GHG-emitting internal combustion engines, private vehicle ownership that contributes to suburban sprawl, and publicly subsidized roads that suck investment away from public transit systems). If moving "beyond mobility" is one solution, a more equitable way to do this would be moving "beyond automobility."

In its place, we find cities experimenting with transit-oriented development, building bicycling infrastructure (bike lanes, bike parking, bike sharing), investing in improved public transit (new metros, bus rapid transit, light rail systems), and promoting active transport (walking, complete streets, new zoning regulations). This includes "redirecting subsidies for gas guzzler vehicles and highways toward promoting public transportation and zoning laws that discourage sprawl and create sidewalks, bike lanes, and public transportation, so people can reach the places they need to go without driving."[40] Such policies have been extremely mobile, traveling to cities around the world, yet there is still much uncertainty about their overall impact. The claimed benefits of improved bicycling infrastructure are that it will reduce car traffic (including its noise and exhaust emissions), it will enhance public space, promote health, potentially contribute to savings in health and infrastructure expenditures, and generally support making "cities for people."[41]

In some cities automobility is already in decline. Across a range of different measures, in the United States from 2004 to 2013, there were fewer car trips per driver, fewer miles driven per driver, and fewer people getting drivers' licenses.[42] "Driving light" (at least temporarily) became a new trend, and the number of annual new car purchases has been slow to return to its 2007 peak. The total number of vehicles on the road did not rise between 2006 and 2013, according to the Bureau of Transportation Statistics, while ridership on subway trains and light rail rose steadily over that decade across the USA, according to the National Household Travel Survey.[43]

There also appeared to be a generational shift in patterns of car use. From 2001 to 2009, the average annual vehicle miles traveled by young people (sixteen to thirty-four years old) decreased from 10,300 miles per capita to 7,900 miles per capita, a 23 percent drop. Even young people from affluent families with incomes of over $70,000 per year, doubled their public transit usage and biking trips. A spate of research reports and media coverage appeared taking stock of these trends, leading many people to ask whether there was in the USA a significant shift among the "millennial" generation away from car driving. Or was this merely a small blip caused by weak employment, high gas prices, and other financial stresses such as student loans?

This trend was found across all developed countries, not just in the USA. A comprehensive study of changes in age composition of drivers in fifteen countries revealed that driving license rates among the younger generations declined significantly between the 1980s and late 2000s in the US, UK, Canada, Germany, Japan, and Sweden. Why? There is weakening commitment by policy makers and car manufacturers to business-as-usual; there is experimentation with alternative charging systems, fuel types and materials; there are new urban design measures and pricing schemes that begin to place limits on car use; and there is much evidence that younger generations consider smartphones a more crucial technology to have than cars.[44]

More recently, the decline in driving has also been linked to the rise of new mobile communication technologies that have facilitated the emergence of car-sharing, ride-sharing, ride-hailing, transport-service networks, and the concept of "mobility as a service." New (and sometimes old) forms of shared mobility are starting to shift some of those assumed cultural discourses and entrenched urban mobility regimes, but it is not clear yet whether they will expand mobility capabilities and lead toward greater mobility justice. Indeed, in many cities, such trends have been linked with rising property prices, high rental costs, and gentrification.

Bike-sharing, car-sharing, carpooling, on-demand ride-sharing, paratransit, microtransit, and for-hire mobility services have all been promoted in cities in various combinations, often drawing on new mobile information and communication capabilities. While some see shared mobility as a potential disruption of traditional forms of automobility and transport injustice, there are also concerns that it will undermine public transit services, increase elite mobilities, and not be fairly distributed to the mobility poor.[45] While some innovative "new urban transport investments largely depart from the expansive, public-subsidy intensive, auto-centric, and environmentally destructive patterns of urban development that prevailed during the past century," according to a study at Harvard's Graduate School of Design, these mobility innovations "risk compounding, if not intensifying, existing socio-spatial inequalities in cities" because they increase gentrification.

Los Angeles, for example, is considered a very car-dependent city. Yet it has also committed to a 2035 Mobility Plan that will "balance the needs of all road users," according to the Los Angeles Department of City Planning. Having implemented policies to enhance cycling and walkability, it saw a 56 percent increase in cycle commuting between 2000 and 2010. It also has the third highest usage of public transport in the United States. Yet these improvements were accompanied by forcible evictions of homeless people and ongoing processes of gentrification. Many people question whether the new cycling culture is inclusive, not only in LA but across the United States. The Untokening project, for example, has highlighted the white biases built into urban planning processes, and raise questions about the inclusivity of recent policy changes and transport plans in cities like Los Angeles:

> Bodily ability, gender presentation, clothing, race, and other elements of appearance limit our access to what privileged groups view as open spaces. Our bodies encounter different risks and have different needs. Many women and trans individuals experience sexual harassment on streets and on public transit. Black and brown bodies experience disproportionate policing. One-size-fits-all approaches to urban design do not respond to the complexity of our different bodies in motion . . . We all have diverse abilities and challenges and, therefore, different bodies demand distinct social, physical, and cultural supports within shared mobility environments. True safety and equitable mobility require radical inclusion in mobility planning and implementation.[46]

In Philadelphia, as young millennials have repopulated the center of the city and brought a new buzz of restaurants and real estate development to once quiet residential neighborhoods, a movement for protected bike lanes and safer streets has challenged the entrenched car culture. Young professionals and the "creative class" (and their ex-suburban retiree parents) want to walk or bike amid Philadelphia's charmingly varied low-rise colonial and nineteenth-century streetscape, and jump into Uber and Lyft when they need a ride. But it has also brought a backlash against gentrification from old-time residents who feel priced out by newcomers planting street trees and installing bike lanes, which they claim attracts more expensive housing development, drives up rent, and raises property taxes. Battles have raged in the City Council over the building of bike lanes, and questions over whether city residents support them.

Urban central business district growth and changing urban transport policies may simply reflect a spatial redistribution of elite mobilities and a retrenching of the automobile industry to incorporate new information technologies, rather than being indicative of some deeper change in car culture. Given the rising property values in central urban cores, lower-income populations are pushed out to areas that lack alternative transport options:

> We must reverse the order of change, first articulating our visions for a more socially inclusive, environmentally sustainable city and then pursuing the complementary mix of urban policies and technological innovations that achieve these aims. Without such a framework, innovations that hover on the horizon, including autonomous vehicles, will likely do little to address the bigger picture of growing socio-spatial inequality.[47]

Even if automated electric vehicles were to lead to increasing efficiencies and lower costs of transportation, it is not clear that this will reduce the number of vehicles on the road. It could also lead to more trips (as already seems to be the case in New York City) and a growing undifferentiated sprawl of quasi-urbanization spreading through the matrix of existing suburbs, now serviced by driverless delivery vans and a proliferating fleet of automated cars traveling "intelligent highways" between such non-places in platoons.

From my vantage point in the US, in contrast to some of the more enthu-siastic proclamations of post-automobility in Europe, cars remain king. Automobility builds on patterns of kinship, sociability, habitation, land use, and work, all of which are relatively stabilized and locked into built environments and social patterns. These car cultures have social, material, and above all affec-tive dimensions that are overlooked in current strategies to influence car-driving decisions. People (and their feelings) are embedded in historically sedimented and geographically etched patterns of "quotidian mobility," which are not easily changed.[48] This attention to what I have called "automotive emotions" also signals the need to pay attention to how an individual's daily routines reinforce the embodied aspects of transport injustice and reproduce elements of race, class, gendered, and (dis)abling embodiment.

Dwelling with or without cars is complex, ambiguous, and contradictory. Car consumption is never simply about rational economic choices, but is as much about aesthetic, emotional, and sensory responses to driving which contribute to locking in a set of individual practices. While some theorists refer to the "psychology" of the car as one of admiration, attachment, and even "addiction," it may be more pertinent to understand individual practices through their social context and the design of socio-material environments.[49] Car cultures are also highly politically charged, and not necessarily subject to rational analysis during legislative processes as demonstrated by the intense backlash against building bike lanes in many instances.

There has even been a cultural phenomenon of the modification of light trucks to belch out smoke and purposely choke pedestrians, cyclists, and drivers of electric vehicles: "There is a new menace on America's roads: diesel truck drivers who soup up their engines and remove emissions controls to 'roll coal,' or belch black smoke, at pedestrians, cyclists, and unsuspecting Prius drivers."[50] Coal rollers, generally white working-class men, claimed a right to the road and to entertainment through a kind of adrenaline-rush, but were also lashing out against Obama administration policies within the Clean Air Act that enforced new engine efficiency standards. Their assertion of a "basic human right to use energy" was a foretaste of the Trump administration's assault on the Clean Air Act and support for coal mining, the building of oil pipelines, and the opening of protected public lands to oil drilling.

Steeped in white nationalism, this kind of backlash suggests the need to pay attention to wider patterns of mobility injustice at the bodily, regional, and global scale, not just as a question of individual psychology or automobile addiction. Coal rollers embody patterns of class resentment, racial supremacy, military power, and global inequalities that support racialized white ethno-nationalism-on-wheels, as well as the needs of the American fossil fuel industry.

There is also an articulation of these (sub)urban and ex-urban American mobilities with transnational mobility regimes that restrict border crossing and depend on the global mobilities of energy and resources associated with planetary urbanization. I return to these issues in later chapters. The point I want to make here is that neither the transport justice movement nor the theory of spatial justice have gone far enough in connecting together these dispersed elements of mobility injustice. It is this multi-scalar entanglement of cascading effects that helps *explain* the persistence of the dominant system of automobility. We ignore this at our peril. Current trends in adjusting automobility to new "smart" technologies and automation may simply reproduce, or even exacerbate, existing patterns of uneven mobility and racialized global mobility injustice.

POST-CAR AND POST-CARBON TRANSITIONS

The IPCC identifies transportation (of both freight and people) as responsible for around one-quarter of energy-related CO_2 emissions globally and notes that despite increases in efficiency of vehicles, transport-related GHG emissions have continued to grow.[51] The IPCC has "high confidence" in the mitigation potential of a combination of actions including avoided journeys and modal shifts due to behavioral change, uptake of improved vehicle and engine performance technologies, low-carbon fuels, investments in related infrastructure, and changes in the built environment. Yet IPCC expertise mostly lies in quantitatively measured technological changes and to some extent infrastructural changes, with little qualitative social science expertise on *how* the far-reaching social and cultural changes that are necessary to limit CO_2 emissions (and other GHGs) will take place.

The IPCC notes that among the knowledge gaps in the transport sector, additional research is needed on "the implications of norms, biases, and social learning in decision-making, and of the relationship between transportation and lifestyle. For example, how and when people will choose to use new types of low-carbon transport and avoid making unnecessary journeys is unknown." Notice that this statement frames the unknowns in terms of individual choices, rather than addressing wider social and material arrangements. The traditional emphasis on personal choices framed by "travel-time budgets, costs and prices" as key drivers of transport decisions is locked within older ways of thinking about transport planning and modeling, including rational choice economic thinking.[52]

The IPCC report admits that current approaches to climate change mitigation lack the basic social science knowledge to incorporate this into GHG mitigation planning and policy.[53] Indeed, they have completely failed to address the kinds of social and political backlash that we have noted against carbon reduction. Nor have they noted the vast resources poured into challenging climate change science by the oil industry.

At the same time, many advocates of mobility transitions and sustainable transportation also approach alternative mobilities as an individual choice, focusing on how to educate, encourage, and support more people to ride bikes, walk more, or use public transit. This is linked to policy ideas such as travel demand management (TDM), which seeks to reduce individual demand for trips by private vehicle. A second approach focuses on technological systems, and emphasizes the continuing demand for private cars, which could be met with low-carbon technological solutions such as electric vehicles, alternative fuel vehicles (such as natural gas or new biofuels), or better systems for car sharing. Both approaches are accompanied by behavioral theories that rely on pricing mechanisms (e.g., gas taxes, congestion charging, subsidies for electric cars) to encourage behavioral shifts, which generally rely on "rational choice" economic models focused on cost or benefit to the consumer for different changes in behavior. A third approach considers wider ranging cultural changes that may affect individual behavior and are often linked to new "smart" technologies, such as the popular appeal of ride-hailing apps.

Many transport analysts have predicted a "revolution" in the way transportation is done in cities. A report by the non-profit Institute for Transportation and Development and the University of California at Davis, for example, argues that "there can be an 80 percent cut in CO_2 emissions if cities embrace 3 revolutions (3R) in vehicle technology: automation, electrification, and, most importantly, ride-sharing."[54] Electrification, automation, and sharing, they argue, have the potential to reduce the number of vehicles on the road by about 75 percent. They point toward the revolution already beginning in cities like Oslo, Norway, where 30 percent of new cars sold are electric; or Vancouver, Canada, which has the largest car-sharing market in the world. Norway's parliament set a goal that by 2025 all cars sold should have zero emissions, and indeed, by 2017 it was reported that half of all new car registrations in Norway were electric or hybrid, according to the Norwegian Road Federation. France and Britain also plan to ban the sale of fossil-fueled cars by 2040.[55]

However, this hopeful scenario still largely focuses on vehicles and transport systems isolated from a wider mobilities context. It ignores the ways in which class, race, gender, and ability might factor into such a transformation of transport. It ignores the larger mobility regimes that articulate with transportation systems and usually redirect them toward hegemonic projects that serve elite interests (such as real estate development, increased consumption, and easier mobility for kinetic elites). When cost of transport falls, people tend to use more of it. Many of the measures still support growth in private vehicle sales. Moreover, Norway's generous subsidies for electric vehicles depend on their vast revenues from oil and gas drilling, distributed from the world's largest sovereign wealth fund, valued at more than $1 trillion.

The 3R vision also centers on the city as an isolated unit, and does not address suburban and extra-urban transport issues, where shared mobility systems have been much more difficult to implement. When lower income groups are pushed out of the increasingly expensive urban center (as seen in Vancouver, for example, which has some of the highest real estate prices in the world), they will not have access to electric vehicles and shared mobility services. Cities might stop investing in mass public transportation systems. And such visions ignore the even larger scales of extended urbanization and planetary energy circulation: Where will we get the lithium for batteries and all the other metals and energy to fuel this system?

Such "smart" mobility services aim at the young, healthy, middle-class, implied white consumer who has the "mobility capital" and capabilities to "give up" driving. Other groups may not have such capabilities or may already be using public transit, or, as seen across America, may come from cultural groups who simply assert their right to the road and to automobility. The pricing mechanisms approach, meanwhile, falls more heavily on the working poor and the lower middle class, who already spend greater proportions of their income on transportation, while not impacting the kinetic elite who drive luxury vehicles. This feeds into class-resentment and fuels the white anti-environmental backlash seen among Trump supporters in the USA, or among the white working class in Australia or parts of Europe.

Building out the infrastructure for electrical vehicle charging or natural gas refueling, for example, will require not just individual consumer demand, but quite large public or private investments that will likely need public subsidies or changes of regulation that allow public utilities to apply energy rate payments to such new infrastructural investments. Yet both the racialized "mobility poor" and white, working- and middle-class rural and suburban car drivers are very unlikely to benefit from the use of these (relatively expensive) electric vehicles or alternative fuel vehicles, so tax-payers will effectively be paying for public subsidies to the infrastructures used mainly by the urban kinetic elite. As we have already seen, American mobility cultures are deeply distorted through the lens of white supremacy, white nationalism, and racialization of subaltern "others" who are not afforded access to free mobility, and these policies for "mobility transition" do nothing to change that.

Any mobility transition is a systemic question that transcends individual choice models, technological availability, or econometric models. Mobility behaviors, and more widely *mobility cultures*, are more fundamentally embedded in and performed with and through spatial patterns of racialized urbanization (and suburbanization)—which also effects rural areas. Urban forms are racially uneven and contested, both locally and globally. Changes in mobility systems concern micro-level changes in embodied inequalities and privileged mobilities, as well as meso-level changes in systems of urban and regional governance. But they also involve macro-level changes in energy systems such as oil extraction and pipelines, or electric infrastructure for vehicle charging and batteries, and in wider political discourses around things like "energy independence" and "resource sovereignty."

To better understand such systemic changes scholars in the Netherlands developed the idea of "multi-level transition theory."[56] This situates "niche level" changes in individual mobility in relation to meso-level "regime" changes in institutions such as car-manufacturing and regulation, and broader "landscape" level changes such as oil prices or climate change that might influence transitions to sustainable automobility. While alternative mobility choices can demonstrate that certain things are possible—such as sharp reductions in individual carbon footprints for people who give up cars—it is still necessary to consider the "regime" and "landscape" levels at which larger urban (and national) mobility systems are slowly shaped.

Mobility regimes are embedded in entrenched repertoires for political interaction, transport planning and urban governance. And urban governance itself does not occur in a vacuum but relies on the extended "operational land-scapes" of resource extraction, connected to energy generation, food systems, water systems, mining, oil extraction, military power, etc.[57] Transitions in mobility systems depend, therefore, not just on individual choices, technological transformations, or even economic "disruption," but also on transitions in entire kinopolitical cultures.

Such kinopolitical practices produce and perform the mobility space of the city, the region, and the nation, as well as its extended infrastructure space. Mobility systems persist and combine into local, national, and even transnational cultural assemblages. This generates interlocking constellations of mobilities that remain very durable over long periods of time. The introduction of cleaner vehicles, alternative fuel vehicles and refueling stations, or bicycling lanes and infrastructure might help to promote sustainability, but only in a very limited sense if it is not coupled with wider reconfigurations of this kinopolitical landscape of mobility systems and discourses that shape the built environment and its everyday practices.

Cultural change in mobility regimes takes time. Disruptive startup companies with their new technologies do not change the world, nor do urban planners with their TOD standards, unless everyday users appropriate new technologies, incorporate new practices, and mobilize politically to counter the power of kinetic elites. Only then will the dominant mobility regime of automobility lose its power and give way to new actors seeking collective justice. Even when technological transformations are driven by social innovation "for profit, and for good," such as the European Union's shift toward "decarbonization," they may benefit already empowered groups more than those who are marginalized. Even when informed by principles of inclusion, deliberative and procedural extensions of decision-making and planning often still face limitations in practice. And in many cases, people simply are not able to change entrenched patterns or do not recognize what changes can and should be made.

A paradigm shift is therefore needed to understand the complexity and practices that drive transportation shifts and sustainable mobility transitions. Tinkering with travel-time budgets, transit-oriented development, transportation demand management, and fuel costs will not be sufficient to generate the massive global infrastructural and behavioral changes needed to dislodge the existing system of gendered, classed, racialized (im)mobilities and the governance of global kinopolitics. Mobility justice calls for a far more wide-ranging analysis of complex relational systems of infrastructural and social interaction across multiple scales, which the IPCC only barely begins to address in section 8.4 on "Infrastructure and Systemic Perspectives."[58]

Can such transitions toward more sustainable *and equitable* mobilities be accelerated, directed, guided, or fostered? And what can we learn from the current transitions that are taking place in some cities? Where are the openings for new transportation systems or more widely conceived mobility regimes to emerge? And what are the kinopolitical relations that must be mobilized to make this transition happen?

There is already work incorporating mobilities theory into urban design, as well as sophisticated qualitative analyses of travel-time use, the emergence of mobile lives, and the impacts of new information and communication technologies on urban space and mobility.[59] But mobilities research also focuses on questions beyond urban transport and travel behavior to encompass topics such as historically embedded systems and embodied experiences of air travel, cultural histories of metals and mining, and climate change itself.[60] This expansiveness of the new mobilities paradigm suggests that a kinopolitical transition will happen only with a scalar jump in transforming the wider energy cultures and the everyday social practices that sustain the dominant mobility regime.

GLOBAL TRANSPORT JUSTICE AND JUST CITIES

Energy is not only consumed in the act of moving; it is also materialized in objects, infrastructures, and distributions of ways of living that depend on specific global mobilizations of energy. None of the proposed "sustainable" transitions or "revolutions" in smart transportation consider the extended operational landscape from which the resources for urban life must be sourced, with all the attendant uneven impacts of pollution, waste, mining, and energy production. Low-carbon, post-car, and *just* transport transitions require a more holistic mobility justice perspective. For this we need a kinopolitics that can span multiple scales at once.

Changes in automobility in US cities pale in comparison to what is happening in other parts of the world where urban growth is more rapid, and transport and infrastructure investments are happening by necessity. We know that there is a major expansion of urbanization occurring globally, as well as a huge expansion of automobility in many countries, and especially China, where car ownership increased with the fastest rate of growth ever.[61] David Tyfield assesses that the hoped-for switch to cleaner electric cars in China faces a number of barriers and is unlikely to occur on a large scale. However, there is a large and potentially "disruptive" uptake of electric two-wheelers and three-wheel micro-vehicles, which could advance an e-mobility transition among the middle classes (if supported by the government).

In many parts of the urbanizing world there are indeed trends such as the rapid increase in motorcycle use and in some cases, electric two-wheelers, as well as the expansion of public transit systems. Accompanying these changes has been a new focus on using transportation improvements to foster more "just cities" that overcome historical patterns of urban sprawl and avoid the re-creation of informal neighborhoods which lack transport, access, and public space.

In Latin America, for example, there has been much development of Bus Rapid Transit projects, led by Colombia's TransMilenio system in Bogotá, which opened in 2000/2001, along with the later addition of other BRT-type projects in cities such as Pereira, Medellin, Cali, and most recently the TransCaribe system in Cartagena. In many cases BRT has extended access to transport, reduced travel times, introduced wheelchair accessibility, and brought in alternative fuels such as compressed gas. Such systems are also trying to improve bicycle and pedestrian accessibility. It is worth noting that in cities such as Cartagena there has been a rapid increase in the use of motorcycles, which grew from 30 percent to 60 percent of registered vehicles between 2008 and 2017, and are especially used as moto-taxis.[62]

Robert Cervero's previous work on "Progressive Transport and the Poor," about Bogota's Metrovivienda Project, was far more directly critical of automobility than his recent book, *Beyond Mobility*. It shows how an equitable transit-oriented development project combined a buildout of 440,000 units of affordable housing clustered around the termini of the successful TransMilenio Bus Rapid Transit System. This was only possible because of the acquisition of cheap land before the extension of BRT services was known. This suggests a strategy that was not about place-making, but about a strategic intervention in real-estate markets that are directly linked to mobility improvements.[63]

In contrast to current "place-making" policies that claim to shift our focus "beyond mobility," a mobility justice approach means revealing the power relations inherent in city and regional planning processes. It means challenging more directly the dominance of automobility and fossil fuels, not to mention real estate developers and so-called place-makers. Mobility justice requires including all affected communities in urban and regional planning processes, not just through token "stakeholder" consultations, but through meaningful epistemic inclusion. Finally, we must not be afraid to name and call out elite privilege, vested interests, and dominant paradigms that have benefitted the kinetic elite—whether through the uneven impacts of (auto)mobility or through processes of gentrified place-making.[64]

There are also cases of dire failures in the implementation of new BRT systems, as infamously occurred with the launch of the Transantiago bus system in Chile.[65] Transantiago was an attempt to reform and expand access to the public bus system in Chile while reducing air pollution by overhauling the bus and metro systems with an all new BRT system and electronic fare cards. However, it was implemented in such a short space of time that it led to chaotic scenes of confusion, insufficient buses, overcrowding, and impossible wait times of up to four hours. It also exacerbated existing social inequalities because already marginalized groups such as poor migrants who lived in the periphery, women whose bodies were literally crushed in the crowds, and people with disabilities experienced decreased access to the system.[66]

The City of Santiago has nevertheless found success in implementing other changes such as improving walking conditions, implementing transit priority streets, and opening many miles of new cycle lanes. In 2017 it won ITDP's Sustainable Transport Award and hosted the MOBILIZE Summit. Low-carbon inclusive modes of transport (including walking and bicycling) are increasingly seen as one of the best ways to address social inequalities in how people travel and how goods are delivered, and this, it is argued, will result in more just cities.[67] On the other hand, a relatively new toll-highway through the heart of Santiago also points toward the "splintered" provision of exclusive transport systems, and suggests how many cities in the Global South (which already exhibit high income inequality) will likely build spatially uneven and unequally accessible systems for the upper and lower classes (as noted in Graham's discussion of flyovers).

Organizations such as the non-profit Institute for Transportation and Development (ITDP), founded in 1985 in the United States, works with developing cities around the world to improve transport and urban street design. It is one of the leading organizations promoting environmentally sustainable and equitable transportation policies and projects worldwide. In China, for example, they partnered on a Child Friendly City program in Changsha to improve road safety for children. They report that 18,500 children under fourteen die in traffic accidents in China each year, 2.5 times the number in Europe and 2.6 times the number in the USA. Changsha has now implemented improvements including refuge islands at road crossings, parking demand management, rush hour traffic organization, sign integration, and public space upgrades. This, of course, must be placed in the context of the large increase in car use in China, as a new middle class adopts automobility. China has also, however, built many new underground metro systems and rail networks on a huge scale, as well as supported investment in these around the world. So, there are many simultaneous transformations happening in the country's transport systems.[68]

Of most importance for our arguments here, ITDP has promoted transit-oriented development (TOD) as a social justice issue around the world. They suggest that:

> The TOD Standard stands for the rights of all to access the city: to walk and cycle safely, to easily and affordably reach the most distant destination through rapid and frequent transit, and to live a good life free of dependence on cars. It stands for access to opportunity, education, services, and all the resources available via no- or low-cost mobility options.[69]

The Ford Foundation's support for this initiative—ironically coming from a private foundation founded in 1936 by Edsel and Henry Ford, founders of the Ford Motor Company, which has become one of the largest and most influential foundations in the world—explicitly calls for more "Just Cities" and social inclusion: "Inclusionary objectives need to be embedded in policies and in planning and design processes to actively protect and bring along people and social groups who might otherwise be excluded, marginalized, or not afforded the same full privileges as others." This kind of language advances a capabilities approach to justice based on measures of human well-being as well as advocating deliberative and procedural justice in urban planning.[70]

The TOD Standard is a planning and design tool developed by ITDP that is used to measure and evaluate projects on eight core principles. These include indicators of safety, vibrancy of neighborhoods, well-connected pedestrian and cycling networks, density, and minimal car traffic and parking. Transit-oriented development, they argue, "is an answer to the unsustainable, car-dependent, and transit-poor urban sprawl that has characterized the growth of cities around the world in the last century. It also . . . complement[s] and actively support[s] the use of transit."[71] The latest standards explicitly link TOD to the creation of affordable housing and preservation of local businesses, thus seeking to mitigate the gentrification effect that TOD has often had when implemented in cities in North America, for example, where housing prices have risen around "good" transit areas both in Canada and the US.

Policy tools such as the TOD Standard, which itself travels around the world, seek to implement some of the concepts of transport justice within actually existing cities. While Karel Martens' notion of transport justice sets certain thresholds or minimum standards of fairness for sufficient accessibility, as noted above, it still leaves unanswered the political problem of how such a utopian ideal might be achieved under existing conditions.[72] Even within a system of democratic governance there are serious unresolved issues of recognition, deliberation, and procedural justice that are lacking in this approach. The Capabilities Approach (CA) emphasizes not only the need for fairness in the distribution of transport and accessibility, but also calls for greater attention to justice in transportation decision-making and participatory processes.[73]

Yet transport planning tends to be a very technocratic undertaking, and even when it involves some public consultation does not truly allow for the opening up of planning to wider questions of justice such as reparative justice and epistemic justice. Within urban planning there is a movement advocating "communicative planning" or "collaborative planning" as a more inclusive approach that seeks to represent various interests and reach consensus through deliberative processes.[74] It would be desirable to implement such processes in order to deal with new issues such as the regulation of networked transport services and app-based shared mobilities, or pricing policies such as reducing private car parking and "coding the curb" to capture the costs of using public streets for private pick-ups or deliveries. Collaboration and communication, though, will remain challenging. As the Untokening project urges, we should:

> Join urban planning discussions from a perspective of respecting and valuing the assets inherent and abundant in marginalized communities, rather than their deficiencies, and develop data tools that measure community vulnerability and the impacts of gentrification to serve the current community. Development's success should be measured by its effects on existing residents, not by its economic return for absent investors. The benefits of neighborhood changes must accrue most to those who historically have experienced the most neglect.[75]

This requires listening to others, combatting institutional racism, checking privilege, and valuing local knowledge.

Therefore, we can build on some of the insights of the field of transportation justice and, more broadly, the emerging movement for mobility justice, to call for the following principles, which also extend to what might be called infrastructural justice:

- Public systems of transport must not arbitrarily deny access nor impose undue burdens, externalities, or limitations.
- Cities should ensure equitable provision of public transportation through a social benefit analysis based on population-level measures of social exclusion and minimum thresholds of accessibility (as described by Martens), and should seek to reverse the historical subsidies and other preferential treatment given to private automobility.
- Complete Streets policies should ensure that all modes of moving are afforded space and that streets are not dominated by one mode, such as cars.
- Cities should preserve public space, support multi-modal shared space, and must not develop splintered infrastructures that systematically advantage some groups with superior levels of service and disadvantage others with inferior levels of service.
- Transit-Oriented Development standards should be used to evaluate and measure social impacts of urban transport plans on accessibility, affordable housing,

and social inclusion, and all communities should be included in decision-making processes.

Against the current policy trends of simply adjusting the system of automobility by promoting alternative fuel systems (such as electric vehicles and charging stations) or imposing congestion charges, road pricing, and other limits on use, Daniel Newman further argues that we need to truly re-think how the mobility needs of all people can be met. Pricing policies that seek to make automobility scarcer will inevitably price out the poor rather than the wealthy, and will disadvantage those who need car services (including the disabled, the elderly, etc.). Technological fixes that merely reduce the environmental harms of automobility (such as electric power systems) will simply perpetuate the many other inequalities and forms of exclusion that an overreliance on automobility produces.

Instead, Newman argues that "issues of socioeconomic justice [need to] be brought into discussions of sustainable transport," to bring an end to transport poverty and automobile dependency. He has drafted a very easily understood Mobility Bill of Rights that lays out some of the basic principles, and calls on others to share it, discuss it, promote dialogue, and to take action. With that in mind, I include it here:[76]

MOBILITY BILL OF RIGHTS

1 The right to affordable transportation to meet our basic needs.
2 The right to transportation that does not harm us, the environment, or the climate.
3 The right to transportation that does not threaten health, safety, water, air, or the local environment of a community.
4 The right to a fair transport pricing system that does not penalize those that use less.
5 The right to not be cut off from society.
6 The right to not be forced to use a car.
7 The right to a public transportation system that is owned by us and run in our interests.
8 The right to efficient, inviting mobility options that do not adversely contribute to resource depletion.

I believe these rights are in line with the mobility justice principles outlined in this book, although I find it hard to understand how items 6, 7, 8 could be ensured since geographical choices to live far from alternatives might "force" car use, public transport systems are sometimes fairly run by private companies or public-private partnerships, and whether a mode of transport is "efficient" and "inviting" seem like rather subjective and relative qualities.

However, more fundamentally, I also believe that it is not enough to isolate transportation systems from the wider social and physical relations out of which they are assembled, nor can we bracket transportation from wider kino-political struggles around unjust (im)mobilities. Rights-based approaches are also limited by their individualistic framing, which draws attention away from relationality and competing political ontologies (such as those that are anti-individualistic, or assert the autonomous rights of non-human entities such as plants, animals, or rivers). Nor does this tell us how such rights might be achieved, or whether they are even achievable in any actually existing context.

Hard decisions on limiting some forms of environmentally and socially harmful mobility will need to be made. What kinds of kinopolitical movements are necessary to ensure the protection of such mobility rights? as well as ensuring basic mobility capabilities.

More just mobility transitions will require a wider transformation of larger urban infrastructures and kinopolitical spaces, to encompass the full array of bodily (im)mobilities and planetary urbanization. We need both a deeper historical view of unequal mobilities in terms of colonial histories, global geographies, and understandings of neoliberalism, as well as a deeper ecological vision of the material resource bases of mobility in extractive industries and extended infrastructural spaces that take us far beyond the city limits. I turn to these dimensions in the next chapter, on infrastructural justice.

Chapter 4

Smart Cities and Infrastructural Justice

Mobilities are organized in and through mobility regimes and uneven infrastructure spaces that simultaneously presuppose and reproduce immobile "others." Mobilities are never free but are in various ways channeled, tracked, controlled, governed, under surveillance, and always unequal. They are striated by gender, race, ethnicity, class, caste, color, nationality, age, sexuality, differential abilities, etc.—both in the past and today. Mobility regimes can be defined as systems "of disciplining and channeling movements and mobility by way of principles, norms, and rules," which shape movement, space, behavior, and conduct.[1] Often such norms and rules take a material form, built into the very infrastructure of cities and streetscapes.

Cities rely upon an exceptional scale of connections, networks, and flows, with "infrastructure" being the "basic physical and organizational structures and facilities (e.g. buildings, roads, power supplies) needed for the operation of a society or enterprise."[2] Mobility regimes generate dynamic topologies of the infrastructural spaces of movement, enabling some people to speed through without a glance, while others are slowed, detained, or expelled.[3]

Infrastructure has recently become a key topic of critical social theory. Deborah Cowen writes of the need for alternative infrastructures of hope and infrastructural repair that would help produce different social futures. "What might it mean," Cowen asks, "to ground citizenship in the material architectures and social relations of alternative infrastructure, instead of the gate/ways of corporations and nation-states? Could repairing infrastructure be a means of repairing political life more broadly?"[4]

Lauren Berlant even more broadly describes infrastructure as "defined by the movement or patterning of social form. It is the living mediation of what organizes life: the lifeworld of structure." A war, a disaster, or even more ordinary day-to-day failures of infrastructure can open up potentials for "new organizations of life" through what she calls "glitchfrastructures." Insofar as anti-austerity, antiracism and antixenophobic movements all condense around "the infrastructural breakdown of modern practices of resource distribution, social relation, and affective continuity," she finds hope here for new potentials.[5]

In the Global South, on the margins of global cities everywhere, and in the regions that James Ferguson calls the "global shadows" of the neoliberal world order, the challenges of precarious access to mobility (and unsafe or risky mobilities) produce the sharpest contours of uneven infrastructure. Mobility justice, from this perspective, is concerned with which "moves"—and resting places, dwellings, gatherings, or assemblies—are allowed or denied, who gets to decide, and whose mobility is valued and self-determined. A mobility justice perspective informed by feminist, postcolonial/Indigenous, critical race, and disabilities theories leads one to ask how some people's freedom of mobility impacts and depends on others' coerced mobilities, slowed mobilities, uprootings, and re-routings.

Focusing on infrastructural justice empowers us to ask questions about the relation between larger scale mobilities and local, situated access—i.e., the material connections between distributed sites of mobilization and demobilization, the circulations that connect production and consumption, the borders and walls that enact inclusion and exclusion. There has been a recent renewal of global/local struggles over infrastructural justice organized around the conflicts over hydraulic fracturing, oil and gas extraction, and the building of pipelines and megadams (both of which export energy elsewhere and damage the land). Sometimes these struggles come to the foreground especially after breakdowns, disruptions, and natural disasters.

At other times, we find the activation of mobility justice in political struggles such as Occupy, which reclaim public spaces and forms of assembly in the heart of cities, or in Indigenous peoples' movements, which have taken the lead in connecting local and global movements that demand that we move across the Earth differently.

As one group of Water Protectors expressed this regarding Indigenous infrastructural blockades across Turtle Island (aka North America):

> Pipelines are pieces of critical infrastructure produced to satisfy the energy needs of the global capitalist world. There isn't a way to have operating freeways, stores full of the latest electronic gadgets, military occupations of foreign countries, or Super Wal-Marts full of food grown by wage slaves in the global south without the oil infrastructure. To be against pipelines is to be against the very world we inhabit. No struggle that sets out to permanently destroy the possibility of all future pipelines imposed on this Earth can ever be successful without radically transforming the society that produces them through its energy needs.[6]

How can we rebuild broken infrastructural space more justly, when so often it deepens uneven geographies of super-accumulation by a few and theft of common goods (such as clean air, rivers, and oceans) from many? Critical approaches to infrastructure building, and more generally "development," demand that we ask: Who is connected? Who moves? Who is displaced? Who benefits? And is there any reason to be optimistic about the possibility for hacking or bending infrastructures toward greater social justice?

Cowen notes the important role that infrastructure systems play in "profoundly material" crises, reminding us how "relations of power and of force rely on socio-technical systems, that are themselves increasingly the object of struggle." She writes eloquently about the connection between movements such as the protests against oil pipelines across Indigenous communities in North America, the increasingly frequent blockades of dams, ports, highways, and rail infrastructure, and the politics of airports and the detention of migrants that are another kind of mobility infrastructure:

> Infrastructure connects a range of political conflicts which might otherwise seem disparate and discrete: crises surrounding the rights of refugees and the provision of asylum in a world of thickening borders; crises of indigenous peoples' lands and sovereignty in the face of transnational extractive industries; crises regarding local livelihoods in an economy organized through speed and flexibility in trade across vast distances; crises of water infrastructure in Black and Indigenous communities; crises of police and carceral violence that breed profound distrust in the core institutions of the state for communities of color.[7]

Most importantly, her work teaches us how "infrastructure may entrench injustice in systems that seem technical rather than political, instead of technopolitical, and thus can serve to naturalize those relations. And infrastructure does not simply reflect existing inequality but may engineer and entrench new forms."[8] Indeed, nature itself can become infrastructure, as anthropologist Ashley Carse argues in his study of the Panama Canal as a transit zone, where the management of forests, agriculture, and the movement of water on a vast scale inextricably entangle the technopolitics of man-made infrastructure (e.g., the canal itself and the 35–45 ships that pass through it daily) and the environmental politics of resource management and distribution (e.g., forest conservation and watershed regulation).[9]

Not only is infrastructure technopolitical, I would add, but it is kinopolitical. The politics of infrastructure concerns the politics of movement. Changing infrastructure, therefore, will require kinopolitical struggle. We already see emerging struggles over critical infrastructure politics, and movements for "infrastructural justice" which have sought, for example, to stop the building of oil pipelines, to tear down urban highways that divided communities, or to demand public funding for clean water or, for that matter, public WiFi and net neutrality. This chapter draws on theories of "infrastructuring" as an active practice, materialist approaches to media, and critical logistics studies, as well as critical mobilities theory, to trace the contours and possibilities of infrastructural justice through a series of mobile realms of infrastructural politics.[10]

As Brian Larkin observes, infrastructures serve not only a technical function (moving water, electricity, or data), but also have a poetics that operates via fantasy, desire, and speculative investments in the future plans of states or corporations.[11] In this chapter, then, I want to treat infrastructure as not only a mundane conveyor of mobilities but also as an often inspiring conveyor of fantasies, desires, and speculative futures. Whether those desires inspire awe or terror may depend on how we are positioned. The struggle over different visions of infrastructural forms and functions is one of the key ways in which alternative futures are shaped. And such struggles may especially come to the fore after the disruption of existing systems, when decisions need to be taken about how to rebuild.

Infrastructure, therefore, is also a space of contestation, protest, and mobile kinopolitics. Dynamic constellations of global and local mobility and communication can be said to exhibit various kinds of uneven topologies, turbulence, disruptions, differential speeds, and frictions, which at the same time offer handles, channels, and frequencies for interruption "from below" or glitches from within.

It is through kinopolitical struggles over "infrastructuring" that the excluded majority potentially can create fissures in existing systems and new possibilities for connection. This could have important effects on urban space, on national space, on scalar relations, and on their governance and control. What kinds of "mobile utopias" can we imagine? Can we use speculative futures and "utopia as a method" to bring about kinopolitical transformation in infrastructure space and mobility regimes?[12]

CITIES AND MOBILITIES

Cities are formed by mobilities as well as moorings. Located at the confluence of rivers, roadways, ports, rail termini, highways, and airports, cities have long been understood as a space of flows of people, goods, information, and ideas. They are places of intense infrastructural density founded upon the energy and resource-dependent movements of people, data, and objects: "Much of the city's existence is concerned with energy flows taking place on different levels: from water and sewage through to electricity and information, from people and animals, to machines and vegetables."[13] The material turn in mobilities research highlights these geoecological underpinnings and spatial questions surrounding infrastructures, including the global political economies of oil, carbon, and the mining of metals.[14]

Cities and mobilities are inextricably linked, and have been changing together throughout history through a series of largescale technological transitions in infrastructures for transport (e.g., from sail to steam ships, from wagons to rail freight, from horses to bicycles and internal combustion engines, and the addition of air transport) and communications (e.g., from codex to print, from newsprint to telegraph, telephone and fax, from radio and television to internet and satellite communication, and most recently mobile hand-held devices). Many of these infrastructural systems, and the practices that produce them, persist and combine into local, regional, and national cultural assemblages of mobility—such as highways, fossil fuels, and internal combustion vehicles that feed into suburbs, freight trucking, and global manufacturing—that remain very durable over long periods of time, even as they are constantly updated.

Geographer David Harvey has dedicated much of his work to showing how these physical infrastructures (or "fixed capital embedded in the land") exist to enable capital accumulation. "Spatially fixed and immobile physical infrastructures of transport and communications systems (ports, airports, transport systems)," he suggests, "are required in order to liberate other forms of capital and labor for easy spatial movement."[15] Over time this generates a "powerful centripetal force" of "uneven geographical developments," and it is this contradictory pull between fixity and movement that heightens inequality and deepens mobility injustice across expanding spatio-temporal horizons.

Infrastructure projects such as the building of highways and airports, whether financed by national budgets or international development banks, often serve the interests of global investors, multinational companies, and military needs. Space, cities, and infrastructures are not only fixed in place by these movements of capital and labor but are also constantly put into motion—they are mobilized and mobilizing.

Infrastructural systems are governed by mobility regimes, including the assemblage of legal regimes and everyday practices that govern who and what can move (or stay put), when, where, and under what conditions. Barriers to access and controls over mobility, whether physical or digital, biometric or algorithmic, limit the right to move. Legal and regulatory regimes of "risk management" filter entry and exit, and selectively apply the protection of the state. These uneven terrains bring socio-technical infrastructures to the social and political foreground, for they depend not only on the design of the built environment but also on the social practices in which delay, exclusion, turbulence, blockage, and disruption are an everyday experience. Such forms of immobilization and exclusion, moreover, are built into the infrastructures that support the mobilities of tourism, business travel, and even humanitarianism.

Contemporary urban systems are places not just of human surface transportation but also vast movements of energy through pipelines and cables, long-distance travel of freight by air and rail, and communication networks that reach into aerial and orbital space. While transport studies have largely been interested in horizontal movements over the face of the earth, we need to include vertical mobilities from the deep sea and underground mines to the aerial spaces of aviation and low earth-orbiting satellites.[16] Mobility justice on the ground must take into account these extended "operational landscapes" and "vertical dimensions of human world-making."[17]

The bundling of "network architectures" of "critical infrastructure" such as energy grids, pipelines, and communications cables is also part of an infrastructure of empire.[18] Contemporary cities can in fact be understood as *nodes* in transnational networks of critical infrastructure, that also manifest deeply colonial and imperial forms. Infrastructure is not simply proximate to urban centers; it is literally constitutive of the city—and the modern metropolis is almost inevitably a global imperial formation because it must source its life-support systems from around the world. Critical urban infrastructures shape and control mobilities in highly uneven ways, not just locally and regionally, but also transnationally and globally.

Infrastructure space is not mere background but takes active forms. Keller Easterling describes the "political character of infrastructure space" based on "accidental, covert, or stubborn forms of power" that hide in its folds.[19] Infrastructure space has "dispositions" that take active forms, she argues, through the organization of components into dynamic mechanisms including multipliers, switches and remotes, wiring and topology, and interplays and governors. The car, for example, is a multiplier that determines the shape of the road, highway, suburb, housing forms, and exurban development. The elevator is a multiplier that shapes the vertical densities of cities. The cell phone is also a multiplier that can expand dimensionally without a point-to-point centralized network. A highway interchange, a dam, or a landing-point for an undersea cable are all examples of "switches" that control flows.[20]

These infrastructural switches are in motion, changing the spatio-temporal format. The Port of Philadelphia, for example, has ordered two giant cranes from Shenzen, China, to increase its capacity to unload the super-size container ships now coming through the expanded Panama Canal. By dredging the Delaware River and expanding capacity, the port hopes to compete with New York and Baltimore. Business leaders are lobbying to build a pipeline across Pennsylvania to bring natural gas, fracked from the Marcellus Shale in the western part of the state, to the refineries along the Delaware where it can be turned into LNG liquid fuel and shipped around the world. More visible are the long black cylindrical CSX freight trains carrying heavy Bakken Shale oil, like caterpillars creeping through Philadelphia over badly rusting bridges, heading to the Sunoco refinery on the outskirts. There they will make fuel for the legions of drivers on Interstate 95, often slowed in traffic as they pass through an apocalyptic landscape of flaring towers, behemoth holding tanks, and metal-encrusted industrialized wetlands, not far from the growing Philadelphia International Airport, the expanding container port, and the historic Navy Yard that is being repurposed as a business campus for "resilient" green design, with its own micro-grid and soon-to-be extended subway line.

In other words, not only do people and things move through cities, but urban forms and infrastructures are on the move, changing the extended operational landscapes of urbanization across huge geographical areas. These extended operational landscapes are as much a concern of struggles for mobility justice (and environmental justice) as questions of accessibility. Indeed, moving beyond automobility will require interventions at this scale.

Everyday Infrastructural Exclusions

At the same time, everyday mobility practices and associated mobility regimes are in turn formed by cities and infrastructures: by public policies concerning urban migration, urbanization, and rights to the city; by forms of urban governance and policy that shape transport and communication infrastructures, and access to them; and by urban technological innovation and regional agglomerations that shape the spatiality and scale of mobility systems.

Movement through cities depends on the laws, regulations, and the everyday practices that hold such cultural-material assemblages together. The right to mobility exists only in relation to exclusions from national citizenship and urban access, governed by mobility regimes that include some people and exclude others, and controlled via policing, fungible borders, gates, passes, and surveillance systems. These restrictions are manifest in architecture, design, and everyday practices that limit the right to the city, splinter access to infrastructure, and selectively apply the protection of the state.

Even for those within the gates of citizenship and urban access, fragmented public services, hostile policing, and gentrified city centers push the poor, the racialized minority, and the undocumented migrant to the margins, where infrastructure is patchy and vulnerable to damage or failure. In the glistening metropolises of densely packed corporate sky scrapers, only the commodified tourism spaces that are urban playscapes and the exclusive zones of "elite mobilities" and cocooning may occupy the best, cleanest, greenest locations and make use of the newest, fastest infrastructures of transport and communication.[21]

When a homeless pan-handler or a migrant street-vendor, or even an entire tent camp appears here (as they often do), they are quickly shunted aside. As legal scholar Risa Goluboff shows, vague anti-loitering laws and highly flexible vagrancy laws have been used to police not only the poor, but also single women, racial and sexual minorities, and political dissenters, restricting their access to urban public space.[22] These uneven terrains depend not only on legal restrictions and the design of the built environment but also on the social practices in which delay, exclusion, turbulence, blockage, and disruption are an everyday experience for those who must dwell in and move through marginalized spaces seeking livelihoods, passage, and asylum.[23]

If critical infrastructures are not just physical but also communicational, then the reconfiguration of complex mobility, communication and information systems is crucial to generating new sites of political struggle. Mobile communication technologies span local and global scales of urbanization that connect cities to distant networked sites of resource extraction, but also to sites of leisure, tourism, and "places to play" that mobilize space in various ways including through media and visual representations.[24] This sense of planetary infrastructure as a matrix for mediatized processes has been enriched especially by anthropologists working on ethnographies of media in as varied locales as Nigeria, the Caribbean, Mongolia, and Zambia.[25]

The mobile phone, for example, affords one kind of multiplier that can potentially reconfigure the public itself, its meanings, its spaces, its capacities for self-organization and political mobilization, and its multiple and fluid forms. Mobile phones can help people enact alternative desires and speculative futures, for example in the hands of a Caribbean small trader trying to import commercial goods to sell at a street market, or an African farmer trying to transport agricultural crops to urban markets with the best prices. The mobile phone's ubiquity can also help bridge public and private spaces, and create new hybrid spaces, in ways that are crucial to political mobilization—in Cairo and Rio de Janeiro, as much as Manila or Kingston.[26]

Easterling holds out hope for "messiness" and "interplay" as found in heterogenous informal urban settlements.[27] How do the denizens of urban informal districts or global city peripheries outrun control and build "cities from scratch"? Can networked infrastructures be extended and appropriated by subversive kinopolitical movements who build their own network capital and tactical counter-media?[28] If infrastructural dispositions shape everyday lives, uneven and differential mobilities, then how can we use the struggle for mobility justice to imagine and make more just infrastructure? If subaltern publics have already appropriated infrastructural possibilities, how might these mobile publics be refashioned and built on to strengthen and democratize existing modes of social and political action and urban mobilities governance?

Mobile materialities and infrastructural struggles produce forms of uneven spatiality and new kinds of mobile subjects, while also perhaps offering glimpses of forms of collective mobile resistance. The creation of informal infrastructures for working around uneven mobilities, and do-it-yourself means of access might leverage urban infrastructure for a politics of empowering the marginalized. McFarlane and Vasudevan refer to these mobile planning practices as "insurgent urbanism" (like squatting, or informal neighborhood water/sewage systems).[29]

Insurgent urbanism can be found in a "green favela" in Rio de Janeiro where squatters grow their own food, in a community-run water and sanitation system in Port-au-Prince, Haiti, or in the creation of an urban garden, community radio station, or mesh network in a semi-abandoned neighborhood of Detroit or Philadelphia. We should cherish and grow these small spaces of infrastructural experimentation, for they may hold the seeds of the future.

DISASTER (IM)MOBILITIES

While everyday situations are important, sometimes more extreme events can help reveal some of the usually hidden actions of infrastructural space, including their repair and maintenance in the face of disruption.[30] Natural disasters bring to the fore the astounding interdependence and fragility of the complex mobility systems and infrastructural moorings that make up contemporary cities, regions, and transnational geographies of planetary urbanization. How do questions of mobility justice play out in these messy post-disaster situations?

Recent approaches to the geography of disasters and post-disaster recovery emphasize how prior distributions of advantage and disadvantage lead to uneven reconstruction and redevelopment, often exacerbating preexisting inequalities and reinforcing their spatial forms. One crucial element of "uneven redevelopment" concerns the role of im/mobilities in re-shaping space and delimiting forms of access. Insofar as "urban crises lay bare the underlying power structures, long-neglected injustices, and unacknowledged inequalities of contemporary cities," then uneven mobilities are a prime example of the social mechanisms by which such inequalities are reproduced in the wake (and in the name) of such crises.[31] In the face of large-scale systems failure, we see laid bare the institutional scaffolding and regulatory regimes that leave some groups most vulnerable to harm.

Natural disasters demobilize and remobilize. They strike at mobility systems but also engender their own unique mobilities (and immobilities) as people seek to flee the onset of an impending catastrophe, to get resituated in its bewildering aftermath, or to locate their dispersed families, food, water, and shelter. At the same time, emergency responders, relief workers, and armed peace keepers and soldiers begin to move into the affected area and take control of infrastructures of mobility such as roads, airports, ports, and communication networks. Given the already splintered provision of infrastructure in less developed countries and their cities, collapsing mobility systems are likely to have very different effects on the wealthy and the poor, on urban and rural populations, and on racialized elites and subaltern groups.

Natural disasters are thought to hit all people alike, yet there is always an uneven unfolding of disasters as man-made catastrophes that aggravate social vulnerabilities due to class, gender, and racial inequality. Disasters also often reinforce the unequal legacies of colonialism, imperialism, and neoliberalism. Although Hurricanes Irma and Maria hit the rich and the poor across the Caribbean with equal force in September 2017, for example, it was the poor who were more likely to lose everything, who often live in more fragile homes, on lower ground more subject to flooding, and are less able to mobilize network capital to seek resources after the devastation. In the weeks after the hurricanes, it was the collapse of provisioning and supply chains that left the elderly, the impaired, and the poor without fuel, water, electricity, or food, with deadly outcomes.

We can see how problems of environmental justice, spatial justice, climate justice, and more particularly mobility justice all come together to produce vulnerability to disasters. Poorer people often live closer to unmitigated toxic sites that can quickly contaminate entire water supplies; they generally have fewer or no emergency supplies of food and water, and are not equipped with back-up generators, emergency radios, and satellite phones; they have less access to transportation and cannot afford the great expense involved in evacuation; and their neighborhoods are often the last to be rescued. After a storm, poorer people may find it harder to reach extended networks of family, friends, or employers who might offer assistance, they may lack passports or visas that allow for travel, and may face responses of a different nature from police and military forces.

Cities and entire islands suffering catastrophic events are illustrative of how the dynamic intertwining of transportation, communication, provisioning, and scheduling systems can rapidly unravel, and along with them civic order, markets, and everyday life. Natural disasters cut off roadways, electricity, and communication networks, but more than that they also deepen uneven spatialities. Such differences are not arbitrary but are shaped by colonial and imperial histories that have left behind multiple kinds of territorial jurisdictions with differential forms of citizenship and unequal racialized boundaries. As Yarimar Bonilla argues, "Vulnerability is not simply a product of natural conditions; it is a political state and colonial condition."[32]

An approach highlighting mobility (in)justice in post-disaster situations focuses our attention on who can exercise rights to mobility and who is not capable of mobility within particular situations such as post-earthquake Haiti or post-hurricane Puerto Rico. While the "informal infrastructures" of "insurgent urbanism," described above, might promote resilience, they are also at highest risk, when disasters strike socially vulnerable populations in physically vulnerable locations.

Based on my own research in post-earthquake Haiti, I have argued that there is an *islanding effect* in which mobility regimes in post-disaster situations bring highly motile foreign responders and assistance to some of the affected population, while holding the 'internally displaced' in place, in an ongoing process of marginalization, displacement, and forced containment.[33] In post-disaster Haiti, there existed a connected mobility for kinetic elites (including journalists, humanitarians, and foreign researchers like myself) traveling within the disconnected infrastructural spaces of the disaster-affected region, alongside diminished network capital for those they purport to help.

The very same logistical efforts that enact post-disaster recovery simultaneously produce disconnections and diminish capabilities for mobility for people affected by earthquakes, hurricanes, and other natural disasters if they are not included in decision-making processes and supported in access to communication networks. As anthropologist Mark Schuller and Lambi Fund collaborator Jessica Hsu argue, in the forgotten aftermath of the devastating Hurricane Matthew in Haiti in 2016: "It is no coincidence that higher climate vulnerability communities are largely communities of color and disenfranchised communities within the Global South. To achieve climate justice requires making sure that communities most directly affected are directly involved in discussions, as well as solutions."[34] Even in Puerto Rico, which is part of the United States, or in independent Caribbean Commonwealth countries such as Antigua and Barbuda, or Dominica, that have far higher employment rates and income levels than Haiti, hurricanes Irma and Maria had the most devastating impacts on the mobility poor.

Those with high network capital are able to appropriate their own potential for mobility whether to flee disaster, or to come to the rescue. Those with low network capital, in contrast, are usually caught in a vortex of displacement, temporary shelter, and containment within the disaster zone. Or they may be subjected to forced evacuation, such as the de-peopling of Barbuda, whose entire population was moved to Antigua after Hurricane Irma wiped out more than ninety percent of its buildings and infrastructure in September 2017.[35] Meanwhile, property developers and tourism investors may already be moving in on prime beachfront land throughout the region.

By the end of November 2017, in the wake of Hurricane Maria, over 200,000 Puerto Ricans had left for Florida alone, with predictions that between 500,000 and 750,000 people (out of a population of around 3.5 million) will leave the island over the next five years. There are worries that the ongoing exodus of population will clear the way for further land grabs, as distressed real estate is bought up by foreigners and "vulture funds," not to mention quite a few billionaires, who are intent on techno-utopian experiments, from Elon Musk's arrival in Puerto Rico with solar panels and Tesla batteries, to "crypto-currency" traders building their own vision of a libertarian, tax-free "Puertopia" built on Bitcoin.[36]

Schuller and Hsu call for a climate justice perspective to expand the debate about climate change beyond simply adaptation, and toward more equitable decision-making in emergency situations such as these. I would add to this a mobility justice perspective that enables us to connect the full range of uneven mobilities across multiple scales, from the bodily, the local, and the urban, to the regional, national, and global. But it is not only after disasters that we should pay attention to such concerns. The slow transformation of urban infrastructure space, whether in the Global North or Global South, through the spread of digital information and communication technologies is equally a site of uneven reproduction of (im) mobilities, and emerging kinopolitical struggles over networked urbanism.

NETWORKED URBANISM

The late twentieth century was associated with grand narratives of globalization, acceleration, liquidity and mobility. Yet there were also quite different dispositions of unequal access, software sorting, and remote control built into the new materialities of global circulation and spatializations of mobile media.[37] New internet technology companies poetically valorized narratives of speed, acceleration, connectivity, and openness even as they politically entrenched infrastructural multipliers, switches, and topologies that supported highly uneven access to the WiFi-enabled urban spaces that networked technologies were making. To understand such networked urbanism, we need to pick apart its material affordances for uneven mobility and communication.

As John Urry and I argued in our introduction to *Mobile Technologies of the City* (2006), the mobility systems that constitute urbanism include "ticketing and licensing [of drivers], oil and petroleum supply, electricity and water supply, addresses and postal systems, road safety and public safety protocols, station interchanges, websites, money transfer, luggage storage, air traffic control, barcodes, bridges, time-tables, CCTV surveillance, and so on."[38] Some of these systems engage physical infrastructure while others concern informational systems; some involve moving things like bodies, vehicles, oil, or water while others involve moving things like data, code, and images. These physical and informational mobility systems are being tightly coupled into complex new configurations, such that mobility systems are becoming more complex, more interdependent, and more dependent on computers and software.

Media and communication infrastructures are deeply embedded into specific physical and material contexts, as seen in recent work on the invisible infrastructure of mobile networks and computer servers, on the laying of under-sea cables, and the geography of satellites and signal transmission.[39] Increasingly, the 'Internet of Things' will permeate all of these layers, connecting together physical flows with data flows and controlling circulation through algorithmic methods. The Internet of Things (IoT) refers to the network connectivity of physical devices, such as vehicles, web cameras, home appliances, and infra-structure such as traffic lights or electric meters, all of which are embedded with sensors, actuators, and software that enables the devices to exchange data and carry out actions.

These systems are part of a larger set of cyber-physical technologies that are described as "smart": i.e., smart grids, intelligent transportation, smart homes, and Smart Cities. They are smart in the sense of taking the human operator "out of the loop," so to speak, enabling the technologies to work autonomously, based on massive data collection and processing, complex algorithmic calculations, and automated transactions that they are programmed to perform.

Automated systems are also increasingly using machine-learning tech-niques to improve their performance. Geographer Nigel Thrift calls this the production of "enacted environments" because space is animated and brought into being by this pervasive background of calculation and computation. Such algorithmic systems are anticipatory rather than reactive. Pervasive data–surveillance and forms of continuous real-time calculation—"qualculation"—create an artificial world that is said to be increas-ingly sentient, and potentially adaptive.[40] More bluntly, Adam Greenfield calls this "the colonization of everyday life by information processing," whether embedded in Fitbits, smartphones, smart homes, Smart Cities, or more gener-ally the Internet of Things. These processors enmesh us all in "an urban fabric furiously siphoning up information," but one that he worries is a "project of a technical elite that aspires to universality."[41]

Media is more than an image, message, or content to be relayed from one point to another. And computational infrastructure is more than a neutral carrier and collector of information. Rather, these are embodied techno-spatial practices that produce space/time and are constitutive of social orders.[42] The pervasiveness of location-aware connected technology has made it possible to locate oneself and be socially networked while on the move. This affects not only the way we connect to other people and to information while moving through connected physical places, but also the ways that spatial infrastructures connect to us and keep our traces. Urban mobility inequalities thus become virtual as much as physical.

We no longer enter so-called "cyberspace" as a virtual realm—instead we carry it with us and are potentially immersed in it, especially with the emergence of augmented reality and 'hybrid space,' which combines physical and virtual realities.[43] Indeed, we are distributed in and through hybrid space, just as it is distributed in and through everyday life.

For example, as user-generated maps and location-aware mobile devices become commonplace for smartphone users today, one's position, defined by latitude and longitude coordinates, also becomes the entrance to the internet. According to this logic, location works as a filter that determines the types of information we access and the way we interact with the spaces around us. Some (but not all) can access its diverse affordances even while moving. Others (without smartphones or credit cards or billing addresses) are excluded, falling through the cracks of technology, though perhaps picked up by the occasional CCTV camera.

Locational awareness is increasingly integrated into transportation networks, including cars, airports, transit networks, and a range of new applications for accessing and sharing vehicles, determining walkability, or navigating among location-based transport options.[44] Ultimately, there is a hybrid interface between physical and digital mobilities in the "transduction" (or making) of "code/space" which is increasingly automated, ubiquitous, and pervasive. Kitchin and Dodge define "transduction" as "the constant making anew of a domain in reiterative and transformative practices."[45] Software (or code) is designed to advance particular ideologies of transformative practice such as enhanced ease and convenience of consumer capitalism, or enhanced reach of state surveillance. Thus, we should ask what kind of world this technology is transducing—and is it one we want to live in?

Prognosticators of the end of capitalism see the potential for new postcapitalist economies to emerge out of these technological potentials. Jeremy Rifkin believes that new technologies such as IoT and an emerging "collaborative commons" will enable shared economies of "zero marginal cost." Paul Mason rather optimistically sees pervasive computation and peer-to-peer organizations enabling societies to harness sustainable energy sources and carbon-neutral technologies.[46] But others tend to see more pessimistic outcomes of these new techno-spatialities.

Thrift describes five key socio-technical characteristics of the contemporary moment, which he describes as "Lifeworld Inc.": 1) "a structured continuity which always privileges the appearance of movement"; 2) gesture-awareness and interactive surfaces; 3) "awhereness" in which "the continuity of motion becomes locative as the world is tagged with an informational overlay"; 4) constant feedback, enabling "interactive composition" in real time; and 5) that "cognition becomes even more of a joint experience between persons and things."[47] These five processes become more and more noticeable in the emerging "Smart City" where cars, phones, homes, refrigerators, and toys communicate with each other, and where voice-activated devices like Amazon Echo and other increasingly popular "Alexa" devices listen in to every conversation.

These forms of continuous movement, interactive surfaces, informational overlay, and augmented reality are epitomized by imagined futures of automated driving, in which software delegates coordination to smart vehicles rolling through intelligent environments. Referred to as vehicle-to-vehicle (V2V), vehicle-to-infrastructure (V2I), or, ultimately, vehicle-to-everything (V2X) connected systems, the idea is that people riding in such connected vehicles will be able to hand over control to the system. The sensor-rich system will be constantly self-monitoring, gathering data, and reacting in real time to multiple informational inputs, building "fleet learning" from roving platoons of similarly connected vehicles and infrastructures.

However, the control of algorithmic pervasive software by both private corporations and the policing apparatus of the state, with little regulatory oversight, raises crucial concerns about the protection of citizen rights, labor rights, privacy, and justice.[48] If "Smart Cities" are being built, whose needs are they serving and whose capabilities are they extending? How much power are we handing over to automated technologies or to data mining operations?

We enact the networked city, but it also enacts us. Many people today live "mobile lives." They are dependent on such stretched but uneven infrastructures that seduce or coerce a juggling of attention, an intensification of work, and a fragmentation of time.[49] There is also a constant barrage of news, ads, and social media updates—another kind of reiterative and transformative practice—that are increasingly linked to on-demand shopping and delivery services.

On-demand mobility-based services such as Uber and Lyft for ride-hailing, or other companies specializing in courier delivery, promise to connect independent drivers and couriers with customers, improve efficiency, and bring down costs. Yet some analysts suggest that private corporations' algorithmic manipulation of temporary contract workers' schedules, jobs, and pay rates simply undermines worker autonomy and labor rights protections such as overtime pay or health insurance.[50] The "gig-economy" offers flexible work, but also a high degree of precarity, especially given the push to replace human drivers and couriers with self-driving machines. How does this connected, autonomous, sharing economy affect the class, gender, and racial inequalities already embedded in existing transportation systems?

Meanwhile, software systems developed for immigration control, crime databases, and predictive policing are being integrated into a continuous immersive and pervasive presence of the security state's apparatus of surveillance and anticipatory anxiety. Predictive policing software such as PredPol is being adopted by police forces across the United States, along with the use of body cameras and blanket CCTV coverage of cities. The justification is that technology will take the bias out of policing, reducing the unfair use of stop-and-frisk powers or other police abuses of power. Yet in practice, as communications scholar Aaron Shapiro argues, such technologies may actually reinforce inherent biases in policing by feeding biased data into the predictive algorithms, if the predictive alogorithms are "trained" based on already existing patterns of racial segregation, the historical concentration of violent crime in lower-income areas, and biased policing of those areas.[51]

In highly political ways, then, mobility systems become crucial points of anxiety, fear, and securitization—whether to keep on-demand drivers and couriers moving, or search out terrorists, smugglers, undocumented migrants, or even detect people with contagious fevers at airports. Terrorist attacks on airplanes, and the growing use of cars and trucks for violent terrorist attacks on pedestrians in multiple cities around the world, only intensifies this suspicion of mobility, leading to ever more invasive checkpoints, barriers, surveillance, integrated databases, and predictive policing.

Networked urbanism is not simply about "building a better world," as some corporations describe it, but is part of the production of spaces of uneven livability that enroll differentiated bodies into unequal modes of locational control and racialized, gendered mobility regimes. Smart Cities as imagined in the retrofitted post-industrial Global North enact a fantasy of total data and total control of mobilities. This reaches an apogee in the built-from-scratch Smart Cities in places such as Songdo Internationl Business City in South Korea or Masdar City in Abu Dhabi. Here fully planned automated "intelligence" is built into the architecture, infrastructure, and centralized coordination and computerized control systems of the city. Such cities seem to leave no room for unmonitored public space, open streets, and the urban life that was once the origin of civil society. Some urban theorists suggest that American cities have already gone that way, with their privatization of once-public spaces for the sake of security and shoppers: "This anti-urbanism succeeds to the degree that it is profitable for some, often at the expense of others."[52]

Against some of the current visions of automation as a purely technological system, mobilities research also reminds us that culture, lived experience, and meanings are all crucial elements of technological systems, including infrastructure. Cities are made up of technologies, practices, infrastructures, networks, and assemblages—as well as narratives, images, and stories about such technologically enhanced urbanism—which together inform their mobility cultures. Critical mobility thinking in the field of urban studies calls for "re-conceptualizing mobility and infrastructures as sites of (potential) meaningful interaction, pleasure, and cultural production," where people engage in "negotiation in motion" and "mobile sense making."[53] Negotiation and sense making, though, are not always peaceful or consensual.

Such cultural production of the city might also involve political conflict and forms of "dark design" that purposefully seek to exclude the "unwanted" using fences, spikes, unwelcoming sounds, and various kinds of barriers on benches, streets, and walkways.[54] Infrastructure, in other words, is culturally produced, actively shaped by and shaping human staging, and therefore always politically in play. It has both ideologically intended consequences (such as exclusion and surveillance) and unintended consequences (including hacking), with significant kinopolitical implications for not only our potential mobilities, but also our potential political mobilizations.

OFFSHORING AND ELITE SECESSION

Mobilities, it must be emphasized, are not just about moving people or goods from A to B—there are also financial mobilities, virtual mobilities and various imaginary mobilities that are combined into infrastructural assemblages. Moving capital "offshore" is crucial to orchestrating many elite mobilities at a transnational scale for, as both Featherstone and Urry note, it involves the significant capacity to escape the state and its forms of regulation. Fast-moving global financial markets and information networks, and the capital-intensive performance of elite lifestyles that they enable, have wide-ranging social, spatial, economic, environmental, and political impacts. Informational and financial mobilities are as crucial to the study of unequal mobilities as are transportation infrastructures. In this case, recent huge data leaks have helped expose the secret circulation of capital and the hiding places of wealth.

The Paradise Papers—an anonymous exposé of 13.4 million files from a law firm known as Appleby, containing detailed information about offshore bank accounts held in tax havens in the Caribbean—have revealed that many billionaires, politicians, celebrities, and ruling elites are using offshore banks to hide their wealth. The Queen of the United Kingdom has millions of pounds from her private estate invested in a tax-free Cayman Islands fund; the world's largest mining company Glencore made secret loans of millions of dollars that were used to secure a controversial mining deal in the Democratic Republic of Congo; the US commerce secretary, Wilbur Ross, had a stake in a Russian shipping venture linked to Vladimir Putin's son-in-law; and the billionaire owners of Premier League football clubs Arsenal and Everton had questionable financial links. Following the money leads to surprising maps of the global financial world.[55]

Yet "offshore" is also part of a discursive imaginary of spatial isolation, using the island imagery as metaphor and semiotic index of elite mobility. With private jet travel, especially, and private islands where luxury foods are flown in and water resources monopolized, there are crucial environmental impacts. There is a need, as Budd notes, "to quantify the environmental impact of business aviation operations at all stages of the service chain, from aircraft manufacture to disposal, and identify how best to improve the sector's environmental performance and help it adjust to an increasingly oil-scarce world."[56] Yet we might ask tougher questions of such business operations. Beyond the service chain and its direct ecological footprint, there is a more indirect impact of these high-carbon lifestyles on wider geographies. Elite "secession" to enclaves, islands, and hidden locations has become a significant indicator of the recent growth of mobility injustices.

The deterritorialized networked spaces of elite mobility and high-security access offer insulation from the outside world. Mobile global elites benefit from the protections and secrecy that Urry describes in relation to the enclaves of offshore capital. The mobilities of offshore capital and luxury travel often converge in the postcolonial micro-states (or in some cases still colonized) Caribbean territories that offer the benefits of "low taxation and up-market tourism." The Paradise Papers included corporate registries maintained in secret jurisdictions such as Antigua and Barbuda, Aruba, the Bahamas, Barbados, Bermuda, the Cayman Islands, the Cook Islands, Dominica, Grenada, Labuan, Lebanon, Malta, the Marshall Islands, St. Kitts and Nevis, St. Lucia, St. Vincent, Samoa, Trinidad and Tobago, and Vanuatu. Of course, not all these jurisdictions are equally secretive, or corrupt, and US States such as Delaware are equally significant low-tax jurisdictions. Yet in one example, 9,469 companies were registered offshore in Bermuda alone.

With their diverse modes of secrecy, hidden flows, tax avoidance and dodging, these safe enclaves are the spatial formation of elite mobilities as movement-space, in which the "good façade involves a singular assemblage of stability *and* mobility." Robert Frank refers to the mobile space in which these elites exist as "Richistan," observing the ease with which they can travel the world and purchase "Special Investor Visas" for residency in Australia (one of the most popular destinations), Canada, the US or Portugal, and even citizenship in several "offshore" tax havens in the Caribbean on the basis of designated business investments. In contrast to the refugees and migrants who are kept out, these "Millionaire Immigrants" get a "Global Welcome Mat."[57]

So-called "Golden Visa" residency and citizenship programs are offered to "high net worth" families in exchange for investments of between 250,000 and 500,000 Euros. This can be done through "citizenship by investment" in several

Caribbean countries, through "immigration investment" in the UK, USA, Australia and New Zealand, or through the "acquisition of residency by investment often in an EU country through the purchase of real estate, but without the requirement to emigrate permanently."[58] The very same countries that offer this kind of access to the kinetic elite are often the same ones that are increasing restrictions on general migrant naturalization and residency policies, and increasingly refusing refugees and asylum seekers, as discussed below.

Easterling likewise suggests that there is a growing "extrastate urban space" that is beyond the reach of state jurisdictions, including labor law, environmental law, and taxation. These offshore zones profit from the uneven mobilities of people, data, and objects. Global elites can move easily through secured corridors and borders that operate as a kind of spatial sieve, moving in and out of special zones as tourists, investors, managers, non-governmental organizations, and even humanitarians. Offshore untaxed accounts are often used to purchase private aircraft, yachts, investment property, and hidden stocks and shares. Some use these hidden financial flows to fund investments in polluting (yet lucrative) businesses such as mining, fossil fuels, and other companies with questionable environmental and human rights records. Indeed, such businesses are lucrative because they are able to ignore the costs of pollution, leaving it for governments and tax payers to clean up.

The same corridors and borders that enable such financial flows simultaneously prevent the movement of captive pools of labor and service work. Data flows can also be hidden offshore, through the opacity of financial transactions hidden in offshore accounts, shell companies, and tax-free status. Objects and materials can also be moved around freely under a kind of offshore camouflage which hides them from taxation and tariffs. Thus, there emerge forms of "hypocritical sovereignty" or "variegated sovereignty" in which states of exception secure some actors yet expose others.[59] Cynical security is constructed via uneven mobilities: checkpoints, enclosures, detention, demobilization, and waiting serve as forms of friction and exclusion, whereas being a member of "Richistan" greases the wheels of travel.

Offshoring is therefore deeply founded on regimes of secrecy, argues Urry, including hidden mobilities. Secret mobilities are by definition unjust, because they remove certain kinds of mobility from public scrutiny and potential access while benefiting those who make use of it. Smugglers and traffickers, of course, use secret mobilities to hide activities from the law; but many powerful state actors also hide mobility, blurring the boundaries of legal oversight. There is an undertow of illicit mobilities in underground economies such as smuggling, trafficking, and the narcoeconomy—what we might call narcomobilities—that often intersect with the secret state or corrupt agents of the state (a popular topic of television dramas).

While illicit economies (such as weapons smuggling) sometimes involve state actors, they more typically involve extra-state actors whose access to wealth and concern for secrecy overlaps with the performances and spaces of elite mobilities in the legal economy. In reality, it may be difficult to distinguish between legal tax avoidance and illegal money laundering, or private jet vacations and private plane drug drops, and both may share the same getaways, runways, and offshore banks. We need to better understand how the criminal underworld thrives on the extra-territorial movement-spaces and injustices of elite mobilities, whether physical, virtual, or hybrid.

This is perhaps the realm with the least well developed principles for mobility justice, yet we can at least fall back on fundamental democratic principles of state accountability, transparency, and international systems of regulation. But we also need greater infrastructural accountability and corporate transparency. We need to know who is collecting data and for what purposes it is being used. We need to beware of technological fixes and keep tabs on tax avoidance. We need to protect public space, the civic realm, and freedom of information. Without these things, we will lose any pretense of equitable freedom of mobility, as it becomes solely a prerogative of the offshore kinetic elite. Here are some initial suggestions for some principles of infrastructural justice, especially as it pertains to data mobilities:

- Public infrastructure for transport, communication, and information sharing shall be publicly funded and made accessible to all people.
- Information and communication technologies used in disaster recovery, and in general in any situations of digital divide, should be made as accessible as possible to those trying to recover, aiming to strengthen their capabilities.
- Net neutrality and open data repositories should be maintained to ensure public access, and all publicly funded research should require open source publication.
- There should be legal protection for data privacy, and states and corporations shall not have the right to search, seize, take, or use unauthorized private data.
- There should be regulation of so-called "offshore" banking, and enforcement of requirements for financial reporting and taxation in places of residency.

The imagery of "borderless" mobilities that was associated with the late twentieth-century age of globalization, with its rhetoric of a technologically-connected, post-national "flat world," in some ways began to give way in the early twenty-first century, especially after the 9/11 terrorist attacks. Global flows were associated with the unfettered movement of transnational capital and corporations around the world, the proliferation of free trade zones and "offshore" financial centers, the huge expansion of tourism, and the extension of cultural connections and communications networks across national borders.

Simultaneously, though, this sense of opening and acceleration of globalization—a kind of freedom of mobility—was always already belied by the continuing reality of limits on migration, the stark deaths of refugees in many borderlands, the "war on drugs" and its skyrocketing rates of imprisonment, and the violent control of various illicit economies such as human trafficking and the drugs trade. Globalization (and its legitimating discourses) were also heavily challenged by anti-globalization movements in the late 1990s and early 2000s, and the subsequent emergence of actions to release hidden information such as WikiLeaks. Movements for infrastructural justice must therefore also be offshore, global, and mobile, turning the elite strategy of escaping the state (and its regulation) into a tactic of resistance.

Algorithmic pervasive computing presents new challenges to the scope and scale of infrastructural mobility justice not only within the city, but also across extensive mobile borders. If networked urbanism has helped transduce new code/spaces of the Smart City and the offshore enclave, it has been equally implicated in the making anew of the "smart borders" of the state, which are increasingly dependent on connected data systems for citizen monitoring, crime prevention, migrant interception and refugee detention. Cross-border mobilities and mobile borders remain some of the thorniest problems of any contemporary kinopolitics.

1 5475 — 65 MILLION FORCIBLY DISPLACED FROM HOME
25 MILLION ARE VERY COUNTRY
40000 KILLED BY BORDERS, 2006-2015 (IMO)
2 ENORMOUS INCREASE IN STATE SURVEILLANCE & REPRESSION

3 IMMOBILITIES = RELATIONAL & MOBS = POLITICALLY GOVERNED BY MOB. REGIMES

Chapter 5

Mobile Borders and Migrant Justice

4 INFRASTRUCTURE BLOCK / CONTROL / NECROPOLE F. MUN & BORDERS
5 UPP — CITIZENSHIP = KEY SITE FOR DIFFERENTIAL MANAGEMENT OF TRANSNATIONAL MOBS
CROSS-BORDER MOBS = KEY SITE FOR PRODUCT OF THE NATION (+ STRATIFY CITIZENSHIP)

There are an estimated 65 million people who are today forcibly displaced from their homes, including those internally displaced, and 25 million who are living outside their home country, said to be more than at any time since World War II. Approximately 28 million children were driven from their homes in 2017 alone due to conflict, according to the United Nations Children's Fund. The International Organization for Migration has calculated that between 2006 and 2015 more than 40,000 people died trying to cross borders around the world.[1] This has been attributed to the consequences "of states expanding the reach of their security and detention practices to capture, intercede, or make intentionally perilous the movement of people." Such efforts include the growth in construction of border walls, with almost seventy such around the world now, as well as a "much wider set of state practices to control movement such as deployments of more border guards, seaborne patrols, and investments in new technologies to monitor more comprehensively events within state space, at the edges of their territories, and beyond."[2]

Debates over sustainable urbanism, transport justice, Smart Cities, and urban accessibility must be placed in the context of wider transnational mobility regimes, including borders, tourism and migration. Urban, national, and transnational im/mobilities are always relational. Mobilities are politically governed by mobility regimes, including legal regimes that govern who and what can move (or stay put), when, where, how, and under what conditions. The figures above, for example, do not count people displaced by climate change since there is no international treaty regarding climate refugees as potential asylum seekers. The violence of mobility is as crucial here as the freedom of mobility. This demands a wide-ranging agenda for the study of mobility justice, taking us far beyond accessibility or the right to the city, to instead interrogate the biopolitics, the geopolitics, and the necropolitics of movement and borders.

Citizenship has become a key site for the differential management of transnational mobilities, and cross-border mobilities have become a key site for production of the nation itself. The late sociologist Zygmunt Bauman observed in 1998 that differentiated citizenship regimes were "the metaphor for the new, emergent, stratification" in which "it is now the 'access to global mobility' which has been raised to the topmost rank among the stratifying factors." As early as 2001, Ginette Verstraete argued that in Europe the "freedom of mobility for some (citizens, tourists, business people) is only made possible through the organized exclusion of others forced to move around as illegal 'aliens,' migrants, or refugees."[4] Since the turn of the millennium, the exercise of state powers stopping some people from crossing international borders, even while allowing others to speed through easily, has only intensified.

Scholars studying the history and uses of the passport and other travel documents issued by nation-states point out that citizenship has increasingly become a way for states to manage mobility by monitoring travel by citizens and non-citizens, with new technologies emerging for regulation, scrutiny, and tracking.[5] Weber's definition of the state as a monopoly of legitimate violence was extended by John Torpey in his *History of the Passport* to an understanding of the state as the monopoly of legitimate mobility. Border studies scholar William Walters argued that the border is a kind of sorting device, used to differentiate the presumed good from the so-called bad, and anthropologists of borders Hilary Cunningham and Josiah Heyman suggest that borders have become paradoxical sites of both mobility and immobility in which movement is delimited and restricted.[6] Borders are complex assemblages of movements *and* moorings, and it is never simply a matter of the world being more mobile now.

In the European Union, the migration crisis—which some refer to as a reception crisis or a humanitarian crisis—took acute form with the Syrian refugee crisis of 2015–16, when hundreds of thousands of people fleeing war in Syria (as well as Afghanistan and Pakistan) attempted to reach Greece via Turkey. Others escaping violence in places such as South Sudan, the Central African Republic, and the Democratic Republic of Congo have transited through Libya and attempted to make the sea crossing from North Africa into Italy, with thousands drowning en route. Over 10,000 migrants perished trying to reach their destinations in 2014 and 2015, according to a 2016 report from the Geneva-based International Organization for Migration.[7] Five thousand people died in 2016 alone trying to cross the Mediterranean into Europe. The circulation of the tragic photo of the death of Syrian toddler Alan Kurdi on a Greek beach in September 2015 mobilized worldwide protests. In the face of such deaths, some activists in the migrant justice movement have begun advocating a world with "no borders."[8]

Crucial to the contemporary management of mobilities are the roiling political questions surrounding migration, refugees, asylum, and the granting of citizenship to undocumented migrants. The European migration crisis contributed to the Brexit vote, as many ethno-nationalist politicians decried the free mobility within the Schengen area that was allowing more and more EU citizens to settle in the UK as well as the growing pressure to accept refugees and migrants from beyond the EU. In Germany, the far-right Alternative for Germany party won seats in the Bundestag for the first time. In Austria, the Freedom Party, founded by ex-Nazis, was successful enough in recent elections to be involved in the formation of a coalition government. In Poland in November 2017, marchers chanted "White Europe!" during Independence Day celebrations. In Italy, neo-fascists in the CasaPound party won a seat in the Roman suburbs. And in Hungary the increasingly authoritarian government of right-wing Prime Minister Viktor Orbán is finding success with an ethnonationalist anti-immigrant agenda (while also making homelessness a crime). While some Europeans seek to welcome refugees and asylum seekers (a policy which is said to have led to the political weakening of German chancellor Angela Merkel), others try to keep them out.

Meanwhile the United States has long intercepted refugees at sea and turned them away. European countries have started to build walls to keep out refugees. And in one especially troubling development, in Australia (a country itself built on the dispatching of British convicts to a faraway place, where they displaced and stole the lands of the Indigenous Aboriginal people), controversy erupted over the diversion of hundreds of asylum seekers to Manus Island in Papua New Guinea and Nauru in the South Pacific. Intercepting Indonesian smugglers' boats of asylum seekers from Burma, Sudan, Somalia, Lebanon, Pakistan, Iraq, Afghanistan, Syria, and Iran, before they could reach the shores of Australia, Australian forces brought the first refugees in 2013 to the Lombrum Naval Base, established on Manus Island by United States forces in 1944. Imprisoned in these former colonies and denied access to Australia, there were ongoing reports of refugee illness, suicide, and maltreatment. In 2014, a drunken mob attacked the refugees inside the Manus detention center injuring more than 170 people: "Dump men in the middle of nowhere, confine them, abuse them, suspend them in limbo, this is what you get" wrote *New York Times* journalist Roger Cohen, who visited the island in 2016.

In 2015, still hopelessly trapped there, hundreds of the detained men went on hunger strike, and several sewed their mouths shut. Cohen notes that "Australia has relied on the remoteness and secrecy of its program: out of sight, out of mind. Keep the press out. Impose draconian nondisclosure clauses in contracts for everyone who works there. Even pass a federal law that can send whistle-blowers to prison. On the whole, it has worked." In April 2016, the Papua New Guinea Supreme Court ordered an end to "the unconstitutional and illegal detention of the asylum seekers or transferees at the relocation center on Manus."[9] In the fall of 2017, Australia attempted to shut down the center by cutting off all services (including the delivery of medication), while seeking to transfer the men to other nearby holding centers, and ultimately hand over control of the detention center to the government of Papua New Guinea. United Nations officials declared that "they had never seen a wealthy democracy go to such extremes to punish asylum seekers and push them away."[10]

But one group refused to leave even after water, food, and electricity were cut off, turning the detention center into a protest camp where they survived on smuggled goods. They demanded safe passage to a third country as their right under international law. In December 2017, the United Nations High Commission for Refugees accused Australia of abandoning the refugees and

1 GLOBAL mobility Always suppbard by COERCED MOBILITY/INVOLUNTARY IMMOB/ DEPORTNID
2 INCARO/ FORCIBLE translation G/ DISPLACEMENT 3 UNEVEN mobilities & the PRODUCE of
118   MOBILITY JUSTICE   CONTEMP. MOBILE GLOBAL INEQUALITIES
4 UNEQUAL GLOBAL MOB. REGIMES + KINDS OF GLOBAL MOBS

asylum seekers, and declared that Australia must take responsibility for them.[11] As they are still existing in limbo, what rights to mobility do these men have? And what human rights are powerful nations obliged to respect?

[CONSTRUCTING MIGRATION CRISES]

Global mobility patterns have always had an underside of coerced mobility and involuntary immobility, deportation, and detention. Histories of human migration are crucial starting points for thinking about the relation between racial projects and mobility especially in white-settler nations. Studies of the transatlantic slave trade emphasize that from the fifteenth to the nineteenth century there was an interconnected transoceanic economy connecting Africa, the West Indies, North America, and Europe, into a world economy that led to the displacement of Indigenous populations, the massive coerced transport and enslavement of Africans, and the migration of Europeans into the New World, Asia, and Oceania.

The concept of mobility justice takes our attention beyond the uneven geographies of transport, urbanism, and the imaginary of the networked city toward a wider terrain of uneven movement and managed mobilities grounded in colonial histories, with all their resistances, backlashes, and violence. Uneven mobilities are crucial to the forms of elite secession, territorial appropriation, and resource extraction that built colonial worlds, and were braided into ongoing forms of power that underwrite the mobile production of contemporary global inequalities. *cf AMADE MUNNON*

Unequal global mobility regimes today include the carbon-intensive use of air travel, the logistics of borders, walls, and ports of entry, and the rights to cross-border mobility of refugees and migrants. Mobility is therefore relative, with different historical contexts being organized through specific constellations of uneven mobilities that may include migration, tourism, commuting, educational travel, medical travel, return visits, temporary work, smuggling, military deployments, offshoring, sex work, or emergency evacuation, among others. And these varied forms of mobility always bear some relation to their flip side: incarceration, detention, deportation, expulsion.

As Julia Sudbury argues in the introduction to *Global Lockdown*, a book written by activists working at the forefront of the prison abolition movement, "The global prison is a local manifestation of transnational flows of people, products, capital, and ideas . . . [So that] both the fabric of the prison and the people caged within it are shaped by global factors, from free trade agreements and neoliberal restructuring to multinational corporate expansion."[12]

Most American narratives tend to erase the origins of settler colonialism in the theft of Native lands.[13] Racialized mobility systems in the United States (as in Canada, Australia, the Caribbean, and much of Latin America) originate in this genocide and expulsion of Native peoples, as well as in the system of slavery and its coercive and violent controls over black mobility. But modern unequal mobility regimes in the US are also grounded in the reactions against the abolition of slavery and the backlash to the Reconstruction era, which produced efforts at segregation codified as Jim Crow laws that protected white supremacy. Historian Cotten Seiler describes the "racialization of mobility" as the ways in which "the modern practices and institutions of mobility have been and remain highly racialized."[14] This racialization of white mobility and black immobility has contributed to the modern "prison-industrial complex" of mass incarceration in America.

In the mid nineteenth century, the Fugitive Slave Act allowed bounty-hunters to chase runaways from the South up into the Northern States where they could be captured and forcibly returned to slavery, even though these were nominally "free states," where slavery was not legal. Such efforts, of course, did not go uncontested. The famous Underground Railway became a kind of subversive mobility, helping guide people to free states or beyond the United States to Canada. Runaway slaves also joined the Seminole tribe in Florida, or disappeared into the Great Dismal Swamp, a marshy region on the coastal plain of southeastern Virginia and northeastern North Carolina. Maroon communities fought European colonization and resisted enslavement throughout the Americas. Freedom of movement in the United States, and more widely the Americas, has always been racialized.

The notion of racial politics posits that a wide variety of unequal relations of power shape, and are shaped, through the racialization of some groups and not others in different contexts, eras, and encounters. In white-settler nations such as Canada, the United States, South Africa, Australia, and New Zealand, the notion of racial politics further posits that differential racialization is mapped onto a racial ascendancy based on a hierarchy of white over black and brown. A racial ascendancy endures in white-settler nations centuries after Europeans colonized Indigenous territories and after other peoples from many corners of the world have migrated to these nations. For example, starting in the nineteenth century there were strict limits on Chinese migration into the United States, which endured until the Hart-Celler Act of 1965 ended the system of national quotas.

This racialization of mobility continues to inform contemporary attitudes toward immigration into white-settler societies. It results in the steady rotation of temporary workers into the USA (and Canada) from Mexico and Central America, the Caribbean, and the Philippines, who labor in homes as nannies, domestics, and gardeners or work in rural areas as seasonal farm laborers, agricultural and fisheries processors, and as service workers in tourism. The Australian economy likewise relies on tens of thousands of low-wage temporary workers, many from Asia.

In the United States, the most recent "migration crisis" began when President Obama's administration stepped up border enforcement and undocumented

1 Attempts to criminalize undoc migra & assistance to them
2 DREAM Act & DACA (2012)   3   ▬▬ Manufacture
120   MOBILITY JUSTICE —   border crises, from Clinton
L 2006–2012   to Trump

immigrant deportations. The House of Representatives Bill HH4437 in 2006 proposed to criminalize undocumented immigration, to build a 700-mile militarized border wall on the US–Mexico border, double the size of the border patrol, and apply criminal sanctions against anyone caught assisting undocumented immigrants to enter the country, including churches, humanitarian groups, and social service agencies. It passed the House, but not the Senate, and was not signed into law, in part because of massive protests against the Bill, marches for migrant justice, and sit-ins across the country.

From 2006 to 2012, there were numerous Congressional efforts to pass the so-called DREAM Act (Development, Relief, and Education for Alien Minors), legislation which sought to legalize the rights of undocumented young people who had spent most of their lives in the US. It would allow these eligible young people, known as Dreamers, to remain in the United States if they had entered the country before the age of sixteen, were under thirty years of age at the time of application, had lived in the US for at least five continuous years, had no criminal record, and had earned a high school degree or GED, or had served in the military. After a period of conditional residency, they would be allowed to apply for permanent residency if they either completed two years of college or served two years in the military. When this failed to pass, President Obama's executive order in June 2012, allowing for "Deferred Action for Childhood Arrivals" (DACA) gave roughly 800,000 affected young people two years of protection from deportation if they registered in the program, and ability to work while they sought eligibility for residency; however, it was overturned by President Trump in September 2017, with a six-month delay in enforcement.

Today the fate of these Dreamers remains in the balance, as the Trump administration seeks to force Congress to make a deal to protect these young people from deportation only in exchange for legislation approving the building of a border wall. Lives and futures are being held hostage by political gamesmanship over immigration policy.

The media (and right-wing politicians) intensified ongoing rhetoric about a "migration crisis" around 2014 to 2015, as reports indicated more and more people were dying as they tried to cross the Mediterranean into Europe or to cross the most dangerous parts of the northern Mexican deserts into the United States. This included a wave of Central American women and unaccompanied children, who were largely rejected as asylum seekers by the Obama administration despite fleeing extreme violence in their countries of origin. The building of a "beautiful" border wall took hold in the US political imagination through the rhetoric of Donald Trump as he campaigned for the presidency, employing anti-Mexican rhetoric during the Republic primaries. The Trump Administration continues these efforts to restrict legal immigration and build a border wall, which will undoubtedly contribute to a further rise in the number of deaths on the US–Mexico border and at sea in the Caribbean.

1 Trump's violations of mobility Justice 2 Continued anti-immigrant ampaign work

3 Four sections again   MOBILE BORDERS AND MIGRANT JUSTICE   121
   └ + Sanctuary cities part   4 Gary Younce car Dapper us Global food us
                                                                              Right
                                                                                C
                                                                               (c)

Many principles of mobility justice were violated by the executive orders on migration and border controls issued by President Trump in the first month of his administration. His January 2017 ban on accepting Syrian refugees and the immediate halt on travel from seven predominantly Muslim countries (Iran, Iraq, Libya Somalia, Sudan, Syria, and Yemen) were seen as a violation of due process (especially as the ban affected not just foreign nationals but also in some cases US citizens and permanent residents), a violation of the Fifth Amendment equal protection clause (which prevents discrimination on the basis of religion), and a violation of the 1965 Immigration and Nationality Act (which prevents limiting entry to the USA based on nationality). This led to immediate mass protests at airports across the country and numerous suits charging that the ban violated all these acts and protections of the law, not to mention international human rights conventions.

President Trump's two February 2017 directives concerning border enforcement, control of illegal entry into the country, and the exercise of sweeping powers of detention and deportation, revived the earlier bill HH4437 to build a border wall and increase migrant interdiction, that had not passed in 2006, and presents a further threat to the rights to mobility and due process of up to 11 million undocumented migrants living in the USA. The federal government has called for an expansion of Immigration and Customs Enforcement (ICE) with ten thousand new employees, the expansion of "expedited removal" processes (with no court hearings for the deportation of "illegal" migrants who have been in the country up to two years and can now be detained anywhere, whether at workplaces, hospitals, schools, or even courts), and the expansion of immigration detention facilities.

As increased raids and detentions have begun, many undocumented migrants have already moved into the shadows, hiding in their homes, keeping away from public places, and especially avoiding driving cars, which can easily lead to police encounters related to traffic violations. At the same time, there have been numerous reports of US citizens being stopped and interrogated about their citizenship and religion during routine domestic travel. In opposition, some American cities such as New York, Chicago, San Francisco and Philadelphia have declared themselves "Sanctuary Cities" and refuse to cooperate with federal immigration authorities. In November 2017, President Trump's efforts to financially penalize such cities was struck down by the courts as an illegal extension of federal powers.

The growth of this massive deportation regime is seen by many as being at odds with basic precepts of the freedom of movement, as well as existing legal protections.[15] As *Guardian* columnist Gary Younge pointedly observes, "It is a fact, rarely stated but generally acknowledged and accepted, that the global poor should not be allowed to travel. That's most of the world. As such, from the refugee camp in Calais to the rickety vessels on the Mediterranean, from Trump's wall to the Berlin wall, the border stands as an ultimate point of confrontation in the broader dystopia we have made possible."[16] It is the sheer inequality of border crossings and their blatant racial and economic exclusions that jump out today as violating fundamental principles of equality and justice.

This has emboldened the "No Borders" movement to contest such kinopolitical regimes. "A No Borders perspective insists that people should not be categorized through inherently exclusionary state forms of identification such as 'migrant' or 'citizen'" in ways that punish non-citizens.[17] Advocates argue that "a No Borders perspective argues for demolishing any kind of citizenship categorization as a precondition of social protection, and, relatedly, for being social."[18] This is a strong rejection of the taken-for-granted monopoly of states to control human mobility in ways that ultimately cause harm through national exclusion. It implies a radical right to human freedom of movement.

MOBILE BORDER PRACTICES

In *Theory of the Border*, Thomas Nail usefully conceptualizes borders not as fixed dividers that prevent movement, but rather as technologies that control and process movement in a kind of fluid dynamics. Unusually, Nail traces the forming of borders all the way back to the Neolithic era, with agricultural settlement beginning with the technology of *the fence*; then the development of the technology of *the wall*, arguing that "it was not political society that builds the border, but [it is] the border wall that is the kinetic condition for the existence of political life itself."[19] Then he traces this politics of mobility through the development of *the cell*, which appeared in medieval Europe to enclose the individual in forms such as the monastic cell or the prison cell, and finally *the checkpoint*, which emerged in the global European empires in the eighteenth century as a technology that transforms movement into data and serves to regulate and rebalance flows rather than to halt them outright.

Nail then applies his theory of the border to a discussion of the US–Mexico border. Focusing on what Saskia Sassen called "expansion by expulsion," he shows how "land grabs" for purposes of agriculture, mining, or the claiming of water resources have driven migration flows and complex circulations in what he calls a "kinopolitics." This reminds us that the kinds of migrations that the US is trying to prevent are driven in large part by economic policies (including globalization, neoliberalism, and the North American Free Trade Agreement) that undermined rural agricultural economies in Central America and Mexico, displacing people from the land, and strengthened the narcoeconomies of international drug cartels, bringing violent gangs into many small towns across Central America. Expulsions are not accidental, they are made, argues Sassen: "The instruments for this making range from elementary policies to complex institutions, systems, and techniques that require knowledge and intricate organizational formats . . . Our advanced political economies have created a world where complexity too often tends to produce elementary brutalities."[20]

Building on arguments by political philosophers Hobbes and Locke, political theorist Hagar Kotef argues that freedom of mobility is the basis of liberal notions of the state, the individual, and civil society. But she also argues that such a model of freedom depends on a notion of limited mobility, hedged in by law and settlement, against which there is an opposite figure of "excessive mobility" represented by the savage or native who lives in unsettled lands that are by definition without law and reason. Native Americans living in the "state of nature" of the Americas were the foil against which liberty was defined as a condition of limited freedom guided by submission to the state. Kotef suggests that both violence and a liberal regime of mobility are two sides of the same coin. Freedom in the liberal state consists of submitting to a limited mobility regime in order to benefit from the security offered by the state, which effectively slows down movement into and out of the state, as well as preventing and excluding the imagined excessive, nomadic, and "jumpy" movements of the "wild" man.

Kotef, however, also highlights the resistance to this power: the practices "from below" of what people "do" with movement. Focusing on the context of Israeli checkpoints, she calls on us to study more closely how people cross checkpoints: "how they move; where they go; in what ways differential movement (prescribed, incited, or transgressive) dictate differential use of space; what strategies people develop when they are stopped; what obstacles do they find to block the violent movement of the state itself (building barricades, burning tires, sitting tight on a road)."[21] To investigate the various modes of meaning, affect, drives, and momentary encounters that arise during such movements, any inquiry "would have to go beyond the movements of people themselves, and incorporate the movements of things and different forms of assemblages forming between them." Borders, then, are a complex assemblage of people and things, data and bodies, objects and representations, all of which are put into relative relations of (im)mobility with each other.

We can situate these arguments in relation to a wider turn in border studies that has found many theorists rethinking the relation between territory and borders, and between mobility and containment. In contrast to theories that distinguish between fixed territorial logics of state power versus the mobility of capital accumulation, relational theorists emphasize that it is through acts of bordering and debordering that a territory is at once produced, stabilized, and sometimes deterritorialized. Borders are not simply edges, limits, or barriers for controlling mobility in and out of adjacent territories, nor does territory preexist the border, but instead the relation between the two terms can be understood as "bordering practices."[22] The "state border is not simply a borderline," Sassen writes. "It is a mix of regimes with variable contents and geographic and institutional locations," including different flows of capital, information, professionals, undocumented migrants, smuggled goods, etc.[23]

Furthermore, despite the current emphasis on state surveillance and massive powers of data collection by new border security regimes, borders are contingent and sometimes even fragile territorial practices that in many ways exceed the control of a single state, overflowing its edges, tunneling beneath its ground, and stretching beyond its institutional capacities to form state space and to govern populations. Thus, Sassen theorizes territory itself as "a complex capability with embedded logics of power/empowerment and of claim-making," which "cannot be reduced to either national territory or state territory."[24] She emphasizes two types of formations that suggest structural rearrangements of territory: first, there is the extension of non-national jurisdictions inside the state territorial jurisdiction; and second, there are new types of bordered spaces that cut across the traditional interstate borders.

Examples of the first kind include the territorial jurisdictions of the World Trade Organization, the International Criminal Court, or the United Nations humanitarian system. Examples of the second kind include what Sassen calls "structural holes, deep inside the tissue of national territory" including informal, underground, and non-legal practices.[25] Non-state performances of the border, moreover, may intersect with state practices of border governance to mutually constitute border regions that are outside state control, yet still implicated in reproducing state power. In Africa, for example, the Kakuma refugee camp in Kenya became a city of nearly two-hundred thousand inhabitants with a mix of twenty nationalities.[26] Thousands of migrants lived in "The Jungle" camp in Calais, France, waiting to smuggle themselves onto trucks or trains making the Channel Tunnel crossing into Britain (until the entire camp was shut down and evicted in October 2016). Meanwhile, elsewhere African migrants attempt to ascend the high barbed-wire fences into the Spanish territory of Ceuta in North Africa, as a kind of anchor point into Europe.[27]

All these processes of bordering, crossing, and mobility management are now crucial to mobilities research, and to understanding the future of uneven mobility in a relational context.[28] Global racialized systems of mobility management continue to inform racialized migration policies. Today the refugee represents the person in between state powers, seeking escape from one state space and possible entry into another, while the border itself has become a mobile technology. As Alison Mountz argues,

> Mobile states at once center and displace the border, reconstituting ports for those on the move onshore and offshore. Interception at sea reflects this movement well. State authorities travel offshore to meet, board, deter, deflect, and detain those trying to reach sovereign territory, there, interception and remote detention is largely concealed from public, media, and human rights monitors . . . the border is obviously moving, proliferating, dispersed.[29]

With Tamara Vukov, I have argued that "smart" border surveillance enables (neo)colonial governance not only through the mapping of territories and the regulation of mobilities across borders, but also through the biopolitical management of disciplined and racialized bodies enrolled in self-disclosure at the border checkpoint, borders which themselves are increasingly mobile.[30]

European border security regimes already deploy technologies that enable "the creation of virtual identities that condition to a large extent the mobility and life chances of their human counterparts, who are first divided into suspect populations, and then disaggregated into more or less risky subjects." These are now evolving further from a precautionary system that monitors only for those requiring visas to enter the Schengen area, through the integration of personal data, digital fingerprints, and photographs within the Visa Information Systems (VIS), toward a forthcoming preemptive system known as the Entry/Exit System (EES) which will put all travelers under surveillance:

> Among the data recorded in the EES will be names, dates of birth, nationalities, types and expiration dates of travel documents, dates and places of entry and exit, facial images, the number of entries and the duration of the authorised stay of all Schengen visa holders, as well as the fingerprints of those who are not required to carry a visa for traveling to the EU . . . If there is no exit record on the expiry date of one's right to stay, alerts will be automatically issued to the Member State's competent authorities, including border guards, national consulates responsible for the authorisation of Schengen visas, as well as national immigration authorities responsible for determining the right of third country nationals to stay in the territory of a Member State.[31]

When the EES is integrated with police agencies and Europol, it will function as a criminal tracking tool and anti-terrorist intelligence gathering instrument applied to *all* non-EU citizens.

US travelers, including citizens, are already subjected to the collection of digital fingerprints, and in some airports the use of facial recognition technology, a security measure that was implemented with no public discussion or legal mandate. In a special issue of the journal *Mobilities* on mobilities and borders, Jorgen Ole Baerenholdt theorizes "governmobility" as a form of governmentality in which self-regulation of mobility becomes internalized within mobile subjects. American border practices are driven by logics of security, performed by travelers every day, a point against which there is also resistance. Thus, he emphasizes that "borders must be studied along with the practices of resistance, with people's tactics and strategies in coping with, transcending, ignoring, overcoming, using, and, not least, building borders. As such, borders are made not the least by way of the various passages crossing them."[32] What would happen if we refused to cooperate with the border and its regimes of surveillance and data processing?

Kinopolitics is suggestive of a multi-scalar politics of mobilization and demobilization of differentiated bodies through uneven infrastructure spaces and mobility regimes. Our struggles for mobility justice begin with the act of calling attention to the injustices of such regimes and showing the uneven mobilities they seem to enforce, normalize, and legitimate. Chinese artist Ai Weiwei, for example, based himself on the frontlines of refugee camps across the world while producing installations in Prague, Berlin, Vienna, and New York City, using the discarded thermal blankets, life jackets, clothing, and text messages of refugees in his artwork. This project also led to extensive photographic documentation, installation of a series of sculptural barriers and thought-provoking gates across New York City in the fall of 2017, and a documentary film, *Human Flow* (Ac Films, 2017), all of which seek to keep the crisis present in the public eye and to generate human empathy.[33]

Migration as a problem of mobility justice must be considered both at a local scale, an urban and national scale, and at a more transnational and even planetary scales, which are not neatly nested but are simultaneous and entangled. Not only does kinopolitics entangle local and global scales, but it also must necessarily entangle histories of racial, gender, physical, and sexual formations that have impaired various embodied movers. It is through these embodiments that mobility is practiced, contested, appropriated, and negotiated.

DETENTION, DEPORTATION AND CARCERALIZATION

Although not all countries are signatories, the Universal Declaration of Human Rights contains Article 13.1, establishing a right to freedom of movement for individuals *within* states. The right to movement across borders has been established within the European Union, going back to Article 3 of the 1957 Treaty of Rome, which first proposed the abolition of obstacles to freedom of movement between European states. Yet consider the rubber dinghies arriving from Turkey on the Greek island of Lesbos and the dismal loss of life as boats leaving Turkey or North Africa sink in the Mediterranean, just off the island shores of Greek and Italian "places to play."[34] These deaths while crossing borders raise the political and moral question: Do people at risk of death have a fundamental right to freedom of movement? Yes, surely they do, we can answer. It should not even be a question.

Part of the debate in Europe hinges on the distinction between refugee and migrant categories, which is firmly embedded in international law and institutionalized in governmental practices. According to different conventions and mandates, the International Organization for Migration (IOM) oversees migration, while the United Nations High Commission for Refugees (UNHCR) oversees matters pertaining to refugees, with each offering different protective rights. Refugees are entitled to an international legal body of rights, whereas migrants are generally subject to national law. However, the distinction between the two categories is never clear-cut, and seems increasingly to be blurred.[35] And what about climate refugees who, it is predicted, will to a greater extent seek to leave unlivable environments, and for whom there are no specific international rights or legal protections?

Even if we accept that states do have a discretionary right to control immigration, moral philosophers such as Joseph Carens have argued that widely accepted democratic norms still place moral limits on their control over members and who counts as a member. Beyond that he, along with others, also argue that there is a case to be made for open borders as a principle of justice within democratic polities.[36] This case is made strongly by Reece Jones in *Violent Borders: Refugees and the Right to Move*, who asks the deceptively simple question, "After centuries of state practices designed to regulate and control movement, why do so many people continue to die at the edges of modern, civilized, and democratic states?"[37] If stopping migration leads to death, and if the distinction between refugees and migrants is not clear, then should not borders be more open and permeable? This is the case made by "No Border" activist resistance.[38]

The open borders argument is made, in part, on the basis of historical injustices in global inequality, which arose out of colonialism and imperialism, and which now leave people in different parts of the world either highly advantaged or disadvantaged in the global economy, and its associated outbreaks of war. Jones argues that "the existence of the border itself produces the violence that surrounds it. The border creates the economic and jurisdictional discontinuities that have come to be seen as its hallmarks, providing an impetus for the movement of people, goods, drugs, weapons, and money across it."[39] To take just one example, more than five thousand refugees lost their lives trying to cross the Mediterranean and reach Europe in 2016, yet "the Med" is also a site of island tourism, yachting, cruises, global shipping and trade moving through the Suez Canal, coast guard patrols, and military naval maneuvers. This is not an accidental coincidence; these mobilities and immobilities, living and dying, are part and parcel of one mobility regime.

Insofar as trans-Mediterranean, trans-African, trans-Asian, or trans-American mobilities are complex, contested, and multi-scalar systems, they remind us that mobility justice cannot necessarily be limited to what Soja called the "meso-geographies" of the urban. We need to understand these mobilities as crossing scales and spaces, spanning inside and outside, as well as past and present. Borders themselves are mobile: they are biopolitical, geopolitical, geoeconomic, and geoecological, being inscribed in and on our bodies, nations, infrastructures, and global ecologies.

Perhaps the point at which a relation between urban spatial (in)justice and (neo)colonial strategies of managed mobilities becomes most apparent is where one bleeds into the other at the border zones and city-like refugee camps. Today more than ever these borderlands are soaked in the blood of white nationalism, ethnic profiling, and enforced death in the no man's land. We also see the violence of the border exposed in the Israeli killing of more than 40 Palestinians, and injuries to thousands of others, during the "Great March of Return" from March 30 to May 15, 2018. More than 30,000 Palestinians marched on the border fence in an act of civil disobedience to reclaim a right to return to their former homes. Israel met them with teargas and live ammunition, claiming a right to defend its borders and protect its citizens.[40] Some suggest that in such instances around the world, and in the deaths of people crossing borders for asylum, the "hardening of the border through new security practices is the source of the violence," as Jones argues, "not a response to it."[41]

In the cases of migrant detention and refugee camps we can see clearly how containment and mobility are co-produced. As Alison Mountz and her collaborators put it: "We find paradoxical issues of containment and mobility, as well as bordering and exclusion built into national and transnational landscapes of detention . . . Detention functions as part of a rationale to *regulate* mobility through technologies of exclusion rather than to end mobility altogether."[42] And so there emerges "a principle of managed mobilities, mobilizing and immobilizing populations, dislocating and relocating peoples," forming a kind of global metabolism of networked urban and ex-urban mobilizations and demobilizations.[43]

The blending of civil policing, national security, and military patrolling is also evidence of this blended geography of mobility (in)justice. In an important series of articles, Alison Mountz, Jena Loyd, and their collaborators have argued that the militarization and carceralization of immigration "enforcement" whether through militarized border enforcement, non-citizen detention and deportation, or migrant incarceration increasingly erodes human rights. They argue that there is a "long-standing connection between US military operations abroad and US immigration at home," with military bases long being used "to police the mobility of migrants and asylum seekers."[44]

At the same time, we have seen the militarization of civilian policing in the USA, and the statutory blurring of civil infractions (such as those connected with driving), criminal law enforcement, and immigration law enforcement, including detention and deportation. All fall within a metastasizing regime of the Department of Homeland Security, which under the Trump government has especially criminalized Mexicans and Muslims, and by extension anyone with brown skin, biopoliticizing the geopolitical. According to legal scholar Anil Kalhan, "The blurring of war powers and domestic policy in the USA also has crept into the securitization policies surrounding 'smart' borders, automated immigration policing databases, and its effects on routine policing through initiatives such as 'Secure Communities.'"[45] It is in part such militarized securing of borders, along with data sharing between federal, state, and local government agencies, that has contributed to pushing migrants toward the most risky and marginal places, via dangerous modes of travel controlled by "coyotes" and "human smugglers."

If we go back to Ann Stoler's arguments about colonies as carceral archipelagos, we find that there is an even deeper history of overlap between "agricultural colonies, penal colonies, resettlement camps, detention centers, island military bases, and settler communities," all of which were "nodes in an imperial network" that ultimately all "depended on strategic mobilities and imposed immobilities of persons recruited, or forced into and out of colonies and camps by imperial design."[46] I believe these are crucial historical insights to better understanding uneven global mobilities around the world today. These colonial histories help us see the ways in which power over im/mobilities and detention are exercised within states and within urban infrastructures, and thus built into contemporary mobility regimes whether physical or digital.

Illegal migrants are expelled from the nation, detained, and deported. The controversy over such practices extends to Great Britain, as well, where in 2016 there was a surge in sudden deportations using charter flights, at nighttime, from isolated terminals, depriving deportees of any legal recourse, with many deportees being sent to places like Jamaica where they had no social ties, no support, and no welcome. In return for Jamaica accepting the deportees, the UK government funded the building of a prison in Jamaica. While relegated "to the outskirts of the nation and on the edges of the former empire," such detainees are "not outside the law," argues Stoler. "They are not outside imperial networks of security, surveillance, and intelligence or the visionary bounds of governing bodies."[47] Nor are they outside the space of the modern, urban, liberal, and civilized city, even though the city seeks to keep them out.

Mountz highlights the mobility of nation-states as they seek to enforce border exclusion in ways that "fix movement on islands" (like Australia's use of Manus Island, or the earlier US use of Guantanamo); nation-states close their borders and control flows through new practices of detention, processing and exclusion "with the port of entry operating as a mobile island that inhibits others' mobility."[48] Islands may appear to be contained spaces *par excellence*, bounded by water on all sides; yet at the same time islanders dwell thanks to many different kinds of coming and going, pausing and waiting, producing a choreography of uneven spatialities and temporalities.[49] An approach highlighting mobility justice in relation to islands, as well as large urban centers, focuses our attention on who is able to exercise rights to mobility and who is not capable of mobility within particular situations and relations of power.

EXPOSING ELITE MOBILITIES

Finally, then, we must put the discussion of the migration crisis in conversation with another form of cross-border mobility: tourism and elite mobilities. It is predicted by the UN World Tourism Organization that there could be 1.8 billion tourists traveling annually by 2030. What is the relation between migration and tourism in relation to the right to travel across borders, and the "accessibility" of other places? What uneven infrastructures are forming to support (or stop) various kinds of tourism and migration? And does the tourism industry itself shape particular flows of both controlled and undocumented migration? Elite mobilities are often hidden or secluded from the public gaze, yet attention to privileged forms of mobility can help us better understand the power inherent in systems of uneven mobility.

Hierarchies of mobility experience have become normalized within commercial traveling practices, expanding on the traditional "class" distinctions going back to the days of first class, second class, and third class rail cabins and passenger ship decks. Airlines commonly use hierarchies of fine-grained categories of privilege to sort travelers into kinetic classes who experience more or less ease of travel—earlier boarding, free baggage, more legroom, choice of seats, private airport lounges, decent food—versus the "economy" traveler who often seems to lose existing rights (or are they just perks?) such as bringing a suitcase onboard, getting any snack at all, or having enough space to even sit comfortably. Further above these slightly privileged groups are the business cabins and first-class travelers, lording it over all with fully reclining beds, private cubicles, luxury food and wine, organic toiletries, and even, on some airlines, showers. Added to this are quick entry systems such as "Global Entry" which allow travelers to pre-register their passport and biometric data, and so bypass the passport check lines at the border.

More broadly speaking, there is a politics of uneven access to all global air travel, that is institutionalized within regimes of air rights, technical expertise, and aviation security, argues geographer of aeromobility Lin Weiqiang. There is, he argues "an overt sense that the air world is a hierarchical, racialized, and unequal one, according differential rights to different people, in terms of their ability to move, consume, and use resources. This renders flying an issue of mobility justice par excellence that is deserving of greater vocalization and activism."[50] Movements for mobility justice should be as concerned with dismantling these systems of privilege, premium access, and differential rights to air mobility, as with protecting the subaltern subject from the injustices of exclusion, detainment, eviction or refusal of entry.

Mobilities theorists have developed the idea of "friction" to classify some of the differentials in mobility capabilities. Michael O'Regan and Kevin Hannam point out the increasing development of "low friction" travel within the tourism industry, where "travel and tourism is rendered 'frictionless' as hotel apps create seamless hotel check-in, transit systems use technology to make journeys more friction free, and online platforms such as Airbnb generate the illusion of 'friction-free' exchange through the absence of paperwork and frictionless payment systems."[51] Such feelings of smooth travel extends even further into the realm of private jets and private airports, where there are no lines to wait in, and efforts are made to hasten entry and exit.

Yet this valorization of friction-free tourism comes at the expense of others, whose class, race, gender, age, or abilities subjects them to slower travel, airport security searches, lack of access to travel documents, or low-waged work in the tourism sector in which their time and movements are monopolized and controlled. Tim Cresswell notes that friction can also become a weapon of the weak, used to enact certain kinds of subaltern mobility or block the ease of movement of the elite. Perhaps that is why terrorists have so often targeted transport infrastructure as points of attack, where they could have the greatest impact on the global elite by slowing down their movements. The price has been slow security checks at every airport in the world. The kinetic elite again try to bypass this friction by turning to private jets, helicopter travel, and, perhaps in the near future, flying drone taxis, which are already under development by several companies.

In a collection on elite mobilities, Anthony Elliott describes some of the lifestyle biographies of a new transnational corporate elite who depend on a combination of mobility systems, "from mobile phones and computer databases to yachts and private jets," that together support the "contemporary global experiences of great wealth, power, and prestige." Through their network capital, these "globals" shape their lives through practices comprised of "detached engagement; floating; speed; networked possibilities; distance from locality and, mapping of escape routes." In other words, there is a movement-space that the global kinetic elites make as they create particular assemblages of mobility, which in turn shapes their subjectivities, their families, and their social milieux through networked possibilities. Elliott depicts how the rootless lives of the "globals" entails "homes dotted throughout the world, endless business travel, and family life restructured around episodic get-togethers, the old social coordinates divided firmly around work and home have somewhat evaporated."[52]

In another chapter, Khan crucially suggests that being at ease in this world is "an embodied interactional resource of the super wealthy," which "has been central to their capacity to navigate a flat world—ease that makes them mobile through space and helps blame those locked in place through impressions of their own failures."[53] Thus the smoothness of elite air travel is an extension of the other kinds of ease of movement that elites are brought up and trained to expect. It extends from the home space, to private schools and leisure clubs, to luxury ground transport, to airport lounges, into the air, and finally to the luxury destination. It is not just a cocooned corridor through which the super wealthy experience life, but almost a bodily forming of an elite pupa within the cocoon, one who emerges to sense himself as a lightly fluttering butterfly. Such elites might fly to the ends of the earth seeking out physical challenges and new bodily and sensory experiences, whether climbing Mt. Everest or taking a flight on Virgin Galactic, but they will never experience a body without ease.

These spaces and places of elite mobilities are supported by precisely orchestrated forms of visible and invisible labor. Spatio-temporal fixes that support elite formations can occur at many scales, whether as an unequal relation between service workers, women-of-burden, and the bodies of mobile elites, or extending out into the world through elite investments of capital, control over ideas via patents, or through mediatized spectacles of luxury consumption. Like the "creative class" described by Richard Florida, higher-income professionals are mobile and can determine where they want to live, leading a move back into once declining city centers. Service and industrial classes, on the other hand, are effectively stuck in place, as their economic fortunes decline around them.

We might also ask of these smooth spaces of ease: Who does the labor to enable ease? How do personal staff, air crews, wives, nannies, chefs, trainers, cleaners, security guards, etc., move around with the rich? And how is the visibility and invisibility of such labor, including its clockwork movement in and out of place, necessary to the production of the illusion of easy ("frictionless") movement? Clearly the apparent ease of elite mobilities require a great deal of work, and that work requires many other kinds of movement, pausing, waiting, stilled readiness. It also requires the just-in-time movement of luxury goods— caviar from Russia, single malt whiskey from Scotland, Maine lobster, etc.—in a bizarre choreography of privileged consumption.

Elliott reminds us that, "Implicated in all global mobile lives are various immobility regimes." Immobility regimes can range in scale from the stillness of a waiter waiting to be summoned, to the fixed capital invested in real estate, to the labor regimes that limit the mobility of workers across international borders. The high mobility of elites and their capital stands in sharp contrast to the lives of average people, which seem to be more fixed in place: "Crucially, the private jets are an indication not only of super-wealth but of the highly mobile nature of globals themselves and of their money," Elliott argues, "shifting as they do between various countries and regions, tax-regimes and legal systems, while living extraordinary sumptuous lifestyles well over and above even the highest standards of 'locals' living in territorially fixed societies."[54]

Yet such elite mobility also depends on creating places of stillness, pauses where the elite have the right to remain in place, and a kind of bubble of privilege in which they are suspended, even as 'locals' are forced to move out, to move back and forth, to move as if caught in a circular vortex. In a study of Dellis Cay in the Turks and Caicos Islands, I argued that the restructuring of Caribbean air travel as well as real estate financing and internet-based advertising, were crucial to new spatial and scalar geographies in the region. Luxury tourists and foreign property owners had incredible capabilities for mobility and dwelling, that built on the immobilities of local workers, the commodification of once-public land, and the creation of offshore tax havens.[55]

In sum, tourism depends on a geography of mobility and interconnectivity that flies foreign visitors in and out of a country, hides capital flows under shell banks, brings local populations to work in tourist areas, and ties places into complex webs of product advertising, place promotion, and information processing technologies for booking reservations, ticketing, and airport or port logistics.

The impact of private jet travel on these uneven spatial relations is even more pertinent to the privatization of air accessibility to islands. There is a differentiation of exclusive spaces, special infrastructural interfaces between elite consumers and remote localities, and new strategies of navigation for both accessing and imagining such spaces. Parcels of territory, especially islands, are re-spatialized and reincorporated into distant geographies of power. And when infrastructures fail, huge asymmetries in the capability for mobility become apparent.

Private air charter services, fractional aircraft ownership, and corporate travel clubs make use of a wide range of light, mid, super-mid, heavy sized private jets, turboprops and helicopters. Described as "luxurious" and "exclusive," such forms of travel are integrated with luxury villa rentals, access to private islands and luxury property ownership, and VIP services such as personal concierge, limousine and yacht rentals, and armed or unarmed security details. "Once the province of high profile executives and rock stars, this type of air travel is becoming more accessible for more travelers," claim websites. Private air travel is also deeply integrated with online networks, including internet-based booking services, virtual airlines, and just-in-time chartering.

While many studies of aeromobility focus on privileged metropolitan arenas of late modern societies, Peter Adey's investigations in *Aerial Life* remind us of the importance of aereality in producing colonial worlds. He draws a parallel between early twentieth-century aerial survey methods (developed in places like Northern Rhodesia, Palestine, British Guiana, and Borneo) and airport biometrics as used today, as two instances of a colonial "aerial gaze."[56] Airports and air travel now serve as one of the most important sites for sorting the legality and legibility of contemporary human and non-human mobilities.

Adey argues that the "emergence of biometrics in contemporary airports, border zones, security spaces, and everyday life sees the systematic use of biological and bodily data as a means to identify and manage risky mobile populations, focusing upon not territory but vectors."[57] These are vectors of global networked urbanism in which forms of enrollment, self-selection into "trusted traveler" programs, and passenger responsibility to present the data-ready body, all build on colonial practices of mapping, visioning, and surveying.[58] Data-veillance enables neocolonial governance not only through the mapping of territories and the regulation of mobilities across borders, but also through the biopolitical management of disciplined and racialized bodies. Here we see a merging together of the bodily scale governance of mobilities with the urban infrastructure space of the airport, and the transnational spatiality of the border crossing.

Vernadette Vicuña Gonzalez's fascinating book *Securing Paradise: Tourism and Militarism in Hawai'i and the Philippines* demonstrates the links between militarism and tourism, which are crucial to many Pacific Islands, but also applies elsewhere. She shows how particular forms of aeromobility (such as helicopter tours) and road-building (such as the H-3 Interstate Highway in O'ahu that connects the major Marine Corps Base Hawaii with the US Naval Station Pearl Harbor) connect histories of military occupation and the tropical island tourist gaze through embodied mobilities and spatial practices. Interstate H-3 was one of the most expensive highways ever built by the United States (at $80 million per mile), and bisected a scenic and culturally sensitive valley despite extensive community protest and halts to construction. In many cases, "offshore" paradise islands have been given over to military occupation, including even their destruction in war games and as weapons testing ranges.

Aerial accessibility of the Edenic tropical island hides its strategic importance, and the "*interoperability* of technologies, visual systems, and logics of tourism and militarism upon which helicopter tours rely," Vicuña Gonzalez argues. These tours of Kaua'i "generate mobilities, fields of vision, and structures of feeling that produce landscapes for tourist pleasure that are profoundly interconnected with past and present military violence."[59] She suggests that in places where "economic austerity measures and structural adjustment policies have disenfranchised and impoverished people, tourism's conspicuous consumption and mobility stand out in almost obscene contrast . . . The tourist was cast as the innocent subject of leisure whose right to move freely and safely exemplified the ideologies of neoliberal governance."[60] Indigenous lands are seized, local mobilities are severely restricted, and access controlled for the benefit of a few. From offshore finance to remote island military bases, there is a perverse relation between elite travel and hidden means of violence (whether military or economic exploitation).

The system of personalized jet travel and private security services intersects with hidden state practices as exposed by artist/geographer Trevor Paglen, such as the routes of secret renditions of prisoners on CIA flights, secret military satellites, and listening stations, illicit arms shipments, and the use of drones for remote surveillance.[61] Ruling elites are often the most "at ease" in this world of super-mobility, but they may also import their own habits and practices of mobility-without-limits into the repertoires of ruling. We increasingly see politicians using a fractal territoriality of hidden but ever present sovereign power to control and disrupt the mobility of others, to detain and imprison. There is no due process or right to habeas corpus for those locked up on former military bases, from the US military prison at Guantanamo Bay in Cuba, to the Australian migrant detention center at Manus Island in Papua New Guinea. These offshore camps are hidden from public scrutiny and have sought to exclude journalists from reporting on conditions there.

In all these cases, mobility justice requires a principle of transparency so that deliberation and procedural justice can be applied. With secrecy, nothing can be fairly deliberated. We need to shine light on the penumbra of extraterritorial activity and "blank spots on the map" where the sovereign freedoms wielded by the super-rich converge with the sovereign powers of the secret state, each unaccountable to any kind of public scrutiny, and the "innocent" tourist floats by with their eyes and ears closed, in search of paradise islands.

MIGRANT JUSTICE

Barriers to access and controls over mobility are implemented broadly through citizenship regimes, border controls, and the shaping of differential infrastructure to serve elite interests. More locally, migrants' and non-citizens' (im) mobilities are controlled via formal and informal policing, gates, passes, clothing, regulation of public space, and surveillance systems that limit the right to move, filter entry and exit, and selectively apply the protection of the state.[62] Unequal global mobility regimes include the carbon-intensive use of air travel, the logistics of shipping and the law of the sea, and how these infrastructure spaces intersect with the cross-border mobilities of refugees and transnational migrants, whether contract laborers, United Nations peace keepers, and sex workers on temporary visits, business people and government officials on private jets, or tourists and deportees on charter flights.

Not only is there an uneven distribution of these capacities for potential movement in relation to the surrounding physical, social, and political affordances for movement, but such uneven network capital also distributes harm unevenly. At its extreme, lacking the capability of mobility can lead to death. But such death may also take slower forms.

The mobilities of the most privileged groups, including the use of larger vehicles, extensive air travel, and greater energy consumption all contribute to global warming that has greater impact on the lower-income regions of cities and lower-income countries around the world. So, flows of energy, waste, and pollution are also crucial to understanding uneven global mobilities, as are natural disasters. Concerns with climate justice call our attention to the inequities of who has caused climate change through excessive energy use, and who most suffers its impacts—such as the small islands of the Caribbean and Pacific struck by cyclones intensified by global warming.

We need to move beyond treating transport justice, spatial justice, migrant justice, environmental justice, or climate justice as separate issues. These are all interconnected forms of struggle over the politics of (im)mobility and each directly impinges on the others. A holistic theory of mobility justice grounded in a mobile ontology can help us perceive the connections across these many different regimes of mobility, spanning from the scale of the racialized body, to the detention of migrants, to the ease of travel for global elites.

In relation to rights of transnational movement, therefore, we must add these additional dimensions to the protections of mobility justice:

- All people have a right to exit and re-enter the territory from which they originate.
- There is a right to refuge for those fleeing violence and loss of domicile by war, but we must also develop new international agreements on asylum for climate refugees.

- There should be fairness and equity in determining the freedom of movement across borders without arbitrary exclusion of entire categories of persons on the basis of race, religion, ethnicity, nationality, sexuality, health status, or socio-economic status.
- No one should be detained or deported without due process, legal protections and the right to appeal, and no detention centers should be created in "offshore" jurisdictions.
- Tourism shall be fairly exercised to ensure that it does not appropriate public or common lands, does not unduly disrupt the mobility rights or block the accessibility of places to those who dwell there, and does not leave behind undue burdens of waste or pollution.
- Those displaced by climate change shall have a right to resettlement in other countries, and especially in those countries that contributed most to climate change.

Finally, there is a crucial environmental dimension to mobility justice at this scale. While splintered island-enclaves might place offshore elites beyond the reach of state institutions and mechanisms of global governance, it does not place them beyond the reach of broken ecosystems, rising sea levels, hurricanes, tsunamis, or volcanic eruptions. The mobilities of the most privileged groups, including the use of larger vehicles, extensive air travel, and greater energy consumption through the use of more energy-intensive luxury vehicles, all contribute to global warming, which has greater impact on the lower-income regions of cities and around the world. Although orbital tourism, trips to the moon, or colonies on Mars may seem within their reach, even the globals, the kinetic elite, and the borderless rich must ultimately reckon with the constraints of life on one shared Earth.

Given their extensive power to shape time-space and control capital flows, a better grasp of the practices of elite mobility may help us to develop future scenarios by which to predict the lock-in of destructive or adaptive processes that may lead to the fragmentation of survivable regions of the globe and the secession of others. As we move beyond stable state-controlled territories, the mobile elites are perhaps ominous harbingers of a new dark age of offshore enclaves, self-provisioning, and flexible escape from the ecological collapse of their own making.

Chapter 6

Planetary Ecologies and Climate Justice

The Earth churns at its core, spins on its tilting axis each day, and completes a full orbit of the sun each year. The sun itself, with its accompanying solar system, spins in the arms of our twirled galaxy within the expanding space-time of the universe, throwing out solar winds, kinetic energy, and gravitational waves. All existence moves. And our planet's movements between light and dark, warmth and cold, generates winds moving through the atmosphere and tides running through the ocean. Weather systems swirl and stream around the planet. Great vortexes of wind form in late summer over the southern Atlantic Ocean and move toward the Caribbean Sea, bringing voracious cyclonic winds that sweep up all before them. On the opposite side of the planet, huge amounts of water vapor build up in the clouds of the monsoon that rain down upon Southeast Asia. The jet stream sways up and down, affecting weather patterns across the northern latitudes, while searing droughts spread across the equatorial middle.[1]

We live in this ever-changing climate, but we also change it through human activity and especially through our movements. The mobility regimes underlying modern infrastructures require constant high amounts of energy to be consumed in producing round-the-clock transport of people, just-in-time delivery of goods, and energized communications and logistics networks. Human mobilities are performed with and through deep geoecologies that are assembled with components that are underground, under the sea, in the air, in space, as well as on land. There is a global scale at which such infrastructure spaces work, consisting of the entire vertical geography of planetary urbanization, from deep mines to outer space, from micro to macro, including the extraction of minerals and metals, and the production, consumption, and circulation of energy and waste. Human activities have changed the Earth's atmosphere and weather patterns during the period now called the Anthropocene, and climate change is crucial to the future of all such mobilities.

In the face of climate change and concerns over greenhouse gas emissions, societies have moved toward reducing energy consumption and increasing energy efficiency in transport systems, distribution of goods, and built environments. Proposals for alternative mobilities rely on energy conservation, reduced mobility, or use of renewable energy. We are "powering down" fossil fuels as well as "powering up" renewable energy.[2] There is also a geopolitical dimension to these struggles over the uneven production and differential consumption of energy. Mobility justice at this scale intersects with questions of global energy flows, distributions, and their uneven accessibility. The study of contemporary "crises" therefore must encompass both global geoecologies (such as flows of resources, energy, and waste) and global geopolitics (such as flows of climate refugees, resource wars, emergency mobilities, and distributions of humanitarian aid) if we are to understand the underlying mobilities at different scales that are remaking planetary space.

There is a raw material basis to energy systems and infrastructures, which in turn shapes geographies of everyday life. Energy is not only consumed in the act of moving; it is also materialized in objects, infrastructures, and distributions of ways of living that depend on specific mobilizations of energy. Energy is consumed by vehicles, buildings, and communication networks, but we can also think of these material objects and infrastructures as temporary embodiments of energy: energy turned into processed metals and combined with other materials (e.g., cement or glass) used in the construction of particular kinds of energy/object assemblages (e.g., coal-fired steam trains and iron railways, oil-based internal combustion engines and roadways, steel-framed glass-and-aluminum skyscrapers, satellites, and cell towers).

Control over energy involves transferring it into a multitude of objects and moving it through various distribution networks and materials. This infrastructure then supports particular materializations of energy that become routinized in the ways people use and access matter in all its forms. Material cultures embed energy in forms that become taken for granted or invisible.[3] This is a point emphasized by science and technology studies of "infrastructuring," of which electricity is the foundational example.[4] All kinds of mobilities—whether corporeal, communicative, imaginative, virtual, or the physical transit of objects—are always grounded in earthly materialities and energy flows.[5] These material cultures have the potential to do calamitous damage to the natural environment, to settled ways of life, and ultimately to drive further urbanization, migration, and displacement.

This brings into view entirely new dimensions of mobility justice that have generally been overlooked in theories of transport justice and spatial justice, but are somewhat touched upon in the fields of environmental justice and climate justice. By seeding the theory of infrastructure space and extended urbanization with an understanding of the making of energy cultures, we can begin to see the co-dependent entanglement of media, mobilities, and energy. The energizing of mobility cultures extends our ways of life across the planet, but also embeds mobilities deeply in everyday life. Ironically, focusing on changing global energy cultures at the largest scale requires attention to how we relate to each other in immediate, embodied ways, in how we build our homes, how we move around our neighborhoods and communities, and even what moves through our bodies. Mobility justice might lead us to a politics of slow mobilities, nanomobilities, and shared space when we situate kinopolitics within a planetary context.

MATERIALIZING MOBILITIES AND ENERGY CULTURES

The analyses of post-automobile transitions in some ways left unexamined the actual technologies for the production of speed, in particular its physical basis in the harnessing of energy and materials, and the uneven mobilities this produces and perpetuates. Any transition toward a global regime of mobility justice will require greater attention to the moving "stuff" that makes up the world out of which both objects—and subjects—are made along with greater attention to the temporalities of energy embedded in that stuff, from the sub-atomic level to the cosmic.[6] The cultural changes needed to transform the underlying socio-technocultures of speed and acceleration require a deeper engagement with the materialization of energy in large-scale energy cultures and materialities: a full-scale technological and political transition involving a new social organization of time, space, matter, territory, and mobility.

If uneven mobilities are shaped by kinopolitics, then the ecological is also political. Unsustainable mobilities crucially build on colonial, neocolonial, and neoliberal forms of environmental power and resource extraction, which embed racial injustices, gender differences, and class inequalities into global mobility systems and uneven energy infrastructures. Uneven mobilities are therefore geoecological at their root as well as geopolitical, and so we must understand mobility justice in relation to planetary motions on much longer timescales, including those that create fossil fuels and those that contribute to global warming.[7]

The use of electricity is a foundational example of how we "background" the consumption of energy: "It is the sheer familiarity of energy use, and its deep embeddedness in taken-for-granted patterns of everyday life that make it so hard for us to 'see' the energy embodied in objects."[8] As described in chapter four, this attention to infrastructuring as an active yet hidden material-cultural process has been extended in recent work to the global infrastructures that enable both physical and informational mobilities, including the laying of undersea cables and pipelines, the energy consumed by servers and data centers, the material geography of satellite transmission and the internet, and more broadly the forms of what Easterling calls "infrastructure space."[9]

We can think of any historical period as involving specific assemblages of human mobility (transport), distribution of goods (logistics), media infrastructures (such as telegraph, radio, or satellite communication), and energy circulation to support these routings (i.e., the current infrastructure for liquid hydrocarbons and electric generation). Such assemblages are shaped by geographies of social relations, lived practices, and cultural meanings. We can refer to these practices and meanings as an *energy culture* that is embedded in ongoing processes of mobilizing, energizing, making, and doing.

The origins of our contemporary energy culture lie in the late nineteenth century. The combination of electricity and electrochemical production of metals, in a period known as the Second Industrial Revolution, brought lighter transport systems, new capabilities for aerial mobility, and ultimately space travel and satellite communication systems—a shift from heavy to light modernity. As I argue in *Aluminum Dreams: The Making of Light Modernity*, control over such mobility resources also ensures military supremacy, because bombers, armored vehicles, weapons, missiles, unmanned aerial vehicles, and satellite systems all rely on primary metals like aluminum and nickel, silicon and rare earth metals, cobalt and tungsten. Materials and metals are assembled into weapons, satellites, and vehicles, which in turn need the global flow of oil and gas through pipelines and tankers and logistics hubs to fuel them.[10]

Technologies of mobility embody (and lock in) energy in their production, in their moment of use (doing particular kinds of work), and in their relation to specific infrastructural 'moorings' predicated on unequal access to particular forms of energy such as liquid petroleum or the energy embedded in the car itself.[11] Likewise, technologies of dwelling embody energy in their construction process, in their moment of use (today dependent on electrification for many functions), and in their relation to geographically unevenly distributed infrastructures such as power generation and communication technologies, as well as access to roadways, private vehicles, and hydrocarbons.[12]

Material histories and geographies must take a transnational approach, following assemblages outside the nation-state, such as the history of operations of US-owned transnational oil companies in Saudi Arabia, and later around the world; or tracing the making of infrastructures for speeding international circulation, such as the shipping container; or following the "stuff" that travels around the world and the wastes that it leaves behind.[13] Transnational mobilities produce technological regimes that embed particular energy cultures as assemblages of energy generation, metals, vehicles, and objects, which then become materialized in everyday life, in nation states, and in international relations.

Perhaps the best illustration of the contradictory pulls embedded within the politics of planetary urbanization is taken from recent work on the coal, oil, and gas industry. Geographer Matthew Huber argues that "Oil is a powerful force not only because of the material geographies of mobility it makes possible but also because its combustion often accompanies deeply felt visions of freedom and individualism."[14] Oil consumption has been "naturalized" as part of "a way of life" in which "fossil energy has provided the ecological foundation for a peculiarly privatized socio-spatial existence." Oil entrenched a kind of "hostile privatism"[15] that gave rise to neoliberal ideals of autonomous mobility, freedom, individualism, and entrepreneurial life. "This particular cultural politics of entrepreneurial life is not possible—is not made common sense," argues Huber, "without the *material transformation* of the everyday life centered upon reproductive geographies of single-family home ownership, automobility, and voracious energy consumption."[16]

Yet we might also flip that around and say that it was the material transformation of everyday mobilities that made American life—and other similar cultures of automobility around the world—take its contemporary form, which came to seem common sense and almost unchangeable. Thus suburbanization, with its basis in automobility, petrochemicals, plastics, and industrial agriculture, was not only a structuration of space—a vast stretching of scale into a sprawling megalopolis, dependent on what David Harvey called accelerated "space-time compression"—but also produced what Raymond Williams called a "structure of feeling," based on fossilized "mobile privatization."[17]

Before we can address the injustices of hydrocarbons, those living in automobile cultures (especially in the Global North) need first to stop living in disregard of our own involvement in producing these injustices. We must acknowledge our own responsibility as "high emitters" of carbon dioxide. We must acknowledge our role in the splintered provision of unequal mobilities, the associated deficits in urban accessibility, and the exposure of the mobility poor to greater climate risk and vulnerability.

Nor will the switch to an information economy and digital culture get us out of this bind. As the field of software studies insists, even information technologies and "virtual" media have a materiality, which is also a temporality that is energy-dependent. Jussi Parikka goes so far as to call for media archaeologies, that is, "a more geologically oriented notion of depth of media that is interested in truly deep times—of thousands, millions, billions of years, and in depth of the Earth." He calls for "a media excavation into the mineral and raw material basis of technological development."[18] As we have seen with the growth of cryptocurrencies, even virtual money can lead to vast demands for energy consumption that outstrips local production capacity.

While a great deal of research on climate change and post-carbon transitions has focused on the need to reduce energy consumption in the transport sector, in buildings, and in how we move goods, if we extend our temporal horizon to this "deep time" of material formation, we should also consider an overall Earth energy budget for communication technologies, as well, and evaluate the efficiencies of basic materials and processes for their production. As Pierre Bélanger asks:

> From gold to gravel, copper to coltan, iron to uranium, geological resources represent the invisible mineral media—below the visible surface of the earth—that supports the technological aspects of so-called modern life. In subway tunnels or on suburban streets, in electronic manufacturing or information media, on stock exchanges or in commodity markets, the geological materiality of contemporary urbanism may seem inescapable, but the marks of technological imperialism seem even more indelible . . . Where do these minerals come from? Who do they belong to? Under whose jurisdiction? How are they moved and removed? Where do they go? Who processes them? What energies are required? What do they leave behind?[19]

These are kinopolitical questions crucial to the problem of moving toward mobility justice. Studies of large-scale socio-technical transitions suggest that energy cultures do change over time, slowly, and will change in the future, through interactions between micro-level changes in people's everyday practices and new niche innovations, changes at the meso level of governing regimes and institutional practices, and at the macro level of broad shifts in the landscape (e.g., energy availability, resource depletion, climate change).[20] I argue that this shift will also entail kinopolitical struggles across interconnected scales that change how we connect, how we move, and how we use both metallic resources and energy.

Given the potential for economic and political turbulence brought on by climate change and associated human vulnerabilities, the material groundings of global energy infrastructures will increasingly come to the fore as sites of transnational conflict over the politics of uneven mobilities. From a dystopian perspective, as mobility is rationed or far more highly priced due to the politics of resource scarcity, austerity policies, and security concerns, the inequalities of mobility and accessibility will be thrown into sharper relief and generate ever greater conflicts. We see such narratives driving current politics, invested in bolstering ethno-nationalist exclusion, hardening borders, strengthening energy independence, and competitive militarization. However, if we take a more utopian perspective, we might begin to imagine more generative ways of changing how we use energy, how we move, and how we dwell together.

SLOW MOVEMENTS AND SHARING ECONOMIES

In the midst of the triple crisis of urbanization, migration, and climate change that seems to challenge contemporary forms of existence, many are trying to seek out better modes of moving, living, and dwelling together with others. A more positive way to think about infrastructural transformation is to go beyond technological infrastructures to engage more fully with social infrastructures. Infrastructures not only shape the material world, but they also shape human relationships and shape us as human beings using them. This has led to efforts to reshape infrastructures by changing how we connect with others, in part by slowing down our movements and learning to share goods to create more civic collectives.

One way to promote greater mobility justice is to intervene in the dispositions of speed by limiting our energy consumption and use of high-energy materials. Building on earlier concerns over the dangers of automobiles, an explicit critique of speed began emerging in the early 1970s along with wider criticism of the injustices of uneven mobility. Critical socialist philosopher Ivan Illich identified the injustices of speed embodied by the car: "What distinguishes the traffic in rich countries from the traffic in poor countries is not more mileage per hour of life-time for the majority, but more hours of compulsory consumption of high doses of energy, packaged and unequally distributed by the transportation industry."[21]

Illich's book *Energy and Equity*, first published in serial form in French newspaper *Le Monde* in 1973, grew out of the energy crisis of that year and contained subheadings such as "speed-stunned imagination," "net transfer of life-time," "the ineffectiveness of acceleration," and "degrees of self-powered mobility." Illich argued not only that cars pollute the physical environment in ways that would lead to the extinction of humanity, but also that "the impact of the industrially packaged quanta of energy on the social environment tends to be degrading, exhausting and enslaving." In a prescient rejection of the harms of automobility, he advocated life at the speed of a bicycle as the most socially just use of energy.

Illich's critique of speed anticipates later proposals for alternative mobilities that also rely on energy conservation, reduced fossil fuel mobility, and the use of renewable energy, producing a slower assemblage of traffic and energy consumption. He called for politically chosen limits on speed (and limits on per capita use of energy) as a matter of social justice:

> Past a certain threshold of energy consumption for the fastest passenger, a worldwide class structure of speed capitalists is created. The exchange-value of time becomes dominant, and this is reflected in language: time is spent, saved, invested, wasted, and employed. As societies put price tags on time, equity and vehicular speed correlate inversely.

He diagnosed this as a problem not only of overdevelopment of the "overindustrialized" world, but also of "underequipment" of other countries, who could not outfit each citizen with a bicycle, good roads for the cycle, and adequate public transport. If we could promote more balanced access to mobility at a slower speed, he argued, we could solve many other problems of local and global inequity.

Slowness, then, is not just a negative opposition to speed, but is a positive promotion of a form of mobility justice and ecological balance based on a different kind of temporality. Japanese philosopher Shin'ichi Tsuji similarly argued that "Modern society, with its emphasis on getting 'more, faster,' has also given rise to grotesque disparities between North and South, developed and developing countries. Isn't it time for those who speak of justice, fairness, equality, and democracy, to start seriously considering ways to live with 'less, more slowly?'"[22] It is a fitting question for our own times.

American philosopher, architect and inventor R. Buckminster Fuller also called for doing more with less and envisioned a technological transition that he called "emergence by emergency." Fuller argued that "anticipatory technologies" will one day be taken up and widely adopted once humanity faces an emergency in which such technologies become necessities.[23] Climate change and the imperative to reduce greenhouse gases may pose precisely such an emergency. Unlike Illich, Fuller thought that advanced technologies and design could promote this social good by embracing technological innovation and pushing materials to their utmost potential for energy savings and resource efficiency. Illich was critical of such an approach, arguing that:

> Certain would-be miracle makers disguised as architects offer a specious escape from the paradox of speed. By their standards, acceleration imposes inequities, time loss, and controlled schedules only because people do not yet live in those patterns and orbits into which vehicles can best place them. These futuristic architects would house and occupy people in self-sufficient units of towers interconnected by tracks for high-speed capsules. Soleri, Doxiadis, or Fuller would solve the problem created by high-speed transport by identifying the entire human habitat with the problem. Rather than asking how the earth's surface can be preserved for people, they ask how reservations necessary for the survival of people can be established on an earth that has been reshaped for the sake of industrial outputs.

A similar debate over technological fixes foreshadows the ongoing criticism of today's technological miracle makers who dream up Smart Cities, automated cars, hyperloop trains, drone delivery systems, and commercial space travel. Whether premised on acceleration or deceleration, both approaches suggest that any move toward post-carbon transition technologies—and more broadly mobility justice—should address not only the problem of reducing energy consumption, but also wider questions of redistributing global energy assemblages to be more equitable, sustainable, and democratic. This would require elements of deliberative, participatory, and procedural justice to determine more fair distributions, and forms of epistemic justice to reach common frames of valuation and make political choices about limits to speed.

It became increasingly clear in the 1980s–90s period identified with "globalization" that expanding global energy infrastructures were exacerbating the problems of speed and uneven development within capitalism. David Harvey's analysis of "time-space compression" and just-in-time logistics which drew on Marx's vision of the "annihilation of space by time" emerged in this moment, as did Paul Virilio's theory of the dromologic society, and Agger's concept of "fast capitalism."[24] All of these theorists linked acceleration in technologies of physical and informational mobility not only to shifting forms of capitalist modernity but also to wider cultural shifts in everyday life and subjectivity within the "economies of signs and space," and to the emergence of what sociologist Zygmunt Bauman called "liquid modernity."[25]

In opposition to dromological modernity, there is today a renewed interest in considerations of "slowmodernity," slow mobilities, and even the valuing of stillness, suspension, and waiting. Have we reached the limits of the fast life and ever more accelerated mobility? Is it possible to transform a culture of energy-consuming speed into a culture of energy conservation and valuation of slowness? There are now a wide range of social movements calling for a slowing of contemporary life such as the "slow food" movement based around less energy-intensive local production; its outgrowth into the "slow cities" or "cittaslow" movement; slow travel movements promoting "staycations"; advocates of walking and biking as alternatives to motorized transport; and other forms of "off-grid" living and "digital detox" that unplug people from high-speed connectivity.

Various kinds of "sharing economies" or peer-to-peer economies have also been proposed as a solution to the inequities of global mobility. Sociologist Juliet Schor has developed the notion of a "plenitude economy" in which "true wealth" circulates through a post-consumer society in which people work fewer hours, and pursue re-skilling, homesteading and small-scale enterprises.[26] She includes various kinds of do-it-yourself activities, ranging from urban farming, to sharing systems such as tool banks and clothes banks, and online systems for recirculating used goods such as eBay or Craigslist, all of which she argues will bring people greater well-being than the market-based economy. When all of these activities are combined with internet-based networks of connectivity we can speak of a "collaborative economy" of peer-to-peer relationships of "connected consumption" or what some call "collaborative consumption."[27] The entire vision depends on many new kinds of mobility cultures, a new logistics of the everyday with many implications for globally uneven mobilities and infrastructure space.

We find experiments with such models not only in the locally-based "transition towns" movement or rural intentional communities that have moved off grid and into a non-monetary economy, but also in urban experiments in co-housing and new models for sharing resources. Designer and urbanist Dan Hill asks, "How do we build upon the best aspects of cooperative development and shared ownership to use these technologies in a way that reinforces the idea of the city as a public good, not a mere collision of private ones?" He finds one answer in the projects of the *baugruppen* [building group] movement in Berlin, which are based on "local shared ownership, shared design, and decision-making suffused with civic values." Their urban co-housing projects involve special lending packages designed for pooled financing, architect-led participatory planning and design meetings, flexible modular design components to meet various needs, shared spaces such as a common room, laundry room, and rooftop summer kitchen, and a wrap-around balcony that allows circulation between residences through a shared outdoor space.[28]

These kinds of shared buildings not only solve problems of predatory lending, real estate inflation, and housing crisis that plague many cities, but also form a new kind of civic infrastructure for everyday life. Shared mobility systems (and energy efficiency) can be easily integrated into such designs, with the addition of bike sharing or electric car sharing, solar powered charging points, and access to public transit systems. Car sharing is used as an important example in this approach of optimizing the use of durable goods, which would help reduce the number of private cars on the roads, but the vision also includes the sharing of services and time, via methods such as time banks and social currencies. Other futurists imagine the integration of locally shared 3D-printing facilities so that residents can produce their own products such as kitchenware, building parts, bike parts, furniture fittings, or toys. Such systems would arguably have transformative effects on logistical systems, manufacturing, waste, and energy consumption.[29]

A related line of thought on approachable utopian potentials is brought together in the concept of "generative justice," proposed by Ron Eglash in contrast to distributive justice. He defines it as: "The universal right to generate unalienated value and directly participate in its benefits; the rights of value generators to create their own conditions of production; and the rights of communities of value generation to nurture self-sustaining paths for its circulation." This concept builds on the claim that there are new opportunities today for "the bottom-up generation and circulation of value in unalienated forms" and for "gift-exchange" within a "knowledge commons" that include phenomena of "peer-to-peer production such as open source software; community-based agroecology; and 'DIY citizenship' ranging from feminist makerspaces to queer biohacking." In addition to labor value, the concept also encompasses non-human ecological value and expressive values such as "free speech, sexuality, spirituality, and other generative performance."[30]

The weakness with any of these alternative sharing economies is that such utopian experiments simply get reincorporated into the mainstream economy where their generative potential is absorbed into corporate profit. As the existing sharing economy has grown, what at first seemed like economic alternatives such as not-for-profit peer-to-peer ride-sharing communities morphed into commercial ride-hailing services like Uber, and peer-to-peer room-sharing communities like Couchsurfing morphed into commercial platforms like Airbnb. Will proximate utopias always remain small experiments on the outskirts, with their transformative hopes just beyond our reach? Are they just the artifacts of comfortable urban elites that will be perpetually reabsorbed into the market?

Other utopian social experiments (or models of social innovation) take a more politically transformative approach that acknowledges head-on the existing systems of class inequality and racial injustice. Robin D.G. Kelley, a historian of African-American working-class radical social movements, has recently pointed toward the social model being developed in Jackson, Mississippi, which he describes as "America's most radical city, where a genuinely revolutionary movement is building our first cooperative commonwealth dedicated to the principles of democracy, human rights, workers' power, environmental sustainability, and socialism." The Jackson Plan is "an initiative to apply many of the best practices in the promotion of participatory democracy, solidarity economy, and sustainable development and combine them with progressive community organizing and electoral politics."[31]

It emerged out of the work of the Malcolm X Grassroots Movement and the Jackson People's Assembly in the wake of the devastation of the US Gulf Coast by Hurricane Katrina. It combines first, people's assemblies using principles of direct democracy, a model that emerged in the Reconstruction era after the Civil War when African Americans were first enfranchised; second, a comprehensive electoral strategy to support candidates committed to "restoration of the commons," creating and expanding "public utilities" (including public transportation and universal health care), and economic democratization; and third, the creation of a "Solidarity Economy," understood as "a process of promoting cooperative economics that promote social solidarity, mutual aid, reciprocity, and generosity." This includes cooperative enterprises and credit unions, local urban farms and regional agricultural cooperatives, and conservation land trusts to reconstruct "the commons" and decommodify land and housing. The plan also calls for expanding public transport using green vehicles, building a renewable power grid, and creating South-South trading networks with CARICOM and Latin America.[32]

This project also takes inspiration from the Mondragón cooperative community economy in Spain's Basque region, which has been held up as an example of a long-lived and successful "intentional economy" with worker-owned industry, retail, service, and banking cooperatives.[33] Such "actually existing utopias" connect across many of the dimensions of justice discussed in this book, including racial justice, reparative justice, and epistemic justice.

Elsewhere in Europe, including Spain, Greece, and the Netherlands, an alliance has been built between advocates for the right to the city and advocates for migrant justice. Alex Vasudevan observes that "across Europe, a number of squats have been set up as spaces of refuge and hospitality for forced migrants who often find themselves in political limbo or unable to access local social services. In Athens, there are currently seven separate squats housing over 1,500 refugees."[34] These building occupations by a coalition of squatters, housing activists, refugees and migrants insist on the right to "habitat and to inhabit" (*a l'habitat et à l'habiter*), as French theorist of space Henri Lefebvre put it. Like other utopian projects of prefigurative transformation, these movements call for the right to habitat ("a place to make a life") and the right to inhabit ("to make a place one's own"), as crucial to expressing "a basic right to be and persist in that place and participate in the production of a different kind of city."[35] This is reminiscent of Escobar's *Designs for the Pluriverse*, where multiple autonomous forms of life could be self-generating and self-defining.

The Untokening movement also call for addressing environmental racism on this wider scale, linking it to the right to stay in place: "Environmental racism and disinvestment have disconnected many urban communities from green spaces and disproportionately created toxic environments. Infrastructure improvements like bike lanes and green space often result in environmental gentrification as longtime and lower-income residents are displaced by more affluent populations." Thus, they call for integrating environmental justice principles into the movement for the right to the city:

> Mobility Justice integrates environmental justice principles to address health disparities, displacement and disconnection from nature. It prioritizes the right of communities who have suffered the harms of environmental racism to stay in place to benefit from access and ownership of green spaces and a cleaner environment. Communities have the right to demand and expect healthy environments, and EQUAL ACCESS to the benefits of green space—and remediation of past environmental harms. Advocates must critically examine the implementation of "sustainable" development, so that healthier environments aren't active agents of displacement and cultural erasure.

All the alternative economies discussed here also cut across the scales of mobility justice, involving new ways of mobilizing the body, rethinking transportation systems, addressing migration and belonging, transforming infrastructures, and transitioning away from fossil fuels at a planetary scale. They bring us closer to a "just" solution at multiple scales of mobilities because they encompass epistemic justice and reparative justice. They seek to change not simply transportation systems, but entire political ontologies.

Ultimately, alternative community economies seek to reconnect communities, redistribute resources, and reduce energy consumption and the kinds of waste and pollution associated with industrial systems and extractive economies by changing how we connect, move, and dwell. Nevertheless, few advocates of technological transitions and sharing economies fully explore how resource exploitation and energy cultures are embedded in technologies and systems that are crucial to military strategy and industries that are closely allied with military research and development such as metal alloys research with direct military applications. Our contemporary energy culture and its industrial capitalist consumer economies are rooted in military prerogatives of acceleration and energy logistics, which have driven modernization and continue to drive "transition" technologies.

ACCELERATION, MILITARY POWER, AND DRONE WARS

Any wholesale shift in energy cultures also means that we must grapple with the imperatives of militarization that drive current energy policy, infrastructure, and logistics. Too often advocates of transport justice, spatial justice, and climate justice have operated in the civil realm, bracketing questions of military power and conflict. When we look at planetary infrastructure space, however, the problems of military competition and "just war" come into focus as well. How can we acknowledge that speed and acceleration have their basis in warfare, military technology, and strategies of armed conflict? And how can we incorporate this knowledge into social and political projects for mobility transition?

Speed and acceleration became key concerns for social theorists and critical geographers in the 1970s, partly in response to the oil crisis which sharpened awareness of the global politics of energy production and consumption. "History progresses at the speed of its weapons systems," wrote Paul Virilio, and such systems depended on the high-speed logistics of lightweight metal and fossil fuels.[36] Fuller traced the continuing investment in the technologies of "ephemeralization" and "acceleration," showing how the accelerating temporalities of technological turnover and "ever-improving metal-alloy capabilities"—in particular involving aluminum—supported military superiority but could potentially be turned toward the common good or what he called "livingry" systems.[37]

Wars in the future will revolve around such resources and the control over the logistics systems that allow us to move materials, troops, and weapons around the world. Yet it is exactly such wars and their new forms of weaponry that are depleting the Earth's resources and contributing to ecological instability, pollution, and existential threats to human and non-human life, the costs of which are falling most heavily on the poorest parts of the world. I have traced the relation between military power, aluminum smelting, electricity generation, and its environmental harms more fully in my book *Aluminum Dreams*. Here, the point I want to make is that uneven speed is the basis of unequal advantage in warfare, and always has been. Those who control mobility increase their power through speed (including data transmission speed), and those with power often control the mobility of others by limiting their speed. Technological advantages in speed have always been the basis of conquest, enslavement, colonial domination, and, as Virilio showed, patriarchy.

Caren Kaplan, moreover, points out that historically the drive for "air power" afforded huge military advantages to those who controlled the "cosmic view" from aerial vision technologies, so that military air power is closely tied to modes of visualization and surveillance.[38] In the "age of the world target," military satellite operators seek to render the world visible from the "ultimate high ground"—in orbit above the Earth.[39] Stephen Graham argues that powerful imaging satellites "now constitute an important part of our public realm" insofar as ever widening "domains of terrestrial life" (and especially mobilities) "are now mediated by far-above satellite arrays" in ways that require far greater public input and critical analysis.

These satellite mobilities, and spinoff visioning technologies such as Google Earth, are shaped by the military logics and dispositions of contemporary infrastructure spaces. Still, though, they are never all-powerful or omniscient. We should therefore ask how they contribute to producing the uneven global mobilities, unsustainability of energy usage, and ecosystem destruction associated with contemporary forms of planetary urbanization, and how these processes might be challenged.[40]

Advocates of "sustainable" technological transitions, Smart Cities, or alternative economies should consider how energy cultures are embedded in technologies and systems that are crucial to military strategy. Everyday artifacts, infrastructures, and the routines they support arise out of industries that are closely allied with military research and development, from satellites and the internet to drones and decentralized energy storage systems. In most cases this military geopolitical underpinning of infrastructure space remains in the background, except perhaps during war, when what Paul Virilio calls "dromoscopy" becomes a crucial mediation of speed. Dromoscopy can be understood as a "means of apprehending speed and its pivotal—and potentially destructive—role in contemporary global society."[41]

Access to energy, and the minerals and metals that make up transportation and communication systems, are therefore a crucial dimension of uneven mobilities and global inequalities. The potentials for mobility and communication are grounded in questions of where energy for transportation and telecommunication is sourced, where it is exported via what means, and who uses most of it. Militarily-backed kinetic elites are increasingly monopolizing control over energy, water, and mineral rights, using their offshore financial power to control global resources that are becoming increasingly scarce.[42] A large percentage of primary demand for oil and metals is driven by military demand (a.k.a. war or war readiness), so the consumption side of the equation is also (in part) an artifact of geopolitics. Low-carbon transitions and uneven patterns of energy consumption should be considered within this wider military context rather than seen simply as an outcome of consumer demand.

Warfare, furthermore, is often concentrated on blowing up the infrastructure for transportation and oil production, thereby destroying supply. That means that oil and metals, the key commodities that currently determine the cost of many other things, are to a large extent functions of military power. Their provision and destruction effectively exist outside of market forces, yet the entire capitalist market economy rests on them since energy, machinery, and transportation (created with metals) are primary cost bases of many other goods and products. Planetary consumption of energy (and its direct relation to climate change) therefore is highly unlikely to change unless military power also changes to a reliance on low-carbon renewable energy. States would then be in a position to stop subsidizing fossil fuel companies, and would instead support the renewable energy infrastructure upholding their military power and hence security.

If we return to the lessons of Virilio and Harvey, we find that military power, and warfare and its fundamental role in capitalist global economies are crucial to the technologies of acceleration. Speed and accelerated mobilities "lock in" energy in the form of complex mobility regimes, spatially fixed infrastructure, industrial plants, logistics systems, and the constantly updated military balance of power which shapes global energy economies. These are all aspects of the contemporary energy regime and wider landscape for energy that are not so easily reshaped by technical efficiencies, consumer choices, or even by national policy such as reducing GHG emissions.

Logistics (or "the management of the movement of *stuff*") is one core system of mobility that concerns the militarized infrastructure of global movement of goods, minerals, metals, and fuels, but also concerns the imaginaries and symbolic meanings that drive such organizations of space and time. Deborah Cowen's work on logistics rationalities shows that logistics have undergone profound changes since World War II, and have since become a driving force of military strategy and tactics, as well as of corporate practices for the global organization of trade.[43] With the rise of the shipping container, the computer, and satellite communications to manage logistics, new forms of systems thinking came to the fore, re-shaping labor relations, landscapes, and forms of security.

Now, in the age of drones, the advantage in physical speed for military superiority is compounded by advantages in data processing and transmission speed. Communication acceleration not only allows for high-speed financial transactions, but also for real-time drone operation, sending visuals instantly around the globe to remote operators who hover over targets for hours, days, and weeks, studying their patterns of movement. In his study of the use of military drones as a kind of "remote control warfare," anthropologist Hugh Gusterson emphasizes that the once spatially proximate relation between weapon, warrior, and target, "formerly a tightly packed and spatially concentrated ensemble," has been disarticulated. Crucially, he interprets this disarticulation of the spatial concentration of warfare as a form of freedom of mobility: "The respatialization dynamics here are profound and asymmetrical. The human targets of drone strikes feel trapped in the local, from which there may be no escape, but the targeters inhabit a space of free movement that has become stretched to global proportions."[44]

Gusterson compares this to labor being locally trapped (when workers do not have freedom of movement) versus capital being "free to move anywhere in the world with a few keystrokes. In the cases of both military conflict and global capitalism, the freedom to move on a global scale affords an important but not necessarily decisive advantage." Not only does drone warfare shape such uneven spatial relations, but it also "scrambles time and speed, too," giving another kind of advantage: "In war, the party that controls the tempo of hostilities has an advantage." These spatio-temporalities undermine the Augustinian tradition of "just war" which were "guided by the principles of distinction, proportionality, and military necessity."[45]

The spatial disarticulation of drone warfare leads to outcomes that are not only unjust but may potentially be seen as war crimes under international law insofar as noncombatants outside of war zones are frequently targeted and, in some situations, civilian populations are terrorized indiscriminately. In short, the combination of dromoscopy with drone-oscopy adds a further dimension to the problem of planetary-scale mobility justice.

Energy consumption and its materialization underlies all forms of mobility; such energy consumption involves global flows of resources such as metals, fossil fuels, and various kinds of energy generation and infrastructure; and such energy flows are the basis of military power and thus for state support for the militarized logistics of the industrial economy. Drone warfare shifts the equation of mobility power toward remote forms of a deadly "strike," which may reduce the energy consumption and logistical demands of some kinds of warfare, but at a heavy moral cost. Drone warfare tips the balance of "just war" toward ever greater mobility injustice because of the highly uneven and differential mobility capabilities involved. The emergence of autonomous weapons, sometimes called "killer robots," only exacerbates such mobility injustices.[46]

Cowen's work on the militarization of logistics, moreover, suggests how logistical spaces are lifted out of sovereign territoriality and legal jurisdictions (labor laws, environmental protection laws, etc.), and are secured as militarized enclaves, and connected corridors of mobility and communication. Cowen argues that militarization drives secured enclaves in which military logics reshape space and employ migrant racialized labor forces without rights of citizenship or collective organization. These subordinate racialized labor forces and enclaved racialized regional spaces contribute to producing the unsustainability of energy usage and ecosystem destruction associated with contemporary forms of unequal mobilities.

A transition toward sustainable mobility therefore requires more than changing how much energy we use in everyday life or in our cities. Individual low-carbon consumption will not change the world unless we tackle the underlying global inequalities which make contemporary ways of life unsustainable. We need to move beyond individual choice models and sedentary theories of justice grounded in place-based localism and "green" consumer economies if we are to understand these multi-scalar transition processes.

To reduce global greenhouse gases depends on shifting the entire material assemblage of modern life, which is increasingly splintered and uneven, and redistributing energies in a more just and equitable way across many scales at once. If "dromology" refers to the logic of speed that is the foundation of technological society, according to Virilio, then contemporary societies are "dromocratic" societies, and we are all complicit in a logic of speed.[47] Responses to climate change and to the wider ills of dromological societies, therefore, should entail not only a reduction in energy demand or a shift to non-carbon fuels (the main current policy measures), but a critical stance involving planned reduction in speed, more reflexive (and less destructive) forms of mobility, and ultimately a rejection of the societal valuation of competitive acceleration and aerial power as a supreme goal. This may ultimately require the *demilitarization* of global mobility capabilities in order to ensure the ecological sustainability and resilience of planetary systems for life.

PLANETARY URBANIZATION

Network capital is increasingly concentrated in the hands of a few, while the majority of humans on Earth are losing their capabilities for potential mobility, including the capacities both to move and to dwell without coercion. This ultimately is what the political struggle for mobility justice must be focused on. Arguably, there has been a fragmentation of territorial sovereignty through the creation of special economic, political, and military zones, with their offshore logics, as Easterling suggests, accompanied by a rise of military control of the orbital exoplanet, the atmosphere, and the primary resources. This privatization and militarization of the global commons has contributed to an erosion of the foundations for citizenship and political dissent. Any movement for low-carbon transitions first needs to take account of the wider geopolitical context of the existing socio-ecologies.

And second, we need to excavate deeper underground histories of mining and metals production to understand the transnational material basis of contemporary built environments, energy consumption, logistics and military power. Planetary resource extraction has concentrated control over resources and energy not only in the hands of transnational private companies, but also in *military hands*, which has extended cross-regional and transnational infrastructure integration on a vast scale, outside the control of urban governance and not subject to political transparency.

The theory of planetary urbanization offers one approach that seeks to get a handle on these multi-scalar mobilities of urban and planetary circulations of energy and military power. Neil Brenner and Christian Schmid have posited that there are "new processes of urbanization that are bringing forth diverse socioeconomic conditions, territorial formations and socio-metabolic transformations across the planet" including:

a) The unprecedented densification of inter-metropolitan networks, requiring colossally scaled infrastructural investments (from highways, canals, railways, container ports, airports and hydroelectric dams to undersea cables, tunnels, pipelines and satellite fleets) stretching across territories and continents as well as oceanic and atmospheric environments;

b) the restructuring and repositioning of traditional "hinterlands" through the installation of new export processing zones, global sweatshop regions, back office locations, data processing facilities, and intermodal logistics terminals;

c) the remaking and spatial extension of large-scale land-use systems devoted to resource extraction, the production and circulation of energy (including fossil fuels), and water and waste management;

d) the profound social and environmental transformation of vast, erstwhile "rural" areas through the expansion of large-scale industrial agriculture, the extension of global agribusiness networks, and the imposition of associated forms of land grabbing and territorial enclosure; and

e) the organization of erstwhile "wilderness" spaces, including rainforests, deserts, alpine regions, polar zones, the oceans, and even the atmosphere itself, to serve the relentless growth imperatives of an accelerating, increasingly planetary formation of capitalist urbanization.[48]

Brenner and Schmid contrast concentrated and extended forms of urbanization, the former being densely settles zones such as megacities and metropolitan regions, the latter consisting of far-flung "operational landscapes" of infrastructure for energy, tourism, telcommunications, transportation, resource extraction, agro-industrial production, and waste management, all of which support cities.

When urban planners speak of moving "beyond mobility" via place-making, they are simply not thinking of these extended operational landscapes of movement that support urbanization. Likewise, when we measure the "carbon footprint" of cities, we need to take into account these vast networks of production and consumption. As sociologist Daniel Aldana Cohen and collaborators argue, "Although prosperous urban residents may commute by bicycle or public transport—the forms of low-carbon living most commonly cultivated by sustainability projects such as Freiburg's eco-neighbourhoods—their carbon footprints are enlarged greatly by their consumption practices and leisure travel. Economic activity and urban density in post-industrial cities are inextricably linked with global networks of production, consumption and distribution."[49]

Planetary urbanization is not just a political-ecological project but also a deeply cultural project organized around discourses of modernization, acceleration, lightness, and speed, which provided the legitimation for massive resource extraction and urban concentration founded on environmental destruction and toxic pollution of hinterlands, peripheries, and remote wilderness areas. This process began in the "Age of Aluminum" when the first truly global transnational corporations connected tropical bauxite mines to mega-hydroelectric projects in order to produce a light metal (exported as "packaged electricity") that remade planetary infrastructures of transport, aviation, logistics, and communication. It continues today when "post-industrial cities highlight their sustainability triumphs in terms of building density, building public-transport networks and the presence of knowledge-intensive, high-tech firms all of which drive down locally produced pollution and carbon emissions." However, they do so by exporting polluting activities elsewhere, and even "information in 'the cloud' has an environmental impact."[50]

Building on this, we need to pay more attention to the interaction between urban infrastructure, land use, and connectivity across these "extended" urban systems and "operational landscapes" including mining, oil production, and water and energy flows, all of which feed into concentrated urban systems via transportation and logistics networks.[51] The long-distance global logistics chains that support extended urbanization are a planetary formation based on resource extraction. They are also secured networks of flow, enabling the intensification of extended urbanization to ever more distant places and its scaling up into ever vaster trans-regional agglomerations.

Extended urbanization is deeply tied to the political organization of military capitalism, which undermines all forms of democratic governance. Operational landscapes, therefore, are not simply artifacts of planetary capitalist urbanization but also of state processes of coercive militarization of resource accumulation and planetary logistics. We need to better identify the genealogy of power struggles between these dominant socio-technical regimes and the extensive resistance movements against it, as well as the contradictions within current efforts to improve energy efficiency, reduce energy consumption, and promote ecological urbanism.

This helps to explain a few problems about sovereignty, democracy, and global justice. First, the so-called "resource curse" is not as magical as it sounds; if control of a key resource is a function of military power, then resource-rich countries will simply tend to play the only game going. Military control of resources such as oil, iron ore, copper, or coltan (either through direct control of the state, or behind the scenes military elite control, backed up by state violence and death squads) is the only way to get a stake at the table—otherwise foreign powers will simply take resources and give little in return. And with military control (and dromocracy) there is little incentive to share the wealth with "the sovereign people," even in a democracy. Resource extraction thrives in and reproduces non-democratic governance.

Political geographer Martín Arboleda notes that even left wing "neo-extractivist" regimes facilitate this expropriation of resources like oil (see, e.g., Venezuela). Arboleda argues that "the commodity boom has also set in motion a process of institutional reconfiguration that has facilitated—and even accelerated—large-scale extractive operations."[52] Energy itself must be moved to the right places at the right times (from source to consumer, across national grids, from direct current to alternating current and back again, smoothing out peaks and dips in supply and demand) to enable many other things to happen. This requires a power grid, built out of various metals including, especially, copper and aluminum. Heavy industrial users of electricity such as smelters also help to balance loads and guarantee purchase over substantial periods of time.

Erstwhile peasants and Indigenous communities around the world have been at the frontlines of this transformation, due to the commodity boom, and sometimes spearheading the effort to stop it. In tracing the making of what he calls the "monstrous territories" of finance capital, Arboleda describes these contemporary processes:

> Rampant deforestation as lands are transformed into financial assets; suicide epidemics afflicting peasants under the burden of predatory lending; severe social anxiety resulting from mass evictions; and extermination of indigenous

communities by death squads in order to make way for speculative investment are but a few of the imprints of money's ferocious logic of infinite progression on planetary natures.[53]

Beyond the pollution directly produced by burning fossil fuels, there are extended lifecycle costs, both environmental and social, to contemporary forms of mobility. How can we account for the pollution and human rights violations caused by the "commodity boom," the mining of metals that are used in transportation and energy storage technologies, and the environmental impacts and injustices of the disposal of waste?

Environmental injustices and economic injustices are two faces of the same problem, each contributing to the other, and they are intertwined with mobility injustices in the form of uneven distribution of access to transport, energy, and the fundamental life requirements of clean air, water, food, and shelter. These human rights are now not only monetized and privatized as "natural resources" but are riskily financialized as tradeable "ecosystem services." Natural ecosystems may or may not be able to survive planetary urbanization, and it is open to question whether clean air and water will be available to entire populations and urban zones in the future; for many they are already gone.

Yet I would argue that the current "massive wave of infrastructure, energy, and mining" developments (often followed by the price crash) is not simply about "capitalist urbanization" on steroids, as Arboleda argues, but is deeply tied to military capitalism or perhaps better: military planetary capitalist urbanization. What we used to think of as "Nature," outside of human control, is not only being financialized, but also militarized and now weaponized through utter destruction and denial of the infrastructures that support life. The history of uneven mobilities and urban infrastructures reveal their relation to military power and logistics, which in turn inform the political character of all infrastructure space.

Global Mobility Justice

To develop a critical mobilities approach, in sum, first we need to take account of the wider geopolitical and geoecological context of infrastructure spaces and their dispositions. Second, we need to excavate deeper underground histories of resource extraction, mining, and metals production to better understand the transnational material and political basis of contemporary built environments and infrastructure space. Third, we need to combine broader dimensions of social equity and ecological effectiveness into more democratic transitions toward urban sustainability. As Wachsmuth, Aldana Cohen and Angelo argue, this requires globally standardizing consumption-based carbon accounting, bringing "the widest range of social movements to the table," as well as "more frequent meetings of larger groups of stakeholders and different metrics of policy success."[54] And lastly, we need to recognize the possible counter-geographies and subversive mobilities through which advocates of mobility justice can challenge the kinetic elite, the security state, and the military-logistical epistemologies driving resource extraction and climate destruction.

Mobility justice requires not only a kinopolitical struggle over infrastructure space, but also a counter-poetics of representational practices and meanings that will help enable a more positive counter-mobilization against the destruction of the global commons. In developing a planetary dimension to the principles of mobility justice, we might begin with the following:

- Principles of climate justice and environmental justice suggest that mobility consumed in one place should not externalize waste or pollution on other regions without legitimately agreed upon deliberation, transparency, and reparations.
- Those industries and countries that have contributed the most to greenhouse gases and other forms of pollution have a responsibility of reparative justice to limit the impacts of their actions and to restore the atmosphere and environments as far as possible: a global trust fund shall be established into which polluters pay in order to meet the costs of urgent global climate change disasters.
- Government subsidies for extractive energy industries should be redirected toward the development of clean, renewable energy, while also banning harmful practices and tracking royalty payments, tariffs, and profits through mechanisms such as the Extractive Industries Transparency Initiative.
- Protection of the planetary commons (aquifers, rivers, oceans, seafloor, mountains, atmosphere, Antarctica, the Arctic, and extra-planetary bodies) shall outweigh any rights to global free trade or private rights to resource extraction.
- All states shall be party to world forums at which carbon budgets (as well as other greenhouse gases) are agreed upon and reductions in greenhouse gas emissions regularly measured and met—and multinational corporations must be held responsible for this.

Yet this is just the beginning point. For it does not tell us what we should be moving toward. If we seek to abide by these principles, what kind of built forms, social practices, infrastructures, and stories will support a more just mobility? Where should we direct our attention in building more just mobility cultures and forms of governance across multiple scales at once?

These are the crucial kinopolitical questions that will shape the future. Until we have a better model for understanding the complex spatial connections between mobility injustices from the bodily scale to the scale of planetary infrastructure space, we will not be able to grasp the deep dispositions that materialize uneven and unequal worlds of mobility and dwelling. We seem a long, long way from utopian experiments, especially in the US with the election of President Trump and the "redemption" of the fossil fuel industry, who have been moving policies in reverse on every issue. But they also help us see the problem more clearly. The new mobilities paradigm points us toward the urgent necessity of paying attention to issues of power, justice, and inequity in post-carbon politics.

The reactionary backlash of fossil fuel–funded politics in the United States, the continuing offshoring of vast amounts of wealth, the escape of elites from taxation and regulation, the ongoing privatization of water and forests across the world, the tragically absurd denial of climate change and refusal of the need to reduce energy demand in the United States, and, of course, the ongoing disaster of the Trump administration's obstruction and dismantling of the state and all of its protections: these are all outcomes of the structured and relational (im) mobilities of people, capital, commodities, information, and energy in the world today. I strongly believe that the best way to achieve a transformation of these global tragedies is through a mobilization for mobility justice and in defense of the mobile commons.

A critically engaged mobility justice approach can help bridge various kinds of political concerns and social movements, whether challenging colonial and neocolonial relations of power, promoting racial, ethnic, and gender equality, standing in solidarity with Indigenous rights movements and self-determination, or fighting for environmental justice and climate justice. The mobility justice perspective is crucial not just to understanding the uneven mobilities of bodies, transport, and cities, but also the wider politics of mobility of infrastructure space, military power, and planetary urbanization. Our planet will need this multi-scalar approach if we are to generate new political visions and build the mobility capabilities to mobilize for a more just world.

Conclusion: The Mobile Commons

The concept of "the commons" has been rediscovered as a powerful organizing principle in recent social movements, socialist political thought, and critical theory. Its embrace ranges from the anti-globalization movement's call for a "reclaiming of the commons," which connected together issues of social, ecological, and economic justice in 2001; to Michael Hardt and Antonio Negri's ongoing political project for building "commonwealth" and "assembly" through "constructing new, mobile constellations of shared life"; to George Monbiot's recent calls for restoring and fortifying the commons. What is the commons? As Monbiot simply puts it:

> A commons is neither state nor market. It has three main elements. First a resource, such as land, water, minerals, scientific research, hardware or software. Second, a community of people who have shared and equal rights to this resource, and organise themselves to manage it. Third, the rules, systems and negotiations they develop to sustain it and allocate the benefits.[1]

A commons in this sense might be a shared pasture, a community forest, or a shared irrigation system, suggests Monbiot, but it might also be shared software, the Linux operating system, Wikipedia, or open access publishing; and it might include housing cooperatives, mutual insurance groups, and other kinds of cooperatives or shared use services. These models all build on the Nobel-prize winning work of political theorist Elinor Ostrom, whose research demonstrated that ordinary people could (and did) create rules and institutions that allow for the sustainable and equitable management of shared resources. Open access and cooperative management and decision-making are central features of these commons.

In their series of political treatises on topics such as *Multitudes*, *Commonwealth*, and culminating in *Assembly*, Hardt and Negri expand on the notion of a shared public good with open access by defining the common more precisely as being that which is in contrast to property, both private and public:

> It is not a new form of property but rather *nonproperty*, that is, a fundamentally different means of organizing the use and management of wealth. The common designates an equal and open structure for access to wealth together with democratic mechanisms of decision-making. More colloquially, one might say that the

common is what we share or, rather, it is a social structure and a social technology for sharing.[2]

Hardt and Negri exemplify potential commons in terms of the Earth and its ecosystems; immaterial forms of wealth such as ideas, code, and images; material commodities produced through cooperative forms of social labor; social territories produced through cooperation (i.e., what we might call sharing economies); and social institutions and services aimed at health, education, housing, and welfare.

Feminist theorists Gibson-Graham (who challenge patriarchal possessive names by sharing a single hyphenated name) similarly describe the commons as "an ethical coordinate of an alternative politics, with the traditional definition expanded to incorporate all manner of (potentially) common 'wealth,'" which might include "agricultural land, a gene pool, an atmosphere, a wilderness, a database, a fishery, the Internet, community facilities and support systems, or even the whole set of relations comprising a community economy."[3] The commons, therefore, in all these accounts, is not an empty unpeopled space or piece of unoccupied land, but is a socially produced shared space and a social infrastructure for all kinds of sharing.

What, then, does the commons have to do with mobility justice? In some ways it seems like a very sedentary idea, tying people to place-based communities and local cultures of sharing. Some have critiqued it as relying on an overly romanticized idea of community, and potentially feeding into forms of ethnocentric localism that are detached from political engagement. Yet others are trying to push its boundaries, and give the concept a more mobile ontological basis. Can mobilizing the concept of the commons get us beyond enclosure and more traditional notions of homogenous community?

The idea of a mobile commons seeks to keep the concept radically open to difference, instability, and momentary enactment. Black and queer critical theorists especially have sought to bend the commons toward less sedentary purposes, drawing on a more mobile imaginary. Moten and Harney's counterpoint notion of the fugitive "undercommons" hints at some ways to mobilize the idea of the commons not simply as a place or a resource to be shared, but as a way of moving through the world, a relational counter-position, an embodied relation with others, and an epistemic perspective from below.[4] The undercommons, as they describe it, is a feeling, an improvisation, a break. It is a poetic concept, linked to notions of the black diaspora such as "the underlanguage, underground, underwater, which is the people's macrophone," i.e. a subversive way of spreading words and sound, connecting across space.[5]

For example, the mobile commons might include migrants, as well as migrant ontologies. Hardt and Negri note the significance of migrants, who they say, play a fundamental role in shaping the contemporary world since they engage in making new commons:

[Those] who cross borders and nations, deserts and seas, who are forced to live precariously in ghettos and take the most humiliating work in order to survive, who risk the violence of police and anti-immigrant mobs, demonstrate the central connections between the processes of translation and the experience of "common-ing": multitudes of strangers, in transit and staying put, invent new means of communicating with others, new modes of acting together, new sites of encounter and assembly—in short they constitute a new commons without ever losing their singularities.[6]

This sense of encounter and commoning as an ongoing effort at translation across difference, rather than communal homogeneity, is crucial to the mobile commons. This non-nationalist vision of commoning differs from the idea of the "common good" described, for example, in former US secretary of labor Robert Reich's new book *The Common Good*. Reich defines the common good as consisting in "our shared values about what we owe one another as citizens who are bound together in the same society." Reich's communitarian emphasis on American "democratic" values that we all hold in common tries to establish an apolitical ideal "above-the-fray" of politics. In contrast, moral philosopher Michael J. Sandel argues in a review of the book that the "best hope for reviving the common good is to invigorate moral argument in the messy, contentious domain of democratic politics."[7]

The assembly of multitudes of strangers described by Hardt and Negri puts even more pressure on the idea of the common good. We might compare this "messy" and "contentious" political approach to queer theorist Lauren Berlant's argument for the commons concept as "a powerful vehicle for troubling trou-bled times." She uses it not as a naïve place-holder for community, but to point toward "the difficulty of convening a world conjointly, although it is inconven-ient and hard, and to offer incitements toward imagining a livable provisional life." Incoherent, ambivalent, and "messed up," she says, the commons concept nevertheless holds out a claim upon us: "Under its name, across the globe, communities tap into legacies of occupation to contest ownership rights and resource justice, and under its name, people project a pastoral social relation of mutual attachment, dependence, or vitality."[8] She poetically describes commoning as an activity, a verb, a movement, a connected mediation: it is a queer concept that holds out the possibility of different kinds of more hopeful political futures.

What interests me most about these projects is the way in which they are push-ing toward a more mobile imaginary of the commons, or commoning, as a political action—and one which the contemporary moment demands. What if the commons were not just about the sharing of a territory, a space, a resource, or a product, but could also refer to the affordances and capabilities for practices of moving, trave-ling, gathering, assembling, as well as pausing and being present? What if we conceived of mobility itself as a commons, and the commons as mobile?

The notion of "commoning mobility" has recently been advocated by a research team of mobilities scholars working on a fourteen-country comparison of low-carbon mobility transition policies. Anna Nikolaeva and research collaborators argue that the "commons lens" can help us to transformatively envision more "inclusive and collaboratively governed" cities as part of a new "politics of mobility" that would allow for fairer, greener, more just mobilities. Beyond the individualized "right to move," therefore, the researchers focus on "how collective social needs are mediated through mobilities."[9] This might mean access to shared vehicles or public mobility systems, it might mean reducing energy consumption for the common good, or it might mean producing shared spaces of communal access; but it might also suggest a different kind of politics.

I want to suggest that such a mobile ontology of the commons can become the basis for advancing mobility justice. In mobilizing the commons, we might generate unexpected shared spaces of movement, like neighbors growing community gardens in empty lots to deliver food to their neighborhood; like riders on a Slow Roll through Chicago who create community around a shared activity in order to build trust and "make their neighborhoods better;" like refugees turning up on the shores of tourist resorts in the Mediterranean who elicit receiving societies to question how we practice forms of hospitality; like squatters in informal neighborhoods tapping into the electric grid and challenging the exclusions of infrastructure built by private multinational corporations. We might find ways to undermine the uneven and differential mobilities that have fragmented, privatized, and militarized our bodies, streets, cities, infrastructures, nations, and planet.

THE ORIGINS OF THE COMMONS IN MOBILITIES

Throughout history people have naturally roamed (somewhat) freely over the earth, in the process of hunting or gathering, seeking new areas for settlement, traveling and trading over long distance. Through these rhythmic and seasonally punctuated (im)mobilities people have left behind traces, trails, paths, and tracks. Some modern roadways originated as pathways carved by animals moving across the land, which were later appropriated as human trails adapted to the land's affordances for movement along ridge lines, around swamps, or across valley bottoms. Such trails are a kind of commons that were later appropriated for automobility, such as the Wickquasgeck Trail of the Wappinger people, now known as Broadway, that transects diagonally across the island of Manhattan's imposed street grid. In some cases, the pathway itself remained common, such as the network of public footpaths crossing Great Britain, accessible to all who pass. Such "rights of way" were once the common right of all, distinct from property rights.

Elizabeth Blackmar traces the emergence of the concept of "the commons" in relation to British property law and political struggle, from the resistance movements against enclosure which transformed the agrarian landscape of eighteenth-century England, to the women's anti-war protest at Greenham

Common that began in 1981 to protest North Atlantic Treaty Organization (NATO) cruise-missiles being based there (at an army base that had previously been a town common). This decade-long peace encampment, which itself drew on non-violent political tactics of the American Civil Rights movement and Ghandism, helped inspire other movements of "occupation" such as Reclaim the Streets in the 1980s–90s, and later the Occupy movements in 2011. Against Hardin's influential "Tragedy of the Commons" essay, Blackmar traces the deeply embedded ways in which commons have always been collectively managed and governed by rules of customary shared usage, as Elinor Ostrom also demonstrated in her work on economics, and were not simply a disorganized free-for-all.[10]

Ivan Illich noted that "the road has been degraded from a commons to a simple resource for the circulation of vehicles."[11] The building of transportation infrastructures such as railways in the nineteenth century was initiated as a publicly subsidized undertaking, often using eminent domain to seize private property for the public good, while also of course clearing "natives" from the land. In more recent times, highway building has decimated communities of color, often tearing through the heart of many poor urban areas, even while denying those communities access to automobility (through physical lack of onramps and high costs of car ownership, as well as biased police stops for "Driving While Black").

Taking land for transport infrastructure, whether for nineteenth-century railways or twentieth-century highways, often relied on arguments about "the public good" and generated political struggles over access. Nevertheless, this, too, was a kind of enclosure of the mobility commons, and was resisted throughout history in the collective repertoire known as "tollway riots," or by acts of appropriation such as hitchhiking, hobos riding the rails, and protestors reclaiming the streets.

The capacity for humans to move about, whether to gather, hunt, and fish, or to communicate, trade, and celebrate together, or to hang out, "loiter" and "lime," pre-exists European colonization and enclosure and continued to be expressed in resistance to it. Even in the colonial settler states, original treaties made with Indigenous groups implied that they would still have right to passage, and to hunt and gather food, across certain lands in perpetuity. But in jurisdictions such as the United States, Canada, and Australia, such Indigenous commons have been lost, having been largely completely seized—through violence—whether as private (individual and corporate) or public (state) property. Most resource extraction takes place on land that has been seized in this way, through settler colonialism, expropriation, and expulsion. This loss is the real tragedy of the commons.

Common land and common passage have been blocked by private property holders, corporations, and the state in various ways. Previously common pathways across shared land eventually became surrounded by private and state-owned property, as enclosures and fences increasingly constricted human mobility. This process continues today. Commons around the world remain under constant pressure of privatization and environmental destruction, whether by corporate or military actions.

Reclaiming the Commons

Perhaps the best way to grasp the idea of the mobile commons is to seek out those times and places where people have mobilized to defend it. If we begin from Soja's meso-scale of the city, we can find a history of struggles over street space as a collective commons. Social movements have sought to reclaim stolen commons, from the street scale to the global scale. Take San Francisco, for example. Jason Henderson has traced the kinopolitical conflicts over the rise of private luxury bus services for tech workers, the battle to reduce GHG emissions in California by restricting automobility, and the spinoff effects on property prices, infill development (which adds urban density using vacant or underutilized parcels), and displacement of the poor and homeless. Tinted-window buses glide darkly through the streets of San Francisco, carrying Google employees plugged into smartphones, from their pricey luxury apartments to the cushy corporate campus in Mountain View; or maybe they are Apple employees heading to Cupertino, or Facebook employees on their way to Menlo Park. These buses reduce car trips taken by such workers and support "walkability", all in the service of reducing GHG. However, when we "downscale" the climate fight to the street level, in terms of who has access to streets, bus stops, and road space, it becomes clear that it is also a struggle over "the right to the city," with only well-paid workers benefiting from environmentally-friendly policies of "livability."

The rise of Google buses, writes Henderson, "foreshadows a potential transit future in which a premium system serves the wealthy in first-class coaches—and in premium livable neighborhoods—and a dilapidated, economy-class system serves the lower classes that are gentrified out of the core."[12] In fact, it may be fair to say this is already the case now. Recent censuses of homelessness reveal more than 7,500 people living on the streets in both San Francisco and Los Angeles, though local organizations serving this population estimate that the true number is closer to 12,000–13,000 people in each city. Some cities in California have taken to buying one-way bus tickets for unhoused people, sending them out of state.

So a new bus system that was meant to reduce car dependence, contribute to California's carbon-reduction goals, and create a "livable city" with walkable neighborhoods, can have unintended consequences which hurt the already disadvantaged and mobility poor. When privileged groups design mobility systems to serve their own needs, they may exacerbate existing kinopolitical inequalities. Underlining this is one of the key "Principles of Mobility Justice" emphasized by the Untokening project:

> Mobility Justice includes multi-racial organizing for communities to reclaim power and agency from the structures, policies, and programs that have divided them. It acknowledges distrust grounded in anti-blackness, anti-immigrant sentiments, etc.,

traces resentments to their sources, and uses that process to foster communication, build trust, and forge a common vocabulary and agenda.[13]

Other ways to address the transformation of mobilities have involved either utopian experiments or political mobilization. Mobile utopias offer new experiences and epistemic frames by changing how we do mobility right here, right now. More contentious direct actions foreground the political stakes involved in any kinopolitical transformation. The very terminology we use of "social movements" and "revolutions" already underlines that politics is both subject and object of motion, that it requires mobilization, and that it moves the world in new directions. This is where more experimental "prefigurative" approaches come into play.

One kind of mobile commons that has been embraced in many cities around the world is to implement Open Streets initiatives, which offer the experience of people-centered streets by closing them to car traffic. This began with Bogotá, Colombia's famous Ciclovía, which began in 1974 and grew to include over one million people using the streets on every Sunday and holiday throughout the year. Open Streets initiatives now includes events such as the CicloRecreoVia on Sundays in Santiago, Chile; the CicLAvia in Los Angeles, which ties into the city's Mobility Plan 2035 by using streets targeted for improved biking and walking infrastructure; and a range of Open Streets events in, for example, New York City, Nairobi, Kenya, and Pune, India. These kinds of events were also an inspiration to community cycling events such as Slow Roll Detroit and Slow Roll Chicago.

My own city of Philadelphia recently started a Philly Free Streets program, opening several major central streets to pedestrians and bikes on one Saturday annually, with the first event in September 2016 (inspired by the transformative experience of the closing of the streets for the visit of Pope Francis for the World Meeting of Families in September 2015), and the second in October 2017. The organizers describe Open Streets as promoting fun, recreation, and public health and fitness, rather than specifically targeting car traffic as a problem. In fact, it seems to purposely be trying to avoid antagonizing car drivers and is very limited in scope and time. The city has also long had one street that runs alongside the riverside park open on Sundays to non-motorized recreational uses only. Despite these limitations, ITDP argues that "above all, open streets events let people live briefly in an alternate reality where their city prioritizes streets for people. This alternate reality challenges what people experience in their daily life, and argues that streets where people come first are not only possible but better than the current reality."[14]

Such events, however, lack the political edge of earlier movements such as Reclaim the Streets that began in the United Kingdom in the 1990s, which more aggressively aimed to stop car traffic (and corporate globalization) by reclaiming community ownership of public spaces. I happened to be at one of the first events in Upper Street, Islington, in London in July 1995. The carnivalesque atmosphere, with drumming, dancing through the streets, and the forming of tall tripods onto which people climbed in the center of a major intersection, enacted a new form of kinetic politics. Reclaim the Streets grew out of the squatting movement which also reclaimed property as a commons, and was closely allied with the anti-road-building direct actions in England that occurred around the same time, in which people sought to stop bulldozers by chaining themselves high up in trees or burrowing underground in their path.

These disruptions of automobility also parallel the emergence of Critical Mass bike rides, which started in San Francisco and the Bay Area in the 1980s and early 1990s as direct action, anarchic collective rides that reclaimed roads for cyclists. Critical Mass rides seek to "assert a positive vision of how things should be in order to expose the current injustice of car-dominated public space."[15] These kinds of disruptive subversions of the utilitarian efficiency of horizontal automobile traffic sought to enact a new kind of kinopolitics through direct bodily mobilizations in the spaces of automobility. Historian Zack Furness describes how participants in Critical Mass experienced it as "radically transforming people's collective engagement with, and experience of, urban space (and mobility, for that matter)," and thus it became "a gesture rooted in the positive refusal of constraints, the reconceptualization of urban space and the exploration of desires outside of, or apart from, the framework of consumption and utilitarian mobility."[16]

More recently, there have been all-women cycling brigades doing group rides such as the monthly Luna Rides, annual "Clitoral Mass" rides, and recent "Black Mass" rides organized by a group known as O.V.A.S. (Overthrowing Vendidxs, Authority and the State) in Los Angeles, who describe themselves as supporting "young womxn of color leadership through a credo that believes in feminist ideals with indigena understanding and an urban/hood mentality."[17] Cycling is one way to make a claim on public space by those who have been marginalized. This kind of radical politics is a far cry from more top-down efforts to influence urban cycling through expert-led policy, and illustrates how alternative visions of epistemic justice might be embodied, literally, through bringing different bodies out on the streets. Through such corporeal mobilities, we might begin to generate alternative mobility futures at larger scales, by making intentional moves toward more inclusive and open streets in ways that potentially draw in more people and connect not only with urban planning processes, but also with neighborhood concerns such as health and preventing violence.

Every inch, though, will be politically contested, as there are still other mobility futures being envisioned by the car industry, by automobile driving lobbies, and by politicians who represent these constituencies (many of whose campaigns, at least in the USA, were financed by the oil industry). The path to new mobilities will undoubtedly be a kinopolitical struggle, which is precisely what Reclaim the Streets and Critical Mass explicitly engaged in, and movements such as the Untokening and Equiticity continue to expand upon today. In some US cities, recently there have also been spontaneous "invasions" of public urban highways, especially during Black Lives Matter protests, but also just in random flash mobs (which have sometimes turned violent). These events are less about transport justice than they are about claiming a right to urban space, and to be in the streets often framed in terms of racial justice.

What if we could frame all these kinopolitical movements as mobility justice protests, and by doing so find greater common cause? Rather than the mainstream narrative of an incremental change in daily transportation "choices" supported by the emergence of new "disruptive" technologies leading to a "transportation revolution," we can begin to imagine a broader mobility justice movement that would articulate goals around which diverse groups could coalesce and mobilize. While sustainable transportation is one important focus of social movements for urban spatial justice, the mobility justice perspective can help us see that such movements are also part of a wider kinopolitics associated with global urbanization, labor migration, gendered and sexual spatialities, public health, non-violence, and social protection. We can easily scale up the mobile commons to move beyond the city street and to take on larger planetary mobility politics.

We might say that the "global commons" today refers to all that remains accessible to and shared by all human and more-than-human beings, subject to cooperative democratic mechanisms of regulation and decision-making. Such commons rely on cooperative management to protect and preserve access not just today, but also for future generations. These are not just places that we must share with others and leave intact, but are also common lands that may need protection from human disruption in order to exist, like the Alaska National Wildlife Refuge, or niches within our human-made environments where plants, animals, and children might still thrive. The 2018 US tax bill slipped in the opening of the refuge to oil drilling and prospecting, after years of fighting this off. Oil companies envision the opening of a trans-Arctic passage, abetted by global warming, that will allow new routes for Alaskan fossil fuel markets. This is another privateering off the enclosure of what should be a global commons, to the benefit of transnational carbon capital.

The global commons includes oceans, air, atmosphere, fresh water, rivers, and unenclosed forests, and places such as Antarctica, but could be extended to other kinds of shared entities. The authors of the book *The Cosmopolitan Commons*, for example, also consider the "technologically rich, transnational commons" to include things such as gene banks, radio spectrum, and even weather forecasting.[18] Arguably there is also a communicative commons which is materialized in all human efforts to communicate with each other (printing, telephone calls, text messages, the internet, social media) and these too have been colonized by tech companies, who have commercialized and monetized human communication by gathering data, linking it to advertising, and selling it to all kinds of big data analysts including those like Cambridge Analytica who seek to influence political processes. The loss of "net neutrality" in the United States is also a form of enclosure of what was once "free" and appropriation of what was once "shared," while the "Open Data" movement seeks to keep open the electronic informational commons.

The taking of the global commons, and its degradation by resource extraction and pollution (mining, fracking, oil drilling, etc.), is linked to the production of both climate disruption and human impoverishment and displacement. Yet at the same time, this theft benefits from national borders that prevent the mobility of all people by taking away the mobile commons of human freedom of movement. Borders fix identities in place, deny freedom of movement, and undermine our common humanity.

ANIMATING THE MOBILE COMMONS

The concept of a "mobile commons" first began to appear in the study of migration, where it challenged state-centered approaches with a more autonomous understanding of migrants' own perspectives. Papadopoulos and Tsianos initially characterized the mobile commons as consisting of five main elements: "the invisible knowledge of mobility," such as knowledge about transit routes, shelters, border crossings, etc.; an "infrastructure of connectivity," such as media platforms, word of mouth, and social networks; "a multiplicity of informal economies," including knowledge of how to secure short-term work or engage with smugglers; "diverse forms of transnational communities of justice," such as solidarity groups, shelters, and NGOs; and "the politics of care," such as providing affective support, building trust, caring for people's relatives, etc.

We can see in this description some overlap with the concept of network capital, which also includes forms of knowledge, connectivity, and support systems. Further studies of migration have begun to discuss an "ontology of moving people" in which mobile commons are "generated, used, and extended . . . between people on the move," including the "shared knowledge, affective cooperation, mutual support, and care between migrants" while on the move.[19]

Hardt and Negri likewise argue that "multitudes that cross over, around, and through national boundaries have the potential to undermine fixed identities and destabilize the material constitutions of the global order." They draw on Judith Butler's notion of precarity as "a site of potential," arguing that vulnerability might in fact be a means for securing "forms of life grounded in the common" by exercising "open and expanding networks of productive social cooperation, inside and outside of capitalist economy, as a powerful basis for generating free and autonomous forms of life."[20] The shared mobility commons, therefore, is that which allows for people to exercise such productive forms of autonomous social cooperation outside of capitalism, and beyond or beneath the limits of national borders, existing in the interstices. It can be local, regional, and global at once; bodily, urban, and planetary in scale; spread through neighborhood, regional, urban, rural, national, and transnational networks of activism.

Mobility justice, then, can be conceived of as the interdependent social movement to protect and reclaim the shared mobility commons by "constructing new, mobile constellations of shared life" that can counteract the triple crisis of urbanization, migrant reception, and climate change. Mobile publics, as an active constellation of collective political action, are the way to defend and extend the mobile commons as a more just way of touching others and the world: a haptic kinopolitics. Envisioning new possibilities for mobile publics as protectors of the mobile commons can be a way to "counter the powerful forces of privatization, social exclusion, and enduring inequality that are already aligned against democratic participation and agency."[21]

The mobility commons, then, refers to access to the cooperative social territories and shared infrastructures of movement (both material and immaterial)— i.e., the pathways, ways, and means of moving, sharing, and communicating, which have been cooperatively produced by human relation to others, both human and more-than-human, through common passage, translation, and co-usage over time. This common mobility capability still stubbornly persists in the modern world of walls, gates, machines, property, and territoriality. The commons, in other words, is not land or resources as such, but is an action and a verb—a movement to make life in common, a commoning.

A mobile commons, therefore, does not imply maximizing mobility for all people and it is not simply about access to transport or a right to the city. Instead, it means protecting the capability for human and more-than-human shared mobilities and free spaces for movement by regulating excessive mobilities, limiting unnecessary speed, regulating corporations, pricing the externalities of transportation, and preventing its harms. As I have suggested, this will require a difficult reckoning with military power and its prerogatives of speed. We are temporary visitors and stewards of the global commons, which we must communally protect. The idea of the mobility commons goes beyond a bounded place or shared resource, but also beyond the individual right to freedom of movement. It implies actions that are shared through acts of co-mobilization; it is unbounded and deterritorializing, it is ambiguous and amphibious.

A mobile commons is enacted within shared practices of movement, momentary gatherings, and fleeting assembly, for a time, in a place, without owning it, so long as one does not ruin it, lay waste to it, degrade it, or take it away from the use of others. This implies upholding principles of deliberative justice, procedural justice, reparative justice, and epistemic justice. It is a kind of mindful movement, shared with others, and based upon forms of solidarity, reciprocity, caring, trust, generosity, and stewardship. It is temporally oriented toward maintaining the intergenerational connections between past, present, and future in terms of how we move over the Earth—lightly, carefully, with concern for others, and especially through difficult efforts of translation and accompaniment across difference. It is like carrying a child, to return to Virilio's imagery, but from the kinopolitical perspective of a mother.

The enclosure, securitization, and colonization of the mobile commons—whether by the state, by corporations, by Smart Cities, or by our own technological hypnotization—is equivalent to the de-politicization of humanity, and the dystopian ending of communality. Existing forms of capitalist growth, planetary urbanization, and resource extraction careen toward overheating the planetary atmosphere and disrupting all life on Earth, and local approaches to transport justice and urban spatial justice will not be sufficient to stop these multi-scalar processes. Nor can we place our hope in new technologies or shar-ing economies alone to counteract the interests of carbon capital, the kinetic elite, or the ever-expanding processes of military-industrial planetary urbaniza-tion. It is from the Global South and Indigenous political ontologies, as well as feminist and queer philosophies, that we might begin to find some of the most promising ways out of this bind.

Anthropologist Marisol de la Cadena has proposed the neologism "uncom-mons" to describe "assemblages of life where nature and humans might be beyond the demand for an either/or distinction" between "animate and inani-mate forms of life." Building her account from Andean peoples' relation to the mountain "earth-being" Ausangate, she rejects not only extractivist relations of property (associated with mining), but also "the subject and object detachability that underpins both the common good allegedly sought by extractivist states and the commons that environmentalists rally around to oppose it." She describes extractivism as:

> a geo-techno-financial corporate complex that desiccates lagoons, transforms forests into plantations, redirects and contains rivers, irrigates deserts, replaces mountains with open-pit mines, and builds roads connecting oceans. Extractivism (allegedly) offers resources to development, a common good that (also allegedly) benefits all: mines create jobs, damming rivers produces energy, irrigated deserts become agricultural lands. Yet extractivism destroys commons, from collectively owned resources to the environment.[22]

Yet environmentalists also detach humans from the "nature" that they seek to protect, and often do so by keeping humans out. In other words, while taking "resources" for "the common good" is problematic, even environmentalist ideas of protecting "the commons" assume that resources (or nature) and humans are detachable from each other, an assumption not found in Andean ontologies.[23] How can we think outside these dualisms?

The idea of the mobile commons may help solve this conundrum because it avoids stabilizing the commons as a place or a resource, something to be protected for human benefit. Instead it seeks to transform these kinds of dualistic ontologies by mobilizing commoning as a relational practice of heterogenous coming together in negotiated political alliance. Cadena's idea of the uncommons is reminiscent of Vandana Shiva's classic ecofeminist book, *Staying Alive: Women, Ecology and Development*. It also echoes Escobar's *Designs for the Pluriverse*, which describes multiple "onto-political" projects such as the Latin American movement for Buen Vivir, the Southern African philosophy of *Ubuntu* derived from a Nguni Bantu term often translated as "I am because we are" or "humanity towards others," the Gandhian concept of *Swaraj* focused on self-government through community building and political decentralization, and ideas of "degrowth" and "postextractivism" as transition frameworks for "design of/for and by the South."[24]

The project of mobility justice, finally, is about both the protection of the planet itself through a living process of commoning and the local mobilization of many networked mobile publics for the defense of the mobile commons.

In mobilizing the commons and commoning mobility, we might recognize mobile commoning as a collective activity, a transitive verb, a heterogeneous movement, a connected mediation. We can enact momentary mobile commons together through the difficult work of building more just embodied socio-natural relations and advancing shared movements for mobility justice. Only by actively seeking mobility justice can we protect our common futures.

Following on from this, I share below the list of all of the principles of mobility justice that have emerged from this process of re-thinking transport justice and spatial justice in relation to the complex multi-scalar crises of our age of extremes. I hope that you will read, contemplate, question, share, and translate them across many contexts and locations. And then, together, we must learn how to create the contexts in which we can mobilize to put these principles into action.

Principles of Mobility Justice

- Each person's freedom of mobility shall be constrained by the rule of mutuality: i.e., not trampling, endangering, or depriving others of their capability for mobility.
- Individual mobility shall not be involuntarily restricted by threats of violence, either physical or symbolic, including enforced forms of clothing, segregated means of movement, or unevenly applying temporal or spatial limits on mobility.
- Gender, sexual identity, and other markers of identity shall not be used as the basis for restricting mobility or exclusion from public space.
- Racial, ethnic, religious, or national profiling (including Indigenous identities) shall not be used to police entire groups or stop individuals from exercising freedom of movement.
- Universal design should be required in all public facilities to ensure accessibility to all people and especially access to all modes of public transportation and media.
- Children's rights to mobility and the rights of the elderly, pregnant women, and those needing assisted mobility should be protected and included in design and planning.
- Protections of habeas corpus shall extend to all people, both citizens and non-citizens, and there shall be no forms of state detention without legal representation, due process, and judicial appeal.
- Public transport systems must not arbitrarily deny access nor impose undue burdens, externalities, or limitations.
- Cities should ensure equitable provision of public transportation through a social benefit analysis based on population-level measures of social exclusion and minimum thresholds of accessibility (as described by Martens); and should seek to reverse the historical subsidies and other preferential treatment given to private automobility.
- Complete Streets policies should ensure that all modes of moving are afforded space and that streets are not dominated by one mode, such as cars.
- Cities should preserve public space, support multi-modal shared space, and should not develop splintered infrastructures that systematically advantage some groups with superior levels of service and disadvantage others with inferior levels of service.
- Transit-Oriented Development standards should be used to evaluate and measure social impacts of urban transport plans on accessibility, affordable housing, and social inclusion, and all communities should be included in decision-making processes.
- Public infrastructure for transport, communication, and information sharing shall be publicly funded and made accessible to all people.

- Information and communication technologies used in disaster recovery, and in general in any situations of digital divide, should be made as accessible as possible to those trying to recover, aiming to strengthen their capabilities.
- Net neutrality and open data repositories should be maintained to ensure public access, and all publicly funded research should require open source publication.
- There should be legal protection for data privacy, and states and corporations shall not have the right to search, seize, take, or use unauthorized private data.
- There should be regulation of so-called "offshore" banking, and enforcement of requirements for financial reporting and taxation in places of residency.
- All people have a right to exit and re-enter the territory from which they originate.
- There is a right to refuge for those fleeing violence and loss of domicile by war, but we must also develop new international agreements on asylum for climate refugees.
- There should be fairness and equity in determining the freedom of movement across borders without arbitrary exclusion of entire categories of persons on the basis of race, religion, ethnicity, nationality, sexuality, health status, or socioeconomic status.
- No one should be detained or deported without due process, legal protections and the right to appeal, and no detention centers should be created in "offshore" jurisdictions.
- Tourism shall be fairly exercised to ensure that it does not appropriate public or common lands, does not unduly disrupt the mobility rights or block the accessibility of places to those who dwell there, and does not leave behind undue burdens of waste or pollution.
- Those displaced by climate change shall have a right to resettlement in other countries, and especially in those countries that contributed most to climate change
- Principles of climate justice and environmental justice suggest that mobility consumed in one place should not externalize waste or pollution on other regions without legitimately agreed upon deliberation, transparency, and reparations.
- Those industries and countries that have contributed the most to greenhouse gases and other forms of pollution have a responsibility of reparative justice to limit the impacts of their actions and to restore the atmosphere and environments as far as possible: a global trust fund shall be established into which polluters pay in order to meet the costs of urgent global climate change disasters.
- Government subsidies for extractive energy industries should be redirected toward the development of clean, renewable energy, while also banning harmful practices and tracking royalty payments, tariffs, and profits through mechanisms such as the Extractive Industries Transparency Initiative.
- Protection of the planetary commons (aquifers, rivers, oceans, seafloor, mountains, atmosphere, Antarctica, the Arctic, and extra-planetary bodies) shall outweigh any rights to global free trade or private rights to resource extraction.
- All states shall be party to world forums at which carbon budgets (as well as other greenhouse gases) are agreed upon and reductions in greenhouse gas emissions regularly measured and met—and multinational corporations must be held responsible for this.

Glossary

Accessibility: The design of products, devices, services, or environments for people who experience disabilities. Accessibility is strongly related to universal design which is the process of creating products that are usable by people with the widest possible range of abilities, operating within the widest possible range of situations (whether they have a disability or not). Accessibility has been adopted as a design principle for many public transit systems, and in transportation refers also to measurements of the ease of reaching destinations, including mobility, connectivity, and proximity.

Black Lives Matter (BLM): An international social movement founded by African-American community activists in 2013 to protest against violence and systemic racism toward black people. It campaigns against police killings of black people as well as broader issues of racial profiling, police brutality and racial inequality in the criminal justice system, especially in the United States.

Capabilities Approach (CA): An ethical approach in economics and political philosophy, especially associated with the work of Amartya Sen and Martha Nussbaum, that emphasizes the protection of individuals' functional capabilities to exercise substantive freedoms, measured in non-monetary terms rather than traditional monetary measures of welfare. It inspired the creation of the Human Development Index used by the United Nations.

Climate Justice: An approach to global warming and climate change that frames it as a political and ethical issue concerning equality, human rights and collective rights. Building on environmental justice and social justice frames it suggests that those who are systemically responsible for anthropogenic climate change (e.g., developed countries) have an obligation of repair to those who are least responsible yet often suffer its greatest impacts (e.g. less developed countries, as well as low-income and minority groups).

Commons: Neither state nor market, private nor public, a commons is a shared resource of a community of people with negotiated rules to sustain it and allocate its benefits, according to George Monbiot. According to Michael Hardt and Antonio Negri, the commons "designates an equal and open structure for access to wealth together with democratic mechanisms of decision-making. . . . it is a social structure and a social technology for sharing."[1]

Complete Streets: A transportation policy and design approach that requires streets to be planned, designed, operated, and maintained to enable safe, convenient and comfortable travel and access for users of all ages and abilities regardless of their mode of transportation.

Critical Disability Studies (CDS): An academic field emerging from activism of differently abled people, beginning in the 1970s, that centers the experiences of differently abled people, challenges the ableist assumptions which shape society, and repositions the concept of disability within a social and political definition based on societal power relations. According to the Critical Disability Working Group: "Critical disability studies considers how institutions, cities or societies 'dis-able' people systemically and socially as well as looking into how the body and impairment can critically be incorporated into the discussions of disability and disablement."[2]

Critical Mass: Critical Mass bike rides started in San Francisco and the Bay Area in the 1980s and early 1990s as direct actions, anarchic collective rides that reclaimed roads for cyclists. Critical Mass rides seek to "assert a positive vision of how things should be in order to expose the current injustice of car-dominated public space," according to historian Zack Furness in his book *One Less Car*.[3]

Dromology: The study and analysis of the increasing speed of transport and communications in its relation to the development of land use. The logic of speed became the foundation of modern technological society according to French theorist Paul Virilio, shaping what he calls "dromological societies," in his book *Speed and Politics*, first published in 1977.

Extended Urbanization: Urban theorists Neil Brenner and Christian Schmid contrast "concentrated" and "extended" forms of urbanization, the former being densely settles zones such as megacities and metropolitan regions, the latter consisting of far-flung "operational landscapes" of infrastructure for energy, tourism, telecommunications, transportation, resource extraction, agro-industrial production and waste management, all of which support cities. The concept is elaborated on by political geographer Martin Arboleda to analyze the commodity boom in Latin America and its planetary extension of urban form.

Extractivism: Extractivism generally refers to an economic model based on the large-scale removal (or "extraction") of natural resources for the purposes of exporting raw materials, including industrial-scale agriculture, forestry, fishing, mining and hydrocarbons. Such extractive activity, it is argued, does not benefit local economies, produces high rates of underemployment and poverty, leads to unequal wealth distribution, and leaves behind waste and pollution. Extractivism has become a significant subject of political debate, especially in Latin America, where it is contrasted with postextractivism, neoextractivism, and postcapitalism.

Infrastructure Space: A concept developed especially by Keller Easterling in her book *Extrastatecraft: The Power of Infrastructure Space* (Verso 2014), which describes the way repeatable spatial formulas function as "a spatial operating system for shaping the city." This became the subject of a conference and edited collection, *Infrastructure Space* (Ruby Press, 2017), focusing on the way that such infrastructural systems and networks also determine the structure of buildings, cities, metropolitan regions, nations, and the planet itself.

Institute for Transportation and Development Policy (ITDP): A non-profit organization based in New York City that promotes transport solutions that reduce greenhouse gas emissions and air pollution, while improving urban livability and economic opportunity. Their projects in over 100 cities worldwide seek to inspire cities toward more environmentally and people-friendly transportation, to influence policy, and to direct attention to issues of urban mobility.

Mobile Commons: The enactment of cooperative social territories and shared infrastructures of movement—i.e., the pathways, ways, and means of moving, sharing, and communicating—which have been cooperatively produced by human relation to others, both human and more-than-human, through common passage, translation, and co-usage over time; and which allow people to exercise productive forms of autonomous social cooperation outside of capitalism, and beyond or beneath the limits of national borders, existing in the interstices.

Motility: The potential for mobility, implying a set of mobility capabilities which mobilities theorist Kaufmann and collaborators have defined as "the manner in which an individual or group appropriates the field of possibilities relative to movement and uses them."

No Border network: A loose association of organizations (mainly in Europe) that support freedom of movement and resist state control over human migration by coordinating international border camps, demonstrations, direct actions, and anti-deportation campaigns, See, e.g., *Freedom to Move, Freedom to Stay: A No Borders Reader* (No Borders, 2007).

Open Streets: Community based programs that temporarily make street space available to people by closing them to cars and other motor vehicles. Their aim is to turn streets into places where people of all ages, abilities, and backgrounds can come out and improve their health. See openstreetsproject.org and 880cities.org for examples and planning tools.

Reclaim the Streets (RTS): A collective that promotes collective ownership of public space through direct actions opposed to the car as the dominant mode of transport. Formed in the UK in the 1990s, it joined a wider resistance against corporate forces of globalization.

Slow Roll Chicago: Founded in 2014 by Jamal Julien and Olatunji Oboi Reed, Slow Roll Chicago's mission is "to connect a diverse group of people who utilize bikes and the activity of cycling as vehicles for social justice and social change, transforming lives and improving the condition of communities by organizing community bicycle rides, advocating for bicycle equity and implementing other cycling-related programs throughout Chicago." See slowrollchicago.org.

Transit Oriented Development: A set of standards for compact urban development around transit stations, that maximize walkability, access to residential, business and leisure space, pedestrian and bike facilities, reduced car parking, and protection of affordable housing.

Undercommons: A poetic concept developed in Fred Moten's work, sometimes linked to "the underlanguage, underground, underwater, which is the people's macrophone."[4] It suggests a more diffuse and "fugitive" notion of mobile and subaltern commons, in contrast to more community-based ideas of the common as a resource or place.

Untokening: The Untokening.org is a multiracial collective, founded in 2016, that centers the lived experiences of people, with leaders from marginalized identities as well as leaders who are actively engaging, organizing and advocating alongside people within marginalized communities, to address mobility justice and equity. It has organized "convenings" in Atlanta and Los Angeles, and has published "Principles of Mobility Justice."

Vision Zero: A multi-national road traffic safety project that aims to achieve road systems with no fatalities or serious injuries from vehicular crashes, and refuses cost-benefit analyses that monetize the loss of human life. It started in Sweden and won parliamentary approval there in 1997, and has gradually been adopted in many cities around the world. The concept applies the principle that "it can never be ethically acceptable that people are killed or seriously injured when moving within the road transport system."

NOTES

PREFACE

1. A. Hernández and L. McGinley, "Harvard study estimates thousands died in Puerto Rico due to Hurricane Maria," *Washington Post*, May 29, 2018.
2. N. Smith, "There's No Such Thing as a Natural Disaster," Understanding Katrina: Perspectives from the Social Sciences, June 11, 2006, available at understandingkatrina.ssrc.org/Smith; N. Klein, *The Shock Doctrine: The Rise of Disaster Capitalism* (New York: Henry Holt and Co., 2008).
3. N. Klein, "The Battle for Paradise: Puerto Ricans and Ultrarich 'Puertopians' Are Locked in a Pitched Struggle Over How to Remake the Island", *The Intercept*, March 20, 2018, available at theintercept.com. See also M. Sheller, *Island Futures: Global Mobilities and Caribbean Survival* (Durham: Duke University Press, 2019).
4. M. Sheller, *Consuming the Caribbean: From Arawaks to Zombies* (London: Routledge, 2003); M. Sheller, "The Islanding Effect: Post-Disaster Mobility Systems and Humanitarian Logistics in Haiti," *Cultural Geographies* 20 (2), 2013: 185–204; Sheller, *Island Futures*.
5. A. Dawson, *Extreme Cities: The Peril and Promise of Urban Life in the Age of Climate Change* (London and New York: Verso, 2017), p. 12–13.
6. E. Hobsbawm, *The Age of Extremes: A History of the World, 1914–1991* (New York: Vintage Books, 1994), p. 585.
7. Untokening.org Collective, lead co-organizers Zahra Alabanza and Adonia Lugo.
8. The Untokening, "Principles of Mobility Justice" (2017), available at untokening.org. Many thanks to Adonia E. Lugo for sharing her thoughts on the organization by email and in conversation in May 2018.
9. Personal Communication, Adonia Lugo, May 1st, 2018.
10. SlowRollChicago.org and Equiticity.org. Many thanks to Olatunji Oboi Reed for sharing his thoughts on these organizations during a visit to Philadelphia in March 2018.
11. E. Reid-Musson, "Shadow mobilities: regulating migrant bicyclists in rural Ontario, Canada," *Mobilities*, published online first, October 15, 2017, p. 2; A. Golub, M. L. Hoffman, A. E. Lugo, and G. F. Sandoval, eds. *Bicycle Justice and Urban Transformation* (New York: Routledge, 2016); M.L. Hoffman,

Bike Lanes Are White Lanes: Bicycle Advocacy and Urban Planning (Lincoln, NE: University of Nebraska Press, 2016); A. Lugo, "Decentering whitness in organized bicycling: notes from inside" in Golub et al., *Bicycle Justice*, pp. 180–88; J. Stehlin, "Regulating Inclusion: Spatial Form, Social Process, and the Normalization of Cycling Practice in the USA," *Mobilities* 9 (1) 2014: 21–41.

12. The Untokening, "Principles of Mobility Justice."
13. A. Escobar, *Designs for the Pluriverse: Radical Interdependence, Autonomy, and the Making of Worlds* (Durham: Duke University Press, 2017).

INTRODUCTION

1. S.A. Marston, "The Social Construction of Scale," *Progress in Human Geography* 24 (2), 2000: 219–42; N. Brenner, "The Limits to Scale? Methodological Reflections on Scalar Structuration," *Progress in Human Geography* 25 (4), 2001: 591–614. This description of mobilities as constellations of movement, meaning, and practice draws on Tim Cresswell, *On the Move: Mobility in the Modern Western World* (London: Routledge, 2006).
2. T. Birtchnell and J. Caletrio, (eds.), *Elite Mobilities* (London: Routledge, 2014).
3. M. Sheller and J. Urry, "The New Mobilities Paradigm," *Environment and Planning A* 38 (2), 2006: 207–26; K. Hannam, M. Sheller, and J. Urry, "Mobilities, Immobilities, and Moorings," *Mobilities* 1 (1), 2006: 1–22; M. Sheller and J. Urry, "Mobilising the New Mobilities Paradigm," *Applied Mobilities*, 1 (1), 2016: 10–25; P. Adey, *Mobility*, rev. ed., (London: Routledge, 2017).
4. Cresswell, *On the Move*.
5. R.J. Brulle and R. Dunlap (eds.), *Climate Change and Society: Sociological Perspectives* (New York: Oxford University Press and the American Sociological Association, 2015); J. Urry, *Climate Change and Society* (Cambridge: Polity, 2011).
6. Brulle and Dunlap, *Climate Change and Society*; D. Tyfield and J. Urry (eds.), "Energizing Society," special issue, *Theory, Culture and Society* 31 (5), 2014.
7. R.J. Brulle, "Institutionalizing Delay: Building and Maintaining the US Climate Change Countermovement," *Climatic Change* 122, 2013: 681–94; R.J. Brulle, J. Carmichael, J.C. Jenkins, "Shifting Public Opinion on Climate Change: An Empirical Assessment of Factors Influencing Concern Over Climate Change in the US, 2002–2010," *Climatic Change* 114, 2012: 169–88. On "carbon capital," see J. Urry, *Societies Beyond Oil: Oil Dregs and Social Futures* (London: Zed Books, 2013).
8. N. Klein, *This Changes Everything: Capitalism vs. the Climate* (New York: Simon and Schuster, 2014).

9. G. Monbiot, *Out of the Wreckage: A New Politics for an Age of Crisis* (London: Verso, 2017).

10. M. Featherstone, N. Thrift, and J. Urry (eds.), *Automobilities* (London: Sage, 2004); M. Sheller and J. Urry, "The City and the Car," *International Journal of Urban and Regional Research*, 24, 2000: 737–57; P. Merriman, "Automobility and the Geographies of the Car," *Geography Compass* 3 (2), 2009: 586–89.

11. H. Girardet, *Cities People Planet: Urban Development and Climate Change* (Hoboken, NJ: John Wiley & Sons, 2008); D. Tyfield, *Liberalism 2.0 and the Rise of China: Global Crisis, Innovation and Urban Mobility* (London and New York: Routledge, 2018).

12. D. Tyfield, *Liberalism 2.0*, pp. 169–73; M. Sheller, "Automotive Emotions: Feeling the Car," *Theory, Culture and Society* 21 (4/5), 2004: 221–42.

13. M. Mostafavi and G. Doherty (eds.), *Ecological Urbanism* (Zurich: Lars Müller, 2013).

14. B. Flugge (ed.), *Smart Mobility: Connecting Everyone* (Dordrecht: Springer Vieweg, 2017); and see Tyfield, *Liberalism 2.0*.

15. P. Newman and J. Kenworthy, "Peak Car Use: Understanding the Demise of Automobile Dependence," *World Transport Policy and Practice* 17 (2), 2011: 31–42; K. Dennis and J. Urry, *After the Car* (Cambridge: Polity Press, 2009); P. Newman and J. Kenworthy, *The End of Automobile Dependence: How Cities Are Moving Beyond Car-Based Planning* (Washington: Island Press, 2015); D. Metz, "Peak Car in the Big City: Reducing London's Transport Greenhouse Gas Emissions," *Case Studies on Transport Policy* 3, 2015: 371–76; E. Zipori, and M.J. Cohen, "Anticipating Post-Automobility: Design Policies for Fostering Urban Mobility Transitions," *International Journal of Urban Sustainable Development*, 7 (2), 2015: 147–65.

16. S. Graham and S. Marvin, *Splintering Urbanism: Networked Infrastructures, Technological Mobilities and the Urban Condition* (London: Routledge, 2001).

17. N. Eidse, S. Turner, and N. Oswin, "Contesting Street Spaces in a Socialist City: Itinerant Vending-Scapes and the Everyday Politics of Mobility in Hanoi, Vietnam," *Annals of the American Association of Geographers* 106 (2), 2016: 340–49.

18. T. Schwanen, "Rethinking Resilience as Capacity to Endure: Automobility and the City," *City*, 20 (1), 2016: 152–60, p. 158.

19. N. Brenner (ed.), *Implosions/Explosions: Towards a Study of Planetary Urbanization* (Berlin: Jovis, 2014); S. Sassen, *Expulsions: Brutality and Complexity in the Global Economy* (Cambridge, MA: Belknap Press, 2014).

20. Klein, *The Shock Doctrine*.

21. M. Sheller, "Connected Mobility in a Disconnected World: Contested Infrastructure in Post-Disaster Contexts," *Annals of the Association of American Geographers*, 106 (2), 2016: 330–39; Sheller, *Island Futures*.

22. K. Gotham and M. Greenberg, *Crisis Cities: Disaster and Redevelopment in New York and New Orleans* (Oxford and New York: Oxford University Press, 2014), p. 223.

23. C. Johnson (ed.), *The Neoliberal Deluge: Hurricane Katrina, Late Capitalism, and the Remaking of New Orleans* (Minneapolis: University of Minnesota Press, 2011); S. Graham (ed.), *Disrupted Cities: When Infrastructure Fails* (New York and London: Routledge, 2009).

24. Brenner, *Implosions/Explosions*; N. Brenner and C. Schmid, "Towards a New Epistemology of the Urban?", *City* 19 (2–3), 2015: 151–82.

25. J. Cidell and D. Prytherch (eds.), *Transport, Mobility and the Production of Urban Space* (London and New York: Routledge, 2015); M Grieco and J. Urry (eds.), *Mobilities: New Perspectives on Transport and Society* (Farnham: Ashgate, 2012).

26. On mobile ontologies, see Thomas Nail's forthcoming book, *Being and Motion* (Oxford: Oxford University Press); and P. Merriman, "Molar and molecular mobilities: The politics of perceptible and imperceptible movement," *Environment and Planning D: Society and Space* (2018), online first. I disagree with Merriman's critique of mobile ontology, and understand it in a non-binary way that is closer to what he calls "becoming-molecular."

27. Escobar, *Designs for the Pluriverse*, p. 101.

28. B. Maurer, "A Fish Story: Rethinking Globalization on Virgin Gorda, British Virgin Islands," *American Ethnologist* 27 (3), 2000: 670–701; A. Appadurai, *Modernity at Large: Cultural Dimensions of Globalization* (Minneapolis: University of Minnesota Press, 1996).

29. Maurer, "A Fish Story," p. 672.

30. Sheller and Urry, "The New Mobilities Paradigm"; Hannam, Sheller, and Urry, "Mobilities, Immobilities, and Moorings"; see, e.g., M. Sheller, *Consuming the Caribbean* (London and New York: Routledge, 2003) and M. Sheller, *Aluminum Dreams: The Making of Light Modernity* (Cambridge, MA: MIT Press, 2014).

31. For an overview of the field, see Sheller and Urry, "Mobilising the New Mobilities Paradigm."

32. J. Urry, *Mobilities* (Cambridge: Polity, 2007); J. Urry, *Climate Change and Society* (Cambridge: Polity, 2011); Sheller and Urry, "The New Mobilities Paradigm"; Hannam et al., "Mobilities, Immobilities, Moorings"; K. Dennis and J. Urry, *After the Car* (Cambridge: Polity, 2009); P. Vannini (ed.), *The Cultures of Alternative Mobilities: The Routes Less Travelled* (Farnham, UK and Burlington, VT: Ashgate, 2009).

33. D. Massey, "A Global Sense of Place," *Marxism Today* 35 (6), 1991: 24–9; D. Massey, *Space, Place and Gender* (Cambridge: Polity, 1994); D. Massey, *For Space* (London: Sage, 2005), p. 9.

34. This discussion draws on M. Sheller, "From Spatial Turn to Mobilities Turn," *Current Sociology* 65 (4), 2017: 623–39. And see D. Gregory and J. Urry

(eds.), *Social Relations and Spatial Structures* (Basingstoke: Macmillan, 1985), p. 25; J. Urry, *Sociology Beyond Societies: Mobilities for the Twenty-first Century* (London: Routledge, 2000); J. Urry, "Mobile Sociology."

35. E. Soja, *Postmodern Geographies: The Reassertion of Space in Critical Social Theory* (New York: Verso, 1989); D. Harvey, "From Space to Place and Back Again," in J. Bird et al. (eds.), *Mapping the Futures: Local Cultures, Global Change* (London: Routledge, 1993), pp. 3–29; N. Thrift, *Spatial Formations* (London: Sage, 1996); S. Sassen, *The Global City: New York, London, Tokyo* (Princeton: Princeton University Press, 1991).

36. E. Swyngedouw, "Neither Global Nor Local: 'Glocalization' and the Politics of Scale," in K. Cox (ed.), *Spaces of Globalization: Reasserting the Power of the Local* (New York and London: Longman, 1997), pp. 137–66; E. Swyngedouw, "Excluding the Other: The Contested Production of a New 'Gestalt of Scale' and the Politics of Marginalisation," in R. Lee and J. Wills (eds.), *Society, Place, Economy: States of the Art in Economic Geography* (London: Edward Arnold, 1997), pp. 167–77; K. Cox, "Space of Dependence, Spaces of Engagement and the Politics of Scale, or: Looking for Local Politics," *Political Geography* 17 (1), 1998: 1–23; N. Brenner, "State Territorial Restructuring and the Production of Spatial Scale," *Political Geography* 16 (4), 1997: 273–306; N. Brenner, "Between Fixity and Motion: Accumulation, Territorial Organization and the Historical Geography of Spatial Scales," *Environment and Planning D: Society and Space* 16, 1998: 459–81.

37. Z. Bauman, *Liquid Modernity* (Cambridge: Polity, 2000).

38. P. Merriman, *Mobility, Space and Culture* (London and New York: Routledge, 2012).

39. Sheller and Urry, "Mobilising the New Mobilities Paradigm"; T. Cresswell, "Mobilities I: Catching Up," *Progress in Human Geography* 35 (4), 2011: 550–58; T. Cresswell, "Mobilities II: Still," *Progress in Human Geography* 36 (5), 2012: 645–53; T. Cresswell, "Mobilities III: Moving On," *Progress in Human Geography* 38 (5), 2014: 712–21.

40. A. Jonas, "Rethinking Mobility at the Urban-Transportation-Geography Nexus," in J. Cidell and D. Prytherch (eds.), *Transportation and Mobility in the Production of Urban Space* (London: Routledge, 2015): 281–93, p. 281.

41. C. Johnson, R. Jones, A. Paasi, L. Amoore, A. Mountz, M. Salter, and C. Rumford, "Interventions on Rethinking 'the Border' in Border Studies," *Political Geography* 30, 2011: 61–9; N. Parker and N. Vaughan-Williams, *Critical Border Studies: Broadening and Deepening the 'Lines in the Sand' Agenda* (London and New York: Routledge, 2014); C. Brambilla, "Exploring the Critical Potential of the Borderscapes Concept," *Geopolitics* 20 (1), 2015: 14–34.

42. J. Huysmans, *The Politics of Insecurity: Fear, Migration and Asylum in the EU* (Abingdon, Oxon: Routledge, 2006); V. Squire (ed.), *The Contested Politics*

of Mobility: Borderzones and Irregularity (New York: Routledge, 2011); M. Leese and S. Wittendorp (eds.), *Security/Mobility: Politics of Movement* (Manchester: Manchester of University Press, 2017). And see the special issue of *Mobilities*, Vol. 13, No. 2 (2018) on mobilities and securities.

43. Hannam, Sheller, and Urry, "Mobilities, Immobilities, and Moorings"; Cresswell, *On the Move*; S. Bergmann and T. Sager (eds.), *The Ethics of Mobilities: Rethinking Place, Exclusion, Freedom and Environment* (Aldershot: Ashgate, 2008).

44. M. Sheller, "Uneven Mobility Futures: A Foucaultian Approach," *Mobilities* 11 (1), 2015: 15–31; M. Flamm and V. Kaufmann, "Operationalising the Concept of Motility: A Qualitative Study," *Mobilities*, 1 (2), 2006: 167–89; A. Kellerman, "Potential Mobilities," *Mobilities* 7 (1), 2012: 171–83; D. Kronlid, "Mobility as Capability," in T.P. Uteng and T. Cresswell (eds.), *Gendered Mobilities* (Aldershot: Ashgate, 2008), 15–34; J.O. Bærenholdt, "Governmobility: The Powers of Mobility," *Mobilities* 8 (1), 2013: 20–34; J. Faulconbridge and A. Hui, "Traces of a Mobile Field: Ten Years of Mobilities Research," *Mobilities* 11 (1), 2016: 1–14.

45. T. Nail, *The Figure of the Migrant* (Stanford: Stanford University Press, 2015); T. Nail, *Theory of the Border* (Oxford: Oxford University Press, 2016).

46. Elliott and Urry, *Mobile Lives*, pp. 10–11; V. Kaufmann and B. Montulet, "Between Social and Spatial Mobilities: The Issue of Social Fluidity" in *Tracing Mobilities: Towards a Cosmopolitan Perspective*, edited by W. Canzler, V. Kaufmann and S. Kesselring (Farnham: Ashgate, 2008), 37–56.

47. A. Mountz, "Specters at the Port of Entry: Understanding State Mobilities Through an Ontology of Exclusion," *Mobilities* 6, 2011: 317–34; T. Vukov and M. Sheller, "Border Work: Surveillant Assemblages, Virtual Fences, and Tactical Counter-media," *Social Semiotics* 23 (2), 2013: 225–41.

48. H. Kotef, *Movement and the Ordering of Freedom: On Liberal Governances of Mobility,* (Durham and London: Duke University Press, 2015), pp. 54, 37, 58.

49. Ibid., p. 63.

50. Ibid., p. 100.

51. Massey, *For Space*, p. 7.

52. Kotef, *Movement*, p. 114.

53. R. Clare, "Black Lives Matter: The Black Lives Matter Movement in the National Museum of African-American History and Culture," *Transfers* 6 (1), 2016: 122–5, p. 124.

54. M. Freudendal-Pedersen, *Mobility in Daily Life: Between Freedom and Unfreedom* (Farnham, UK and Burlington, VT: Ashgate, 2009).

55. See N. Glick Schiller and N.B. Salazar, "Regimes of Mobility Across the Globe," *Journal of Ethnic and Migration Studies* 39 (2013): 183–200; V. Thimm, *Understanding Muslim Mobilities and Gender* (Basel: MDPI, 2017); and see the new series, New Mobilities in Asia, from University of

Amsterdam Press, as well as generally the journal *Transfers: Interdisciplinary Journal of Mobility Studies.*

56. Vannini, *Cultures of Alternative Mobilities.*

57. M. Desmond, *Evicted: Poverty and Profit in the American City* (New York: Penguin Random House, 2016); M. Alexander, *The New Jim Crow: Mass Incarceration in the Age of Color Blindness* (New York: New Press, 2012).

58. Elliott and Urry, *Mobile Lives*; J. Bruder, *Nomadland: Surviving America in the Twenty-First Century* (New York and London: W.W. Norton and Co., 2017).

59. J. Shell, *Transportation and Revolt: Pigeons, Mules, Canals and the Vanishing Geographies of Subversive Mobilities* (Cambridge, MA: MIT Press, 2015), pp. 50–51; J.C. Scott, *The Art of Not Being Governed: An Anarchist History of Upland Southeast Asia* (New Haven and London: Yale University Press, 2009), p. 31.

60. P. Linebaugh and M. Rediker, *The Many-Headed Hydra: Sailors, Slaves, Commoners and the Hidden History of the Revolutionary Atlantic* (Boston: Beacon Press, 2001), p. 6.

61. Linebaugh and Rediker, *The Many-Headed Hydra*, p. 6; D. Cowen, *The Deadly Life of Logistics: Mapping Violence in Global Trade* (Minneapolis: University of Minnesota Press, 2014), p. 227.

CHAPTER 1

1. R. Florida, *The New Urban Crisis: How our Cities are Increasing Inequality, Deepening Segregation and Failing the Middle Class—And What We Can Do About It* (New York: Basic Books, 2017).

2. R. Perreira, T. Schwanen, and D. Banister, "Distributive Justice and Equity in Transportation," *Transport Reviews*, 37 (2), 2017: 170–91.

3. Perreira et al., "Distributive Justice," p. 2; and see N. Fraser, "Recognition or Redistribution? A Critical Reading of Iris Marion Young's *Justice and the Politics of Difference*," *Journal of Political Philosophy* 3 (2), 1995: 166–80; W. Kymlicka, *Contemporary Political Philosophy: An Introduction*, 2nd ed. (Oxford: Oxford University Press, 2002); I.M. Young, *Justice and the Politics of Difference* (London: Routledge, 1990).

4. Young, *Justice and the Politics of Difference*; R. Fincher and K. Iveson, "Justice and injustice in the city," *Geographical Research* 50 (3), 2012: 231–41.

5. Perreira et al., "Distributive Justice," p. 10.

6. R. Bullard and G. Johnson (eds.), *Just Transportation: Dismantling Race and Class Barriers to Mobility* (Gabriola Island, BC: New Society Publishers, 1997); R. Bullard, G. Johnson, and A. Torres, "Dismantling Transportation Apartheid: The Quest for Equity" in R. Bullard, G. Johnson, and A. Torres (eds.), *Sprawl City* (Washington, DC: Island Press, 2000), pp. 39–68; R.

Bullard, G. Johnson, and A. Torres, *Highway Robbery: Transportation Racism and New Routes to Equity* (Cambridge: South End Press, 2004).

7. Reid-Musson, "Shadow mobilities," p. 3.

8. T. Cresswell, "The Vagrant/Vagabond: The Curious Career of a Mobile Subject," in T. Cresswell and P. Merriman (eds.), *Geographies of Mobilities: Practices, Spaces, Subjects* (Farnham and Burlington: Ashgate, 2011), pp. 239–54; N. Blomley, *Rights of Passage: Sidewalks and the Regulation of Public Flow* (New York: Routledge, 2011).

9. Kymlicka, *Contemporary Political Philosophy*; A. Sen, *The Idea of Justice* (Cambridge, MA: Harvard University Press, 2009).

10. M.J. Sandel, *Justice: What's the Right Thing To Do?* (New York: Farrar, Straus and Giroux, 2009).

11. Perreira et al., "Distributive Justice," p. 11.

12. J. Rawls, *A Theory of Justice,* revised edition (Cambridge, MA: Belknap Press of Harvard University Press, 1999); J. Rawls, *Justice as Fairness: A Restatement* (Cambridge, MA and London: Harvard University Press, 2001).

13. Perreira et al., "Distributive Justice," p. 6.

14. M. Nussbaum, *Creating Capabilities: The Human Development Approach* (Cambridge, MA: Harvard University Press, 2011); A. Sen, *The Idea of Justice* (Cambridge, MA: Harvard University Press, 2009).

15. Perreira et al., "Distributive Justice," p. 7.

16. J.M. Viegas, "Making Urban Road Pricing Acceptable and Effective: Searching for Quality and Equity in Urban Mobility," *Transport Policy*, 8 (4), 2001: 289–94; Bullard and Johnson, *Just Transportation*.

17. Perreira et al., "Distributive Justice," p. 8.

18. Ibid., p. 8.

19. K. Martens, *Transport Justice: Designing Fair Transportation Systems* (London and New York: Routledge, 2016); K. Martens, "Justice in Transport as Justice in Accessibility: Applying Walzer's 'Spheres of Justice' to the Transport Sector," *Transportation* 39 (6), 2012: 1035–53.

20. See, for example, C. Kaplan, *Questions of Travel: Postmodern Discourses of Displacement* (Durham: Duke University Press, 1996); T. Cresswell, "Citizenship in Worlds of Mobility." In *Critical Mobilities*, edited by O. Soderstrom, D. Ruedin, S. Randeria, G. D'Amato, and F. Panese (New York: Routledge, 2013), pp. 105–24; Cresswell, *On the Move*; Freudendal-Pedersen, *Mobility in Daily Life*.

21. *The Slow Roll Chicago Bicycle Equity Statement of Principle*, Draft Version, Revised August 15, 2017, p. 2, available at SlowRollChicago.org.

22. Perreira et al., "Distributive Justice," p. 12.

23. Ibid., p. 13.

24. Kaufmann and Montulet,"Between Social and Spatial Mobilities," p. 45; V. Kaufmann, M. Bergman, and D. Joye, "Motility," *International Journal of Urban and Regional Research* 28 (4), 2004: 745–56.

25. J. Butler, "Reflections on Trump," *Hot Spots*, Cultural Anthropology, accessed at culanth.org/fieldsights.

26. D. Kronlid, "Mobility as Capability," in T.P. Uteng and T. Cresswell (eds.), *Gendered Mobilities* (Aldershot: Ashgate, 2008), pp. 15–34; R. Hananel and J. Berechman, "Justice and Transportation Decision-making: The Capabilities Approach," *Transport Policy* 49, 2016: 78–85.

27. D. Schlosberg, *Defining Environmental Justice: Theories, Movements and Nature* (Oxford: Oxford University Press, 2007); and see K. Shrader-Frechette, *Environmental Justice: Creating Equality, Reclaiming Democracy* (Oxford: Oxford University Press, 2005).

28. D. Schlosberg, "Climate Justice and Capabilities: A Framework for Adaptation Policy," *Ethics and International Affairs* 26 (4), 2012: 445–61, p. 446; drawing on Nussbaum, *Creating Capabilities*; Sen, *The Idea of Justice*; Young, *Justice and the Politics of Difference*; and N. Fraser, *Justice Interruptus: Critical Reflections on the "Postsocialist" Condition* (New York: Routledge, 1997).

29. J. Dryzek, R. Norgaard, and D. Schlosberg, *Climate-Challenged Society* (Oxford: Oxford University Press, 2013).

30. Escobar, *Designs for the Pluriverse*, p. 207.

31. For a critique of policies based on mobility austerity and scarcity, see A. Nikolaeva, P. Adey, T. Cresswell, J. Lee, A. Novoa, and C. Temenos "A New Politics of Mobility: Commoning Movement, Meaning and Practice in Amsterdam and Santiago," *Centre for Urban Studies Working Paper Series*, WPS 26 (2017), available at urbanstudies.uva.nl/working-papers/working-papers.html.

32. G. Ottinger, "Changing Knowledge, Local Knowledge and Knowledge Gaps: STS Insights into Procedural Justice," *Science, Technology and Human Values* 38 (2), 2013: 250–70.

33. The Untokening, "Principles of Mobility Justice."

34. Sheller, "From Spatial Turn to Mobilities Turn."

35. D. Harvey, *Social Justice and the City*, new ed. (London: Blackwell, 1988), pp. 98, 116–17.

36. E.W. Soja, *Seeking Spatial Justice* (Minneapolis and London: University of Minnesota Press, 2010).

37. Cresswell, "Towards a Politics of Mobility."

38. Soja, *Seeking Spatial Justice*, p. 31. Italics added.

39. Ibid., p. 41.

40. Ibid., pp. 42–3.

41. Ibid., pp. 45–6.

42. Ibid., p. 47.

43. Ibid., pp. 72–3.

44. Ibid., p. 76.

45. Ibid., p. 80.

46. M. Sheller, *Democracy After Slavery: Black Publics and Peasant Radicalism in Haiti and Jamaica* (Basingstoke and London: Macmillan Caribbean, 2000).

47. Sheller, *Consuming the Caribbean.*

48. J. Overing and A. Passes, *The Anthropology of Love and Anger: The Aesthetics of Conviviality in Native Amazonia* (London: Routledge, 2000).

49. N. Brenner, *New State Spaces: Urban Governance and the Rescaling of Statehood* (Oxford and New York: Oxford University Press, 2004), p. 66; and see N. Brenner and N. Theodore (eds.) *Spaces of Neoliberalism: Urban restructuring in North America and Western Europe* (Oxford and Boston: Blackwell, 2002).

50. N. Brenner and C. Schmid, "Towards a new epistemology of the urban?" *City*, 19 (2–3), 2015: 151–82.

51. Soja, *Seeking Spatial Justice*, p. 33–4.

52. Ibid., p. 37.

53. J. Frith, "Splintered Space: The Smartphone as the Screen to the City," *Mobilities* 7 (1), 2012: 131–49; A. De Souza e Silva and M. Sheller (eds.), *Mobilities and Locative Media: Mobile Communication in Hybrid Spaces* (New York: Routledge, 2015).

54. Sheller, "From Spatial Turn to Mobilities Turn."

55. A.L. Stoler, *Duress: Imperial Durabilities in Our Times* (Durham: Duke University Press, 2016), p. 117.

56. Ibid., p. 118.

57. Ibid., pp. 120–21.

58. Ibid., p. 131.

59. Ibid.

60. Sheller, "The Islanding Effect"; and see Sheller, *Island Futures*.

CHAPTER 2

1. K. Sawchuk, "Impaired," in *The Routledge Handbook of Mobilities*, eds. P. Adey, D. Bissell, K. Hannam, P. Merriman, and M. Sheller, (London: Routledge, 2014): 570–84, p. 409.

2. Cresswell, *On the Move.*

3. T.P. Uteng and T. Cresswell (eds.), *Gendered Mobilities* (Aldershot: Ashgate, 2008); M.G. Reyes, *Disability, Mobility and Space* (New York and London: Routledge, 2018).

4. R. Braidotti, *Nomadic Subjects: Embodied and Sexual Difference in Contemporary Feminist Theory* (New York: Columbia University Press, 1994); Kaplan, *Questions of Travel*; Benko and Strohmayer, *Space and Social Theory*, which included Cresswell's early mobilities writing; and see Cresswell, *On the Move.*

5. See, for example, L. McDowell, *Gender, Identity and Place* (Cambridge: Polity, 1999); Massey, *For Space*; N. Puwar, *Space Invaders: Race, Gender and Bodies Out of Place* (Oxford and New York: Berg, 2005).

6. A. Hackl et al., "Bounded Mobilities: An Introduction," in M. Gutekunst et al. (eds) *Bounded Mobilities: Ethnographic Perspectives on Social Hierarchies and Global Inequalities* (Bielefeld: transript Verlag, 2016), p. 23; Schiller and Salazar, "Regimes of Mobility."

7. Stoler, *Duress*; P. Gilroy, *The Black Atlantic: Modernity and Double Consciousness* (London and New York: Verso, 1993).

8. It is at this juncture that my work *Consuming the Caribbean* (2003) and co-edited volume *Uprootings/Regroundings: Questions of Home and Migration* (2003) could be located, building on my earlier work in theorizing freedom and citizenship in post-slavery societies, *Democracy After Slavery* (2000).

9. A. Amin and N. Thrift, *Cities: Reimagining the Urban* (Cambridge: Polity, 2002), p. 26.

10. D. Massey, "A global sense of place," in T. Oakes and L. Price (eds.) *The Cultural Geography Reader* (London: Routledge, 2008), p. 165, as cited in Sawchuk, "Impaired," p. 411.

11. Massey, "A global sense of place," p. 161, cited in Sawchuk, "Impaired," p. 411.

12. Cresswell, *On the Move*; Uteng and Cresswell, *Gendered Mobilities*.

13. P. Virilio, *Negative Horizon: An Essay in Dromoscopy*, trans. Michael Degener (London and New York: Continuum, 2005), p. 37.

14. Virilio, *Negative Horizon*, pp. 38–9.

15. On this point, see also M. Jacqui Alexander, "Not Just (Any) Body Can Be a Citizen: The Politics of Law, Sexuality and Postcoloniality in Trinidad and Tobago and the Bahamas," *Feminist Review* 48, 1994: 5–23.

16. A. Appadurai, *Modernity at Large: Cultural Dimensions of Globalization* (Minneapolis: University of Minnesota Press, 1996), p. 44.

17. Thimm, *Understanding Muslim Mobilities and Gender*.

18. Massey, *Space, Place and Gender*.

19. Personal communication, Esther Figueroa, with Jamaica given as an example.

20. A. Brah, *Cartographies of Diaspora: Contesting Identities* (Abingdon and New York: Routledge, 1996), p. 182. Emphasis in original.

21. Young, *Justice and the Politics of Difference*.

22. Young, *Justice and the Politics of Difference*; L. Murray, "Motherhood, Risk and Everyday Mobilities" in T.P. Uteng and T. Cresswell (eds.), *Gendered Mobilities* (Ashgate, 2008), 47–64; A.J. Jorgensen, "The Culture of Automobility," in Uteng and Cresswell, *Gendered Mobilities,* 99–114.

23. Braidotti, *Nomadic Subjects*; T. Cresswell, "Introduction: theorizing place," in *Mobilizing Place, Placing Mobility*, edited by G. Verstraete and T. Cresswell (Amsterdam: Rodopi), 11–32, pp. 15–18; Urry, *Sociology Beyond Societies*, Ch. 2.

24. B. Skeggs, *Class, Self, Culture* (London: Routledge, 2004), pp. 48–9; Massey, *Space, Place and Gender*.

25. S. Subramanian, "Embodying the Space Between: Unmapping Writing About Racialised and Gendered Mobilities," in Uteng and Cresswell, *Gendered Mobilities*, 35–46.

26. Murray, "Motherhood, Risk and Everyday Mobilities."

27. E. Scheibelhofer, "Gender Still Matters: Mobility Aspirations among European Scientists Working Abroad," in Uteng and Cresswell, *Gendered Mobilities*, 115–28, p. 116, 124.

28. K. Boyer, R. Mayes, and B. Pini, "Narrations and Practices of Mobility and Immobility in the Maintenance of Gender Dualisms," *Mobilities*, 12 (6), 2017: 847–60.

29. R. Law, "Beyond 'Women and Transport': Towards New Geographies of Gender and Daily Mobility," *Progress in Human Geography* 23 (4), 1999: 567–88, p. 575.

30. J.K. Gibson-Graham, *A Postcapitalist Politics* (Minneapolis: University of Minnesota, 2006), p. 127.

31. K. McKittrick, *Demonic Grounds: Black Women and the Cartographies of Struggle* (Minneapolis: University of Minnesota Press, 2006), p. xxvi.

32. McKittrick, *Demonic Grounds*, p. xxvi; Cresswell, "Black Moves"; Sheller, *Citizenship from Below*.

33. K. Kempadoo, *Sexing the Caribbean: Gender, Race, and Sexual Labor* (New York and London: Routledge, 2004).

34. S. Frohlick, "'I'm More Sexy Here': Erotic Subjectivities of Female Tourists in the 'Sexual Paradise' of the Costa Rican Caribbean," in Uteng and Cresswell, *Gendered Mobilities*, 129–42.

35. Appadurai, *Modernity a Large*, p. 39.

36. Reyes, *Disability, Mobility and Space*.

37. G. Anzaldua, *Borderlands/La Fronters: The New Mestiza*, 4th ed. (Aunt Lute Books, 2012); E. Luibheid and L. Cantu Jr. (eds.), *Queer Migrations: Sexuality, US Citizenship, and Border Crossings*, 3rd ed. (Minneapolis: University of Minnesota Press, 2005); K. Chavez, *Queer Migration Politics: Activist Rhetoric and Coalitional Possibilities* (Urbana: University of Illinois Press, 2013).

38. See, e.g., C.J. Nash and A. Gorman-Murrary, "LGBT Neighborhoods and 'New Mobilities': Towards Understanding Transformations in Sexual and Gendered Urban Landscapes," *International Journal of Urban and Regional Research*, 38 (8), 2014: 756–72; C.J. Nash and A. Gorman-Murray, "Sexuality, Urban Public Space and Mobility Justice," in D. Butz and N. Cook (eds.), *Mobilities, Mobility Justice and Social Justice* (London: Routledge, 2018).

39. L. Parent, "The Wheeling Interview: Mobile Methods and Disability," *Mobilities* 11 (4), 2016: 521–32.

40. B. Gleeson, *Geographies of Disability* (London: Routledge, 2006), pp. 129, 137, as cited in G. Goggin, "Disability and Mobilities: Evening Up Social Futures," *Mobilities* 11 (4), 2016: 533–41, p. 535.

41. R. Imrie, "Disability and Discourses of Mobility and Movement," *Environment and Planning A* 32 (9), 2000: 1,641–56, p. 1,641.

42. Cresswell, "Politics of Mobility," p. 21, as cited in Goggin, "Disability and Mobilities," p. 535. And see M. Oliver, *Understanding Disability* (Basingstoke: Macmillan, 1996).

43. Cresswell, *On the Move*, p. 167; Sawchuk, "Impaired," pp. 411, 418.

44. Sawchuk, "Impaired," p. 413.

45. N. Blomley, "Sidewalks," in P. Adey, D. Bissell, K. Hannam, P. Merriman, and M. Sheller (eds) *The Routledge Handbook of Mobilities* (New York: Routledge, 2014), 472–82.

46. O.O. Reed, public talk in Philadelphia, March 26, 2018.

47. The terminology used here draws on M. Omi and H. Winant, *Racial Formation in the United States*, 3rd ed. (New York: Routledge, 2015).

48. S. Wynter, "Unsettling the Coloniality of Being/Power/Truth/Freedom: Towards the Human, After Man, Its Overrepresentation—An Argument," *CR: The New Centennial Review* 3 (3), 2003: 257–337, pp. 260–61; as discussed in McKittrick, *Demonic Grounds*, pp. 131–33.

49. Kotef, *Movement*, p. 121.

50. I. Baucom, *Specters of the Atlantic: Finance Capital, Slavery, and the Philosophy of History* (Durham: Duke University Press, 2005).

51. N. Lightfoot, *Troubling Freedom: Antigua and the Aftermath of British Emancipation* (Durham: Duke University Press, 2015); and see N. Lightfoot, *Fugitive Cosmopolitanism* (Durham: Duke University Press, forthcoming).

52. Patterson, *Freedom*.

53. R. Price (ed.), *Maroon Societies: Rebel Slave Communities in the Americas*, 2nd ed. (Baltimore and London: Johns Hopkins University Press, 1987).

54. Lightfoot, *Troubling Freedom*, p. 47. See also Sheller, *Democracy After Slavery*.

55. Price, *Maroon Societies*, p. 3.

56. McKittrick, *Demonic Grounds*, xxi.

57. F. Moten and S. Harney, *The Undercommons: Fugitive Planning and Black Study* (London: Minor Compositions, 2013), n.p.

58. Gibson-Graham, *A Postcapitalist Politics*, p. 127.

59. Floyd V. City of New York (2013), p. 6, cited in Cresswell, "Black Moves," p. 16.

60. Ibid.

61. Z. Furness, *One Less Car: Bicycling and the Politics of Automobility* (Philadelphia: Temple University Press, 2010), p. 30.

62. S. Browne, *Dark Matters: On the Surveillance of Blackness* (Durham and London: Duke University Press, 2015).

63. C. Seiler, "Racing Mobility, Excavating Modernity: A Comment," *Transfers: Interdisciplinary Journal of Mobility Studies*, 6 (1), 2016: 98–102; and see C. Seiler, *A Republic of Drivers: A Cultural History of Automobility in America* (Chicago and London: University of Chicago Press, 2008).

64. M. Hennesy-Fiske, "Walking in Ferguson: If you're black, it's often against the law," *Los Angeles Times*, March 5, 2015.

65. Alexander, *The New Jim Crow*, p. 133.

66. Dawson, *Extreme Cities*, p. 197.
67. T.L. Langden, "'Public' Transit for 'Every-Body': Invisabilizing Bodies of Difference," *Environment and Planning D: Society and Space*, Forum on Investigating Infrastructures, October 2017, available at societyandspace.org.
68. D. Moran, N. Gill, D. Conlon (eds.), *Carceral Spaces: Mobility and Agency in Imprisonment and Migrant Detention* (London: Routledge, 2013); P. Nyers and K. Rygiel (eds.), *Citizenship, Migrant Activism and the Politics of Movement* (London: Routledge, 2012); Chavez, *Queer Migration Politics*.
69. T. Vukov, "Strange Moves: Speculations and Propositions on Mobility Justice," in L. Montegary and White (eds.), *Mobile Desires: The Politics and Erotics of Mobility Justice* (Palgrave Macmillan, 2015); M. Maldonado, A. Licona, S. Hendricks, "Latin@ Immobilities and Altermobilities Within the US Deportation Regime," *Annals of the AAG*, 106 (2), 2016: 321–9.

CHAPTER 3

1. J. Flink, *The Car Culture* (Cambridge, MA: MIT Press, 1975); J. Flink, *The Automobile Age* (Cambridge, MA: MIT Press, 1988); C. McShane, *Down the Asphalt Path: The Automobile and the American City* (New York: Columbia University Press, 1994); P. Wollen and J. Kerr (eds.), *Autopia: Cars and Culture* (London: Reaktion Books, 2002); J. Urry, "The System of Automobility," *Theory, Culture and Society*, 21 (4/5), 2004: 25–39; S. Böhm et al. (eds.), *Against Automobility* (Malden, MA: Blackwell/Sociological Review, 2006).
2. Association for Safe International Road Travel, asirt.org.
3. Dennis and Urry, *After the Car*; Urry, *Societies Beyond Oil*.
4. Furness, *One Less Car*, p. 52.
5. M. Sheller and J. Urry, "The City and the Car," *International Journal of Urban and Regional Research* 24 (4), 2000: 737–57, pp. 737–8.
6. Statista, "Number of Passenger Cars and Commercial Vehicles in Use Worldwide from 2006 to 2015 (In 1000 Units)," available at statista.com.
7. Elliott and Urry, *Mobile Lives*, p. 133.
8. USDOE, *Transportation Energy Data Book*, Edition 30 (2011) and Edition 36 (2017), Oak Ridge National Laboratory; US Energy Information Administration, eia.gov/tools/faqs.
9. S. Gössling and S. Cohen, "Why Sustainable Transport Policies Will Fail: EU Climate Policy in the Light of Transport Taboos," *Journal of Transport Geography* 39, 2014: 197–207; and see S. Gössling, J.-P. Ceron, G. Dubois, and C.M. Hall, "Hypermobile Travelers," in S. Gössling and P. Upham (eds.), *Climate Change and Aviation* (Earthscan, 2009), pp. 131–49; A. Schäfer, J.B. Heywood, H.D. Jacoby, and I.A. Waitz, *Transportation in a Climate-Constrained World* (Cambridge, MA: MIT Press, 2009).

10. See the series of regular reports on these trends by Sivak and Schoettle at umtri.umich.edu.

11. Sheller and Urry, "The City and the Car"; Urry "The 'System' of Automobility"; Dennis and Urry, *After the Car*; Furness, *One Less Car*; G. Dudley, F. Geels, and R. Kemp (eds.), *Automobility in Transition?: A Socio-Technical Analysis of Sustainable Transport* (London and New York: Routledge, 2011).

12. For example, in April 2018, the Environmental Protection Agency led by Scott Pruitt announced that it would roll back the Obama-era fuel efficiency standards that had required light cars and trucks sold in the US to average more than 50 miles per gallon by 2025. This was widely considered a "win" for the "power of the auto industry." J. Eilperin and B. Dennis, "EPA to roll back car emissions standards, handing automakers a big win," *Washington Post*, April 2, 2018, available at washingtonpost.com.

13. R. Nixon, *Slow Violence and the Environmentalism of the Poor* (Cambridge, MA: Harvard University Press, 2011).

14. D. Hughes, *Energy Without Conscience: Oil, Climate Change, and Complicity* (Durham and London: Duke University Press, 2017).

15. Robert Cervero, Erick Guerra, and Stefan Al, *Beyond Mobility: Planning Cities for People and Places* (Washington and London: Island Press), p. xi–xii.

16. Ibid., p. 220–1.

17. J. Arbib, Plenary on "The Gamechanger: Electric, Shared and Automated," *Geography 2050: The Future of Mobility*, American Geographical Society, Fall Symposium, Columbia University, New York City, November 16, 2017.

18. S. Buckley, Plenary on "Mobility and the City of the Future," *Geography 2050: The Future of Mobility*, American Geographical Society, Fall Symposium, Columbia University, New York City, November 16, 2017.

19. A. Greenfield, *Radical Technologies* (London and New York: Verso, 2017), p. 278.

20. L. Bailey, Plenary on "Mobility and the City of the Future," *Geography 2050: The Future of Mobility*, American Geographical Society, Fall Symposium, Columbia University, New York City, November 16, 2017.

21. B. Schaller, "Unsustainable? The Growth of App-Based Ride Services and Traffic, Travel and the Future of New York City," Schaller Consulting, February 2017, accessible at schallerconsult.com/rideservices/unsustainable.htm.

22. M. Sheller, "Automotive Emotions"; M. Sheller, "The Emergence of New Cultures of Mobility: Stability, Openings, and Prospects," in G. Dudley, F. Geels, and R. Kemp (eds.), *Automobility in Transition?: A Socio-technical Analysis of Sustainable Transport* (London and New York: Routledge, 2012), pp. 180–202; D. Nixon, "A Sense of Momentum: Mobility Practices and Dis/Embodied Landscapes of energy use," *Environment and Planning A* 44, 2012: 661–78.

23. E.g., I. Illich, *Energy and Equity* (1972), available at preservenet.com; A.

Hay, "Equity and Welfare in the Geography of Public Transport Provision," *Journal of Transport Geography* 1 (2), 1993: 95–101; A. Hay and E. Trinder, "Concepts of Equity, Fairness, and Justice Expressed by Local Transport Policymakers," *Environment and Planning C: Government and Policy*, 9 (4), 1991: 453–65; Bullard and Johnson, *Just Transportation*; Bullard et al., "Dismantling Transportation Apartheid"; Bullard et al., *Highway Robbery*.

24. Lucas et al., "Transport and Its Adverse Social Consequences".

25. Kaufmann, Bergman, and Joye, "Motility."

26. N. Cass, E. Shove, and J. Urry, "Social Exclusion, Mobility and Access," *The Sociological Review* 53 (3), 2005: 539–55; Cresswell, "Towards a Politics of Mobility," *Environment and Planning D: Society and Space* 28 (1), 2010: 17–31; J. Preston and F. Rajé, "Accessibility, Mobility and Transport-Related Social Exclusion," *Journal of Transport Geography* 15 (3), 2007: 151–60.

27. S. Graham and S. Marvin, *Splintering Urbanism: Networked Infrastructures, Technological Mobilities and the Urban Condition* (London: Routledge, 2001).

28. P. Gilroy, "Driving While Black," in Daniel Miller (ed.), *Car Cultures*, (New York: Berg), pp. 81–104; D. Mitchell, *The Right to the City: Social Justice and the Fight for Public Space* (New York: Guildford Press, 2003); Cresswell, *On the Move*; Seiler, *A Republic of Drivers*; P. Norton, *Fighting Traffic: The Dawn of the Motor Age in the American City* (Cambridge, MA: MIT Press, 2011).

29. K. Franz, "The Open Road," in Bruce Sinclair (ed.), *Technology and the African-American Experience: Needs and Opportunities for Study* (Cambridge, MA: MIT Press, 2004), 131–54; C. Seiler, "'So That We as a Race Might Have Something Authentic to Travel By': African-American Automobility and Cold War Liberalism," *American Quarterly* 48 (4), 2006: 1,091–1,117; G. Zylstra, "Whiteness, Freedom and Technology: The Racial Struggle Over Philadelphia's Streetcars, 1859–1867," *Technology and Culture* 52 (4): 678–702, p. 685.

30. Henderson, "Secessionist Automobility"; P. Gilroy, "Driving While Black," in Daniel Miller (ed.), *Car Cultures*, (New York: Berg, 2001), pp. 81–104; A. Blake, "Audible Citizenship and Automobility: Race, Technology and CB Radio," *American Quarterly* 63 (3), 2011: 531–53; S. Hutchinson, "Waiting for the Bus," *Social Text* 63, 2000: 107–20.

31. D. Hayden, *The Grand Domestic Revolution* (1984), p. 152, as cited in P. Adey, *Mobility*, new revised edition (London: Routledge, 2017), p. 122.

32. J. Wajcman, *Feminism Confronts Technology* (College Park, PA: Penn State Press, 1991), cited in Adey, *Mobility*, p. 122.

33. S. Graham, "Elite Avenues: Flyovers, Freeways and the Politics of Urban Mobility," *City* (online first, 2018), p. 2; Bullard et al., *Highway Robbery*; J. Henderson, "Secessionist Automobility: Racism, Anti-Urbanism, and the Politics of Automobility in Atlanta, Georgia," *International Journal of Urban*

and Regional Research 30 (2), 2006: 293–307; A.A. Ortega, "Manila's Metropolitan Landscape of Gentrification: Global Urban Development, Accumulation by Dispossession and Neoliberal Warfare Against Informality," *Geoforum* 70, 2016: 35–50.

34. G. Fuller, "Queue," in P. Adey, D. Bissell, K. Hannam, P. Merriman, and M. Sheller (eds.), *The Routledge Handbook of Mobilities*, (New York: Routledge, 2014), 205–13, p. 212.

35. J. Gehl, *Cities for People* (New York: Island Press, 2010); Deutsches Architekturmusuem (ed.), *Ride a Bike! Reclaim the City* (Berline: Birkhäuser, 2018).

36. D. Harvey, *The Condition of Postmodernity* (Cambridge, MA: Blackwell, 1990).

37. R. Imrie, "Disability and Discourses of Mobility and Movement," *Environment and Planning A* 32 (9), 2000: 1,641–56, p. 1,643.

38. R. Wilkinson and M. Marmot (eds.), *Social Determinants of Health: The Solid Facts*, 2nd ed. (Copenhagen: World Health Organization, 2003).

39. M. Sheller, "Racialized Mobility Transitions in Philadelphia: Urban Sustainability and the Problem of Transport Inequality," *City and Society* 27 (1), 2015: 70–91; J. Nicholson and M. Sheller, "Introduction: Race and the Politics of Mobility," *Transfers: Interdisciplinary Journal of Mobility Studies,* 6 (1), 2016: 4–11.

40. IPCC, "Mitigation of Climate Change," *Fifth Assessment Report of the Intergovernmental Panel on Climate Change (AR5)* (Cambridge: Cambridge University Press, 2014), pp. 606, 648.

41. A. Leonard, *The Story of Stuff: The Impact of Overconsumption on the Planet, Our Communities, and Our Health—And How We Can Make It Better* (New York: Freepress, 2010), p. 254.

42. A. Delbosc, G. Currie, "Causes of Youth Licensing Decline: A Synthesis of Evidence," *Transport Reviews* 33 (3), 2013: 271–90; D. Pickrell and D. Pace, "Driven to Extremes: Has Growth in Automobile Use Ended?", John A. Volpe National Transportation Systems Center, Research and Innovative Technology Administration, US Department of Transportation, Washington, DC (May 2013); D. Short, "Vehicle Miles Driven: Population-Adjusted Fractionally Off Its Post-Crisis Low," Advisor Perspectives (September 21, 2013); M. Sivak, "Has Motorization in the US Peaked? Part 2: Use of Light-Duty Vehicles," University of Michigan Transportation Research Institute, Detroit, Michigan, 2013; M. Sivak and B. Schoettle, "More Americans of All Ages Spurning Driver's Licenses," January 20, 2016, available at umtri.umich.edu.

43. National Household Travel Survey, data extraction tool, available at nhts.ornl.gov/det.

44. Drawing on S. Böhm , C. Jones, C. Land, M. Paterson (eds.), *Against Automobility*. (Oxford: Blackwell Sociological Review Monograph, 2006); A.

Millard-Ball and L. Schipper, "Are We Reaching Peak Travel?: Trends in Passenger Transport in Eight Industrialized Countries," *Transport Reviews* 31, 2011: 357–78; D. Tyfield, "Putting the Power in 'Socio-Technical Regimes': E-Mobility Transition in China as Political Process," *Mobilities* 9, 2014: 285–63; E. Rosenthal, "The End of Car Culture," *New York Times,* June 29, 2013.

45. S. Shaheen, A. Cohen, and I. Zohdy, *Shared Mobility: Current Practices and Guiding Principles.* Washington, DC: US Department of Transportation, Federal Highway Administration (2016).

46. The Untokening, "Untokening Mobility: Beyond Pavement, Paint and Place," eds. A. Lugo, N. Doerner, D. Lee, S. McCullough, S. Sulaiman and C. Szczepanski, (January 2018), p. 11–12.

47. "What's the Greatest Risk Cities Face?," *Politico*, July/August 2017, politico.com.

48. M. Sheller, "Automotive Emotions: Feeling the Car," *Theory, Culture and Society* 21 (4/5), 2004: 221–42; Urry, *Sociology Beyond Societies*; Vannini, *Cultures of Alternative Mobilities.*

49. S. Gössling, *Psychology of the Car: Automobile Admiration, Attachment and Addiction* (Amsterdam: Elsevier, 2017); J.P. Huttman, "Automobile Addiction: The Abuse of Personal Transport", *Society* (July 1973) 10 (25): 25–9.

50. H. Tabuchi, "'Rolling Coal' in Diesel Trucks, to Rebel and Provoke," *New York Times*, September 4, 2016, nytimes.com.

51. R. Sims et al., "Transport," in *Climate Change 2014: Mitigation of Climate Change. Contribution of Working Group III to the Fifth Assessment Report of the Intergovernmental Panel on Climate Change.* (Cambridge and New York: Cambridge University Press, 2014), p. 603.

52. Sims et al., "Transport," pp. 605, 612–13; see E. Shove, "Beyond the ABC: Climate Change Policy and Theories of Social Change," *Environment and Planning A* 42, 2010: 1,273–85.

53. Brulle and Dunlap, *Climate Change and Society.*

54. "Three Revolutions in Urban Transportation," ITDP and UC Davis, May 2017, available at itdp.org.

55. C. Knudsen and A. Doyle, "Norway Powers Ahead (Electrically): Over Half of New Car Sales Now Electric or Hybrid," Reuters, January 3, 2018, available at reuters.com.

56. G. Dudley, F. Geels, F., and R. Kemp (eds.), *Automobility in Transition?: A Socio-Technical Analysis of Sustainable Transport* (London and New York: Routledge, 2011).

57. M. Arboleda, "Spaces of Extraction, Metropolitan Explosions: Planetary Urbanization and the Commodity Boom in Latin America," *International Journal of Urban and Regional Research* 40 (1), 2016: 96–112.

58. Incidentally, the IPCC sought input from mobilities theorist John Urry, and cites his work and my own on automobility systems in R. Sims, R. Schaeffer,

F. Creutzig, X. Cruz-Núñez, M. D'Agosto, D. Dimitriu, M. J. Figueroa Meza, L. Fulton, S. Kobayashi, O. Lah, A. McKinnon, P. Newman, M. Ouyang, J. J. Schauer, D. Sperling, and G. Tiwari, Ch. 8: Transport. In: *Climate Change 2014: Mitigation of Climate Change. Contribution of Working Group III to the Fifth Assessment Report of the Intergovernmental Panel on Climate Change* (Cambridge and New York: Cambridge University Press, 2014), p. 613, 618.

59. O.B. Jensen, *Staging Mobilities* (London: Routledge, 2013); O.B. Jensen, *Designing Mobilities* (Aalborg: Aalborg University Press, 2014); Elliott and Urry, *Mobile Lives*; De Souza e Silva and Sheller, *Mobilities and Locative Media*.

60. Adey, *Aerial Life*; Sheller, *Aluminum Dreams*; J. Urry, *Climate Change and Society* (Cambridge: Polity, 2011).

61. Tyfield, *Liberalism 2.0 and the Rise of China*, p. 171.

62. "How BRT TransCaribe Improved Transport in Cartagena, Colombia," Institute for Transportation and Development Policy, September 6, 2017, available at itdp.org.

63. Robert Cervero, "Progressive Transport and the Poor: Bogota's Bold Steps Forward," *Access* 27 (2005): 24–30, as discussed in Cervero et al., *Beyond Mobility*, p. 223.

64. D. Newman, "Automobiles and Socioeconomic Sustainability: Do We Need A Mobility Bill of Rights?" *Transfers* 7 (2) 2017: 100–106.

65. S. Ureta, *Assembling Policy: Transantiago, Human Devices, and the Dream of a World-Class Society* (Cambridge, MA: MIT Press, 2015).

66. P. Jiron, "Unravelling Invisible Inequalities in the City through Urban Daily Mobility: The Case of Santiago de Chile," *Swiss Journal of Sociology* 33 (1), 2007; J.C. Munoz, J.D. Ortuzar and A. Gschwender, "Transantiago: The Fall and Rise of a Radical Public Transport Intervention," in W. Saaleh and G. Sammer (eds.), *Success and Failure of Travel Demand Management: Is Road User Pricing the Most Feasible Option?* (Aldershot: Ashgate, 2008, 151–72).

67. "MOBILIZE Santiago: Just and Inclusive Cities Become the New Normal," Institute for Transportation and Development Policy, August 1, 2017, available at itdp.org.

68. "Child Friendly Cities are Friendly Cities for Everyone," Institute for Transportation and Development Policy, August 8, 2017, available at itdp.org.

69. "The New and Improved TOD Standard," Institute for Transportation and Development Policy, June 25, 2017, available at itdp.org.

70. Ibid.

71. Ibid.

72. Martens, "Justice in Transport"; Martens, *Transport Justice*.

73. Perreira et al., "Distributive Justice"; Kronlid, "Mobility as Capability"; Hananel and Berechman, "Justice and Transportation Decision-Making."

74. P. Healey, *Collaborative Planning: Shaping Places in Fragmented Societies*

(Vancouver: UBC Press, 1997); J.E. Innes, "Consensus Building: Clarifications for the Critics," *Planning Theory* 3 (1), 2004: 5–20.

75. "Untokening Mobility," p. 18.

76. D. Newman, "Automobiles and Socioeconomic Sustainability: Do We Need A Mobility Bill of Rights?" *Transfers* 7 (2) 2017: 100–106.

CHAPTER 4

1. S. Kesselring and G. Vogl, "The New Mobilities Regimes," in S. Witzgall, G. Vogl, and S. Kesselring (eds), *New Mobilities Regimes in Art and Social Sciences* (Farnham: Ashgate, 2013), 17–36, p. 20.

2. Definition of "Infrastructure," *Oxford Living Dictionaries, English,* available at en.oxforddictionaries.com.

3. K. Easterling, *Extrastatecraft: The Power of Infrastructure Space* (London and New York: Verso, 2015).

4. D. Cowen, "Infrastructures of Empire and Resistance," Verso Blog, January 25, 2017, available at versobooks.com.

5. L. Berlant, "The Commons: Infrastructures for Troubling Times," *Environment and Planning D: Society and Space* 34 (3), 2016: 393–419, pp. 393–4.

6. "Disrupt the Flows: War Against DAPL and Planetary Annihilation," December 6, 2016, accessed February 3, 2017 at itsgoingdown.org.

7. Cowen, "Infrastructures of Empire and Resistance."

8. Ibid.

9. A. Carse, "Nature as Infrastructure: Making and managing the Panama Canal watershed," *Social Studies of Science*, 42 (4), 2012: 539–63, p. 539; A. Carse, *Beyond the Big Ditch: Politics, Ecology, and Infrastructure at the Panama Canal* (Cambridge: MIT Press, 2014).

10. S.L. Star, "The Ethnography of Infrastructure," *American Behavioral Scientist* 43 (3), 1999: 377–91; S. Star and G. Bowker, "How to Infrastructure," in L. Lievrouw and S. Livingstone (eds.), *The Handbook of New Media* (London: Sage, 2002), 151–62; J. Packer and S.C. Wiley (eds.), *Communication Matters: Materialist Approaches to Media, Mobility and Networks* (New York: Routledge, 2012); L. Parks and N. Starosielski (eds.), *Signal Traffic: Critical Studies of Media Infrastructures* (Chicago: University of Illinois Press, 2015); D. Cowen, *The Deadly Life of Logistics: Mapping Violence in Global Trade* (Minneapolis: University of Minnesota Press, 2014); Easterling, *Extrastatecraft.*

11. B. Larkin, "The Politics and Poetics of Infrastructures," *Annual Review of Anthropology* 42, 2013: 327–43.

12. These questions arise out of the conference "Mobile Utopia: Pasts, Presents, Futures" held at Lancaster University, UK, November 2–5, 2017, the themes of which built on Ruth Levitas, *Utopia as Method: The Imaginary Reconstitution of Society* (Hampshire: Palgrave Macmillan, 2013).

13. A. Amin and N. Thrift, *Cities: Reimagining the Urban* (Cambridge: Polity, 2002), p. 82; Sheller and Urry, "The City and the Car."

14. Sheller and Urry, "The New Mobilities Paradigm"; Hannam, Sheller, and Urry, "Mobilities, Immobilities and Moorings"; Urry, *Climate Change and Society;* Urry, *Societies Beyond Oil;* Sheller, *Aluminum Dreams.*

15. D. Harvey, *Spaces of Global Capitalism: Towards a Theory of Uneven Geographical Development* (London and New York: Verso, 2006), p. 101.

16. S. Graham, *Vertical* (London: Verso, 2016); L. Parks and J. Schwoch, *Down to Earth: Satellite Technologies Industries and Cultures* (New Brunswick: Rutgers University Press, 2012); Parks and Starsioleski, *Signal Traffic;* N. Starsioleski, *The Undersea Network* (Durham: Duke University Press, 2015).

17. T. Paglen, "Some Sketches on Vertical Geographies," *e-flux architecture,* 2016, available at e-flux.com; E. Weizman, *Hollow Land* (London: Verso, 2007); Graham, *Vertical;* Arboleda, "Spaces of Extraction."

18. Cowen, "Infrastructures of Empire and Resistance."

19. Easterling, *Extrastatecraft,* p. 73.

20. Ibid., pp. 74–5

21. M. Sheller and J. Urry, *Tourism Mobilities: Places to Play, Places in Play* (London: Routledge, 2004); T. Birchnell and J. Caletrio (eds.), *Elite Mobilities* (London: Routledge, 2014).

22. R. Goluboff, *Vagrant Nation: Police Power, Constitutional Change and the Making of the 1960s* (Oxford: Oxford University Press, 2016).

23. B. Fischer, B. McCann, and J. Auyero. (eds.), *Cities from Scratch: Poverty and Informality in Urban Latin America* (Durham: Duke University Press, 2014); A. Mountz, *Seeking Asylum: Human Smuggling and Bureaucracy at the Border* (Minneapolis: University of Minnesota Press, 2010); Graham, *Disrupted Cities.*

24. Brenner and Schmid, "Planetary Urbanization"; Sheller and Urry, *Tourism Mobilities.*

25. B. Larkin, *Signal and Noise: Media, Infrastructure, and Urban Culture in Nigeria* (Durham: Duke University Press, 2008); H. Horst, "The Infrastructures of Mobile Media: Towards a Future Research Agenda," *Mobile Media and Communication* 1 (1), 2013: 147–52; Parks, *Signal Traffic.*

26. De Souza e Silva and Sheller, *Mobility and Locative Media.*

27. Easterling, *Extrastatecraft,* pp. 133–4.

28. Fischer, McCann, Auyero; *Cities from Scratch;* Graham and Marvin, *Splintering Urbanism;* J. Packer, *Mobility Without Mayhem: Safety, Cars, and Citizenship* (Durham: Duke University Press, 2008); Vukov and Sheller, "Border Work."

29. C. McFarlane and A. Vasudevan, "Informal Infrastructures," in P. Adey, D. Bissell, K. Hannam, P. Merriman, and M. Sheller (eds.), *The Routledge Handbook of Mobilities,* (New York: Routledge, 2014), 256–64.

30. Graham and Marvin, *Splintering Urbanism*; Graham, *Disrupted Cities*; S. Graham and N. Thrift, "Out of Order: Understanding Repair and Maintenance," *Theory, Culture and Society* 24 (3), 2007: 1–25.
31. Gotham and Greenberg, *Crisis Cities*, pp. ix, 223; N. Smith, "There Is No Such Thing as a Natural Disaster," 2006, available at understandingkatrina. ssrc.org; Graham, *Disrupted Cities*.
32. Y. Bonilla, "Why would anyone in Puerto Rico want a hurricane? Because someone will get rich," *Washington Post*, 22 September 2017.
33. Sheller, "The Islanding Effect"; M. Sheller, *Island Futures*, forthcoming.
34. K.J. Hsu and M. Schuller, "Dumb and Dumber: Foregrounding Climate Justice from Harvey to Haiti's Matthew," *Huffington Post*, September 2, 2017, available at huffingtonpost.com.
35. J. Sterling and C. Santiago, "For first time in 300 years, no one is living on Barbuda," CNN, September 15, 2017, available at cnn.com.
36. Klein, "The Battle for Paradise;" Sheller, *Island Futures*.
37. D. Wood and S. Graham, "Permeable Boundaries in the Software-sorted Society: Surveillance and the Differentiation of Mobility," in M. Sheller and J. Urry (eds.), *Mobile Technologies of the City* (London and New York: Routledge. 2006), pp. 177–91.
38. Sheller and Urry, *Mobile Technologies of the City*, pp. 5–6.
39. J. Farman, "The Materiality of Locative Media: On the Invisible Infrastructure of Mobile Networks" in A. Herman, J. Hadlaw, and T. Swiss (eds.), *Theories of the Mobile Internet: Materialities and Imaginaries* (New York and London: Routledge, 2015), pp. 45–59; McCormack, "Pipes and Cables"; Parks and Schwoch, *Down to Earth*; Parks and Starosielski, *Signal Traffic*; Starosielski, *The Undersea Network*.
40. N. Thrift, *Non-Representational Theory: Space, politics, affect*. New York: Routledge, 2008.
41. Greenfield, *Radical Technologies*, p. 32, 52, 62.
42. J. Packer and S.C. Wiley (eds.), *Communication Matters: Materialist Approaches to Media, Mobility and Networks* (New York: Routledge, 2012); J. Packer and C. Robertson, (eds.), *Thinking with James Carey: Essays on Communications, Transportation, History* (New York: Peter Lang, 2007).
43. De Souza e Silva and Sheller, *Mobilities and Locative Media*; E. Gordon and A. de Souza e Silva (eds.) *Net-locality: Why location matters in a networked world* (Malden, MA: Wiley Blackwell, 2011); A. de Souza e Silva and D. Sutko (eds.) *Digital Cityscapes: Merging virtual and urban play spaces* (New York: Peter Lang, 2009).
44. De Souza e Silva and Sheller, *Mobilities and Locative Media*.
45. M. Dodge and R. Kitchin, *Code/Space: Software and Everday Life* (Cambridge: MIT Press, 2011), p. 263.
46. J. Rifkin, *The Zero Marginal Cost Society: The Internet of Things, the*

Collaborative Commons, and the Eclipse of Capitalism (London: Macmillan, 2014); P. Mason, *Post Capitalism: A Guide to Our Future* (London: Allen Lane, 2015).

47. N. Thrift, "Lifeworld Inc—And What to Do About It," *Environment and Planning D: Society and Space* 29, 2011: 5–26, pp. 8–11.

48. A. Shapiro, "Design, Control, Predict: Cultural Politics in the Actually Existing Smart City," PhD dissertation, Annenberg School of Communication at the University of Pennsylvania, 2018.

49. Urry, *Mobilities*; Elliott and Urry, *Mobile Lives*.

50. Shapiro, "Design, Control, Predict."

51. Ibid.

52. D. Mitchell, "Against Safety, Against Security: Reinvigorating Urban Live," *The Right to the City: A Verso Report* (iBooks, 2017), p. 134, originally published in Michael J. Thompson (ed.), *Fleeing the City: Studies in the Culture and Politics of Anti-Urbanism* (Palgrave Macmillan, 2009).

53. O.B. Jensen, "Flows of Meaning, Cultures of Movement—Urban Mobility as Meaningful Everyday Life Practice," *Mobilities* 4 (1), 2009: 139–58; O.B. Jensen, "Negotiation in Motion: Unpacking a Geography of Mobility," *Space and Culture* 13 (4), 2010: 389–402; Cresswell, *On the Move*.

54. O.B. Jensen, "Dark Design: Mobilities and Exclusion by Design," in D. Butz and N. Cook (eds.), *Mobilities, Mobility Justice and Social Justice* (London and New York: Routledge, 2018).

55. Examples drawn from "Paradise Papers" report , *Guardian*, November 6, 2017, available at theguardian.com.

56. L. Budd. "Aeromobile Elites: Private Business Aviation and the Global Economy," in T. Birchnell and J. Caletrio (eds.), *Elite Mobilities* (London and New York: Routledge, 2013).

57. R. Frank, "For Millionaire Immigrants, a Global Welcome Mat," *New York Times*, February 26, 2017, Business Section, p. 3.

58. La Vida Golden Visas, goldenvisas.com.

59. Easterling, *Extrastatecraft*, pp. 49, 55.

CHAPTER 5

1. "IOM's Missing Migrants Project," joint initiative of the International Organization for Migration (IOM) and the Global Migration Data Analysis Centre (GMDAC), available at missingmigrants.iom.int.

2. R. Jones and C. Johnson, "Corridors, Camps, and Spaces of Confinement," *Political Geography* 59, 2017: 1–10, p. 1.

3. Z. Bauman, *Legislators and Interpreters* (Cambridge: Polity, 1998), p. 87.

4. G. Verstraete, "Technological Frontiers and the Politics of Mobilities," *New Formations* 43 (2001): 26–43, p. 29; G. Verstraete, "Technological Frontiers and the Politics of Mobility in the European Union," in S. Ahmed, C.

Castañeda, A.M. Fortier, and M. Sheller (eds.), *Uprootings/Regroundings: Questions of Home and Migration* (Oxford: Berg, 2003), 225–49.

5. J. Torpey, *The Invention of the Passport: Surveillance, Citizenship and the State.* (Cambridge: Cambridge University Press, 2000); M. Salter, "The Global Visa Regime and the Political Technologies of the International Self: Borders, Bodies, Biopolitics," *Alternatives: Global, Local, Political* 31 (2), April 2006: 167–89; M. Salter, ed. *Politics at the Airport* (Minneapolis: University of Minnesota Press, 2008).

6. H. Cunningham and J. Heyman (eds.), "Movement on the Margins: Mobility and Enclosures at Borders," special issue, *Identities: Global Studies in Culture and Power* 11 (3), 2004: 287; W. Walters, "Mapping Schengenland: Denaturalizing the Border," *Environment and Planning D: Society and Space* 20 (5), 2002: 561–80; W. Walters, "Secure Borders, Safe Haven, Domopolitics," *Citizenship Studies* 8 (3), 2004: 237–60.

7. T. Brian and F. Laczko (eds.), *Fatal Journeys Volume 2: Identification and Tracing of Dead and Missing Migrants*, Geneva: International Organization for Migration, 2016.

8. B. Anderson, N. Sharma, and C. Wright, "Editorial: Why No Borders?" *Refuge* 26 (2), 2009: 5–18; N. Sharma, *Home Rule: The Partition of 'Natives' and 'Migrants' in the Postcolonial New World Order* (Durham: Duke University Press, forthcoming).

9. R. Cohen, "Broken Men in Paradise," *New York Times*, Sunday Review, December 9, 2016, p. SR1, accessed February 26, 2017 at nytimes.com.

10. D. Cave, "Trapped in a Refugee Camp of Broken Hopes and Promises," *New York Times*, November 19, 2017, p. A15.

11. T. Miles, "UNHCR Says Australia Abandoned Refugees, Must Clear up the Mess it Made," *Reuters News*, December 22, 2017 available at usnews.com.

12. J. Sudbury (ed.), *Global Lockdown: Race, Gender, and the Prison-Industrial Complex* (Abingdon and New York: Routledge, 2005), p. xii.

13. E.g., during the French-Indian War (1754–63), Native peoples were driven out of the Eastern seaboard through warfare and disease; the Indian Removal Act of 1830 drove over 70,000 Native Americans from their homes;, during the California Gold Rush of 1848–55 the Lakota Sioux were forced out of their ancestral lands on the Great Plains, and a purposeful genocide of the Native people of California followed.

14. Seiler, *A Republic of Drivers*, p. 232.

15. N. De Genova and N. Peutz (eds.), *The Deportation Regime: Sovereignty, Space, and the Freedom of Movement* (Durham: Duke University Press, 2010).

16. G. Younge, "End Immigration Controls," *Guardian*, October 16, 2017, available at theguardian.com.

17. D. Baines and N. Sharma, "Migrant Workers as Non-Citizens: The Case Against Citizenship as a Social Policy Concept," *Studies in Political Economy* 69, 2002: 75–107.

18. E. Raithelhuber et al., "The Intersection of Social Protection and Mobilities: A Move Towards a 'Practical Utopia' Research Agenda," *Mobilities,* forthcoming.

19. Nail, *Theory of the Border*, p. 65.

20. Sassen, *Expulsions*, p. 2.

21. Kotef, *Movement and the Ordering of Freedom*, p. 127.

22. S. Sassen, "When National Territory Is Home to the Global: Old Borders to Novel Borderings," *New Political Economy* 10 (4), 2005: 523–41; G. Popescu, "Controlling Mobility," in G. Popescu, *Bordering and Ordering the Twenty-first Century: Understanding Borders* (Lanham: Rowman and Littlefield, 2011), pp. 91–120.

23. S. Sassen, "When Territory Deborders Territoriality," *Territory, Politics, Governance* 1 (1), 2013: 21–45, p. 30

24. Ibid., p. 21.

25. Ibid., p. 23.

26. J. Tegenbos and K. Büscher, "Moving Onwards?: Secondary Movers on the Fringes of Refugee Mobility in Kakuma Refugee Camp, Kenya," *Transfers* 7(2), 2017: 41–60.

27. Y. Jansen and R. Celikates et al. (eds.), *The Irregularization of Migration in Contemporary Europe: Detention, Deportation, Drowning* (London: Rowman and Littlefield International, 2014.

28. P. Adey, *Mobility*, new revised ed. (London: Routledge, 2017).

29. A. Mountz, "Specters at the Port of Entry: Understanding State Mobilities Through an Ontology of Exclusion," *Mobilities* 6, 2011: 317–34. p. 332.

30. Vukov and Sheller, "Border Work."

31. J. O. Baerenholdt, "Governing Circulation Through Technology Within EU Border Security Practice-Networks," *Mobilities* 13 (2), 2018: 185–92.

32. Baerenholdt, "Governmobility," p. 31.

33. M. Sheller, "On the Maintenance of Humanity: Learning from Refugee Mobile Practices, *CARGC Paper 5*, Annenberg School of Communication, fall 2016. And see "The Refugee Project" at artisticlab.forumviesmobiles. org.

34. K. Rygiel, "Bordering Solidarities: Migrant Activism and the Politics of Movement and Camps at Calais," *Citizenship Studies* 15 (1), 2011: 1–19; Sheller and Urry, *Tourism Mobilities.*

35. Tegenbos and Büscher, "Moving Onwards?"

36. J. Carens, *The Ethics of Immigration* (Oxford: Oxford University Press, 2013).

37. R. Jones, *Violent Borders: Refugees and the Right to Move* (London: Verso, 2016), p. 22.

38. Mountz, *Seeking Asylum.*

39. Jones, *Violent Borders,* p. 23.

40. O. Dorell, "40 Hurt as Israel Warns Against Burning Kites at Palestinian Demonstration in Gaza," *USA Today,* May 3, 2018.

41. Jones, *Violent Borders*, p. 24.

42. A. Mountz, K. Coddington, R.T. Catania, and J. Loyd, "Conceptualizing Detention: Mobility, Containment, Bordering and Exclusion," *Progress in Human Geography* 37 (4), 2012: 522–41, p. 524.

43. J. Loyd, E. Mitchel-Eaton and A. Mountz, "The Militarization of Islands and Migration: Tracing Human Mobility Through US Bases in the Caribbean and the Pacific," *Political Geography* 53 (2016), 65–75, p. 68.

44. Loyd, Mitchel-Eaton, Mountz, "The Militarization of Islands," p. 65.

45. A. Kalhan, "Rethinking Immigration Detention," *Columbia Law Review Sidebar* 110 (July 21, 2010): 42–58.

46. Stoler, *Duress*, pp. 78, 113

47. Stoler, *Duress*.

48. Mountz, "Specters at the Port of Entry"; A. Mountz, "The Enforcement Archipelago: Detention, Haunting, and Asylum on Islands," *Political Geography* 30, 2011: 118–28.

49. P. Vannini, *The Cultures of Alternative Mobilities: The Routes Less Travelled* (Farnham and Burlington, VT: Ashgate, 2009); P. Vannini, "Mind the Gap: The *Tempo Rubato* of Dwelling in Lineups," *Mobilities* 6 (2), 2011: 273–99.

50. W. Lin "Aeromobile Justice: A Global Institutional Perspective," forthcoming in D. Butz and N. Cook (eds.), *Mobilities, Mobility Justice and Social Justice* (London: Routledge); W. Lin, "The Politics of Flying: Aeromobile Frictions in a Mobile City," *Journal of Transport Geography* 38, 2014: 92–9.

51. Michael O'Regan and Kevin Hannam, 'The Future Looks Seamless' panel at RGS-IBG 2017.

52. A. Elliott, "Elsewhere: Tracking the Mobile Lives of Globals," in Birtchnell and Caletrio, *Elite Mobilities*.

53. Elliot, "Elsewhere," p. 52.

54. S.R. Khan, "The Ease of Mobility," in Birtchnell and Caletrio, *Elite Mobilities*.

55. M. Sheller, "Infrastructures of the Imagined Island: Software, Mobilities and the Architecture of Caribbean Paradise." *Environment and Planning A* 41, 2009: 1,386–403.

56. P. Adey, *Aerial Life: Spaces, Mobilities, Affects* (Chichester: Wiley-Blackwell, 2010), p. 86.

57. Ibid.

58. L. Amoore, "Biometric borders: Governing mobilities in the war on terror," *Political Geography* 25: 336–51; L. Amoore and A. Hall "Taking Bodies Apart: Digitized Dissection and the Body at the Border," *Environment and Planning D: Society and Space* 27 (3), 2009: 444–64; D. Lyon, "Filtering Flows, Friends, and Foes: Global Surveillance" in Mark Salter (ed.) *Politics at the Airport* (Minneapolis: University of Minnesota Press, 2008), pp. 29–50; M. Salter (ed.), *Politics at the Airport* (Minneapolis: University of Minnesota Press, 2008).

59. V. Vicuña Gonzalez, *Securing Paradise: Tourism and Militarism in Hawai'i and the Philippines*, 2013, p. 149

60. Vicuña Gonzalez, *Securing Paradise,* p. 218.

61. T. Paglen, *Blank Spots on the Map: The Dark Geography of the Pentagon's Secret World* (New York: Penguin, 2009).

62. Cresswell, *On the Move*; Cresswell, "Towards a Politics of Mobility"; Adey, *Aerial Life*; Adey et al., *Routledge Handbook of Mobilities.*

CHAPTER 6

1. For a fascinating description, see B. Szerszynski, "Planetary Mobilities: Movement, Memory and Emergence in the Body of the Earth," *Mobilities* 11 (4), 2016: 614–28. See also Nail, *Being and Motion.*

2. D. Tyfield and J. Urry (eds.), "Energizing Society," special issue, *Theory, Culture and Society* 31 (5), 2014.

3. M. Sheller, "Global Energy Cultures of Speed and Lightness: Materials, Mobilities and Transnational Power," in "Energizing Society," special issue, *Theory, Culture and Society* 31 (5), 2014: 127–54.

4. T.P. Hughes, *Networks of Power: Electrification in Western Society, 1880–1930* (Baltimore: Johns Hopkins University Press, 1983); T.P. Hughes, "Evolution of Large Technological Systems" in W.E. Bijker, T.P. Hughes, and T.J. Pinch(eds.), *The Social Construction of Technological Systems: New Directions in the Sociology and History of Technology* (Cambridge, MA: MIT Press, 1989), pp. 51–82; S. Guy and E. Shove, *A Sociology of Energy, Buildings and the Environment: Constructing Knowledge, Designing Practice* (London: Routledge, 2000).

5. Urry, *Mobilities*, pp. 47–8.

6. D. Miller, *Stuff* (Cambridge: Polity, 2010); H. Molotch, *Where Stuff Comes From: How Toasters, Toilets, Cars, Computers, and Many Other Things Come to Be as They Are* (New York: Routledge, 2005).

7. Szerszynski, "Planetary Mobilities".

8. Guy and Shove, *A Sociology of Energy,* p. 5.

9. McCormack, "Pipes and Cables"; N. Starosielski, "Fixed Flow: Undersea Cables as Media Infrastructure," in L. Parks and N. Starosielski (eds.), *Signal Traffic: Critical Studies of Media Infrastructures* (Chicago: University of Illinois Press, 2015), pp. 53–70; Farman, "The Materiality of Locative Media"; Parks and Schwoch, *Down to Earth.*

10. Cowen, *The Deadly Life of Logistics.*

11. Hannam et al., "Mobilities, Immobilities and Moorings."

12. Graham and Marvin, *Splintering Urbanism*; M. Sheller and J. Urry (eds.), "Materialities and Mobilities," special issue, *Environment and Planning D: Society and Space* 38, 2006.

13. R. Vitalis, *America's Kingdom: Mythmaking on the Saudi Oil Frontier* (Stanford, CA: Stanford University Press, 2007); P. Levinson, *The Box: How the Shipping Container Made the World Smaller and the World Economy Bigger* (Princeton: Princeton University Press, 2006); Leonard, *The Story of Stuff.*

14. M. Huber, *Lifeblood: Oil, Freedom and the Forces of Capital* (Minneapolis: University of Minnesota Press, 2013), p. xi.

15. Ibid., p. xvi.

16. Ibid., p. 23.

17. Ibid., pp. 23, 74.

18. J. Parikka, *What Is Media Archaeology?* (London: Polity, 2012).

19. P. Bélanger, cited in *New Geographies* 9 "Posthuman", M. Gomez-Luque and G. Jafari (eds.) (Cambridge, MA: Harvard Graduate School of Design, 2017), p. 79.

20. G. Dudley, F. Geels, and R. Kemp (eds.), *Automobility in Transition? A Socio-technical Analysis of Sustainable Transport* (London: Routledge, 2011).

21. Illich, *Energy and Equity*.

22. Shin'ichi Tsuji, *Slow is Beautiful: Culture as Slowness* (Surô izu byûtifuru: Ososa toshite no bunk [Tokyo: Heibonsha, 2001]), trans. Andre Haag, n.p., available at keibooiwa.files.wordpress.com.

23. R.B. Fuller, *Critical Path* (New York: St Martin's Griffin, 1981).

24. D. Harvey, *The Condition of Postmodernity: An Enquiry into the Origins of Cultural Change* (Malden: Blackwell, 1990); B. Agger, *Fast Capitalism* (Bloomington: University of Indiana Press, 1989); Virilio, *Speed and Politics*, trans. M. Polizzotti (Los Angeles: Semiotext(e), 1986 [1977]).

25. S. Lash and J. Urry, *Economies of Signs and Space* (London: SAGE, 1994); Bauman, *Liquid Modernity*; Sarah Redshaw, "Acceleration: The Limits of Speed" in H. McNaughton and A. Lam (eds.), *The Reinvention of Everyday Life: Culture in the Twenty-First Century*. (Christchurch: University of Canterbury Press, 2006), 195–206.

26. J. Schor, *Plenitude: The New Economics of True Wealth* (New York: Penguin Press, 2010).

27. R. Botsman and R. Rogers, *What's Mine is Yours: The Rise of Collaborative Consumption*, (New York: Harper Business, 2010).

28. D. Hill, "The Battle for the Infrastructure of Everyday Life," National Gallery of Victoria Triennial (Melbourne, 2017), available at medium.com; J. Bridger, "Don't Call it a Commune: Inside Berlin's Radical Co-Housing Unit," *Metropolis Magazine*, June 20, 2015, available at metropolismag.com. On off-grid rural intentional communities, see M. Sundeen, *The Unsettlers: In Search of the Good Life in Today's America* (New York: Riverhead Books, 2016).

29. T. Birtchnell and J. Urry, *A New Industrial Future?: 3D Printing and the Reconfiguration of Production, Distribution and Consumption* (New York and London: Routledge, 2016).

30. R. Eglash, "An Introduction to Generative Justice," *Revista Teknokultura* 132 (2), 2016: 369–404, quotes from pp. 382, 373.

31. R.D.G. Kelley, "Coates and West in Jackson," *Boston Review*, available at bostonreview.net.

32. Malcolm X Grassroots Movement, "The Jackson Plan: A Struggle for

Self-Determination, Participatory Democracy, and Economic Justice," available at mxgm.org.

33. Gibson-Graham, *A Postcapitalist Politics*, chapter 5.

34. A. Vasudevan, "Re-imagining the Squatted City,," in *The Right to the City: A Verso Report* (London: Verso, 2017), p. 119.

35. Ibid., p. 120.

36. P. Virilio, *Speed and Politics*, p. 90.

37. Fuller, *Critical Path*, p. 216.

38. C. Kaplan, *Aerial Aftermaths: Wartime from Above* (Durham: Duke University Press, 2018).

39. R. Chow, *The Age of the World Target: Self-Referentiality in War, Theory, and Comparative Work* (Durham: Duke University Press, 2006); S. Graham, *Vertical*.

40. S. Graham, "Satellite: Enigmatic Presence," in *New Geographies* 9 "Posthuman," M. Gomez-Luque and G. Jafari (eds.) (Cambridge, MA: Harvard Graduate School of Design, 2017), pp. 90–95.

41. Virilio, *Speed and Politics*.

42. Urry, *Offshoring*, p. 201.

43. Cowen, *Deadly Life of Logistics*.

44. H. Gusterson, *Drone: Remote Control Warfare* (Cambridge: MIT Press, 2016), p. 45.

45. Ibid., pp. 45–6, 85.

46. P. Scharre, *Army of None: Autonomous Weapons and the Future of War* (New York: Norton, 2018).

47. Virilio, *Speed and Politics*.

48. Brenner and Schmid, "Towards a New Epistemology of the Urban?," pp. 152–3.

49. D. Aldana Cohen, "Petro-Gotham, People's Gotham" (and the "Carboniferous" map) in R. Solnit and J. Jelly- Schapiro (eds), *Nonstop Metropolis: A New York City Atlas* (Berkeley: University of California Press, 2016); D. Wachsmuth, D. Aldana Cohen, and H. Angelo, "Expand the frontiers of urban sustainability," *Nature* 536 (August 2016) 391–3.

50. Ibid.

51. Brenner, *Implosions/Explosions*; Brenner and Schmid, "Towards a New Epistemology of the Urban"; Sheller, "Global Energy Cultures"; Arboleda, "Spaces of Extraction, Metropolitan Explosions."

52. Arboleda, "Spaces of Extraction."

53. M. Arboleda, "On the Alienated Violence of Money: Finance Capital, Value, and the Making of Monstrous Territories," in *New Geographies* 9 "Posthuman," M. Gomez-Luque and G. Jafari (eds.) (Cambridge, MA: Harvard Graduate School of Design, 2017), p. 99.

54. Wachsmuth et al., "Expand the frontiers.

CONCLUSION

1. N. Klein, "Reclaiming the Commons," *New Left Review* 9, 2001: 81–9; M. Hardt and A. Negreo, *Assembly* (New York: Oxford University Press, 2017); G. Monbiot, "The Fortifying Commons," December 15, 2016, and "Common Wealth," October 2, 2017, both available at monbiot.com; and see Monbiot, *Out of the Wreckage.*

2. A. Hardt and M. Negri, *Assembly* (Oxford: Oxford University Press, 2017), p. 97–8.

3. Gibson-Graham, *A Postcapitalist Politics,* p. 96.

4. Moten and Harney, *The Undercommons.*

5. F. Moten, *Black and Blur* (Durham and London: Duke University Press, 2017), p.160.

6. Hardt and Negri, *Assembly,* p. 152–3.

7. R. Reich, *The Common Good* (New York: Alfred A. Knopf, 2018); M.J. Sandel, "A Just Society," *New York Times Book Review,* April 7, 2018, p. 21.

8. Berlant, "The Commons," p. 395–6.

9. Anna Nikolaeva has developed the idea of mobility commons through conference presentations at the T2M Conference (Mexico City, 2016), the Sixth World Sustainability Forum (Cape Town, 2017), and the International Sociological Association RC21 Conference (Leeds, 2017). See Nikolaeva, et al., "A New Politics of Mobility."

10. E. Blackmar, "Appropriating 'the Commons': The Tragedy of Property Rights Discourse" in S. Low and N. Smith (eds.), *The Politics of Public Space,* (New York and London: Routledge, 2006), pp. 49–80.

11. I. Illich, "Silence Is a Commons," *The CoEvolution Quarterly* (Winter 1983), p. 3.

12. J. Henderson, "From Climate Fight to Street Fight: The Politics of Mobility and the Right to the City," in J. Cidell and D. Prytherch (eds.), *Transport, Mobility, and the Production of Urban Space,* (Oxford: Routledge, 2015), 101–16, p. 112. And see J. Henderson, *Street Fight: The Politics of Mobility in San Francisco* (Amherst: University of Massachusetts Press, 2013).

13. "Untokening 1.0—Principles of Mobility Justice," accessed at untokening.org.

14. "Philly Free Streets" and the International Open Streets Movement, Institute for Transportation and Development Policy, April 12, 2017, available at itdp.org.

15. Furness, *One Less Car,* pp. 78–83.

16. Ibid., p. 92.

17. See ovarianpsycos.com, and thanks to Anna Davidson, whose PhD dissertation (2018) "Mobilizing Bodies: Difference, Power and Ecology in Urban Cycling Practices," in the School of Geography and the Environment at Oxford University, brought this group to my attention.

18. N. Disco and E. Kranakis (eds.), *Cosmopolitan Commons: Sharing Resources and Risks Across Borders* (Cambridge, MA and London: MIT Press, 2013).

19. D. Papadopoulos and V.S. Tsianos, "After Citizenship: Autonomy of

Migration, Organisational Ontology and Mobile Commons," *Citizenship Studies* 17 (2), 2013:178–96, pp. 191–2; N. Trimikliniotos, D. Parsanoglou, and V.S. Tsianos, *Mobile Commons, Migrant Digitalities and the Right to the City* (Basingstoke and New York: Palgrave Macmillan, 2015), p. 19; N. Trimikliniotos, D. Parsanoglou, and V.S. Tsianos, "Mobile Commons And/ In Precarious Spaces: Mapping Migrant Struggles and Social Resistance," *Critical Sociology* 42 (7–8), 2016: 1,035–49, p. 1,041; C.A. Pasel, "The Journey of Central American Women Migrants: Engendering the Mobile Commons," forthcoming in *Mobilities*.

20. Hardt and Negri, *Assembly*, p. 60.
21. M. Sheller, "Mobile Publics: Beyond the Network Perspective," *Environment and Planning D: Society and Space* 22, 2004: 39–52, p. 50.
22. M. de la Cadena, "Uncommons," *Theorizing the Contemporary, Cultural Anthropology* website, March 29, 2018, available at culanth.org.
23. Ibid.
24. Escobar, *Designs for the Pluriverse*, pp. 206–7; V. Shiva, *Staying Alive: Women, Ecology and Development* (Berkeley: North Atlantic Books, 2016 [1999]).

GLOSSARY

1. Hardt and Negri, *Assembly*, pp. 97–8.
2. See Critical Disability Studies Working Group, "What is Critical Disability Studies?" available at mia.mobilities.ca/criticaldisability.
3. Furness, *One Less Car*, pp. 78–83.
4. Moten, *Black and Blur,* p.160.

INDEX